CW01379305

SMALL FIRMS

NATIONAL SMALL FIRMS'
POLICY AND RESEARCH CONFERENCES

Available from:
Paul Chapman Publishing
144 Liverpool Road
London
N1 1LA

Telephone 071 609 5315/6
Fax 071 700 1057

Towards the Twenty-First Century: *The Challenge for Small Business*
edited by
Martyn Robertson, Elizabeth Chell and Colin Mason
(ISBN 0 9519230 0 5).
Selected papers from the 13th National Small Firms' Policy and Research Conference 1990.

Small Enterprise Development: *Policy and Practice in Action*
edited by
Kevin Caley, Elizabeth Chell, Francis Chittenden and Colin Mason
(ISBN 1 85396 215 5).
Selected papers from the 14th National Small Firms' Policy and Research Conference 1991.

Small Firms: *Recession and Recovery*
edited by
Francis Chittenden, Martyn Robertson and David Watkins
(ISBN 1 85396 249 X).
Selected papers from the 15th National Small Firms' Policy and Research Conference 1992.

SMALL FIRMS
PARTNERSHIPS FOR GROWTH

edited by
FRANCIS CHITTENDEN
MARTYN ROBERTSON AND IAN MARSHALL

PUBLISHED ON BEHALF OF
THE INSTITUTE FOR SMALL BUSINESS AFFAIRS

P·C·P
Paul Chapman
Publishing Ltd

Copyright © 1995, ISBA.

All rights reserved

Paul Chapman Publishing Ltd
144 Liverpool Road
London
N1 1LA

Apart from any fair dealing for the purposes of research or private study, or criticism or review, as permitted under the Copyright, Designs and Patents Act, 1988, this publication may be reproduced, stored or transmitted, in any form or by any means, only with the prior permission in writing of the publishers, or in the case of reprographic reproduction in accordance with the terms of licences issued by the Copyright Licensing Agency. Inquiries concerning reproduction outside those terms should be sent to the publishers at the above mentioned address.

British Library Cataloguing in Publication Data

Small Firms:Partnerships for Growth
I. Chittenden, Francis
338.642

ISBN 1-85396-288-0

Typeset by PanTek Arts, Maidstone Kent.
Printed and bound by
The Cromwell Press Ltd, Broughton Gifford,
Melksham, Wiltshire.

A B C D E F G H 9 8 7 6 5

Contents

Foreword vii

List of Contributors ix

1. Small Firms: Public Policy Issues in Partnerships for Growth 1
FRANCIS CHITTENDEN, MARTYN ROBERTSON AND IAN MARSHALL
Introduction; Finance and the Small Firm; Spatial Influences; Employment Creation; Partnerships: Small Firms and Large Firms; Partnerships: Public and Private Sector; Patterns of Growth; Conclusions; Policy Recommendations

2. Bank Lending to Unincorporated Firms in the UK, 1976–92 14
MICHAEL GODWIN
Introduction; Defining the Variables; Exploratory Factor Analysis; Regression Analysis: The First Series of Regressions; Using Differences in BLSS as the Dependent Variable (CBLPSS); A 'Trickle-down' Interpretation of the Data; Omitting Bank Lending from the Independent Variables; Conclusion; Recommendations for Policy

3. The Equity Gap in the East Midlands: An Initial Assessment of the Operation of a New Venture Capital Fund 31
GRAHAME BOOCOCK, MARGARET WOODS AND KEVIN CALEY
Introduction; Methodology; Background; The UK Markets for Risk Capital; The East Midlands; The New Venture Capital Fund; Initial Enquiries to the Fund; Comments on Existing Sources of Finance; The Business Plans; Incomplete Plans; Risk; Marketing; The Management Team; Is There an Equity Gap in the East Midlands?; Conclusion; Future Research Agenda

4. Finance, New Technology and SMEs: A Comparative Study of the UK and France 49
SARAH AUSTIN, AIDAN BERRY, SUE FAULKNER, JO JOHNSON AND MARK HUGHES
Introduction; Literature Review: SMEs and External Finance; Financing New Technology; Methodology; Key Findings; General Financing; Financing of New Technology; Conclusions

5. An Exploratory Analysis of the Factors Associated with the Survival of Independent High-Technology Firms in Great Britain 63
PAUL WESTHEAD, DAVID J STOREY AND MARC COWLING
Introduction; Previous Research; Factors Associated with Business Survival/Closure; This Research; Methodology; Assumptions/Limitations of the Strategy Adopted; Results; Conclusions

6. Employment Generation and Small Business Growth in Different Geographical Environments 100
DAVID NORTH AND DAVID SMALLBONE
Aims of the Paper; The Data Base; Employment Change and the Growth Performance of Firms; The Employment Generation Potential of SMEs in Different; Geographical Environments; Factors Influencing Employment

Change in Inner London and Rural Firms; Labour Constraints; Labour Productivity; Labour Flexibility; Conclusions

7. Longitudinal Study of Small Enterprises in the Service Sector   116
ADRIAN WOODS, ROBERT BLACKBURN AND JAMES CURRAN
Introduction; Methodological Background; Business Conditions 1992–1993; Turnover Changes; Coping with the Recession; Employment Changes; Relations with Banks; Training and Enterprise Councils; The Outlook for 1993; Summary and Conclusions

8. Quality Assurance and Business Support Organisations: Chaos or Coherence ?   134
HELEN WINNIFRITH
References

9. Small Firms and BS 5750: A Preliminary Investigation   141
JULIAN NORTH, JAMES CURRAN AND ROBERT BLACKBURN
Introduction; Quality and BS 5750; BS 5750 and Small Firms; A New Study on BS 5750 and Small Firms; The Results; Conclusions

10. Multinational/Supplier Linkages in the Scottish Electronics Industry   152
IVAN TUROK
Electronics Growth in Scotland: A Potential Market for Suppliers; The Actual Level of Local Sourcing; The Pattern of Local Sourcing; Towards an Explanation: Demanding Customers and Supplier Weaknesses; Conclusion

11. Small Firm Autonomy Within a Franchise: A Case of Shifting Fortunes   169
ALAN FELSTEAD
Original Franchise Structure; Exposing the Contradictions; Economies of Scale and Technological Advance; Retailer Concentration; Reshaping the Franchise Structure; Consolidation of Production; Contractual Changes; Central Sales Company; Conclusion

12. Supporting Inner-City Firms: Lessons from the Field   182
J MARK FORD AND MONDER RAM
Introduction; The Initiative; Marketing; Why Do Owner-Managers Opt for – or Reject – Business Support?; Delivering the Two-Day Consultancies; Business Problems and Preoccupations; Employer Feedback; Conclusions

13. TEAMSTART - Overcoming the Blockages to Small Business Growth   192
SHAILENDRA VYAKARNAM AND ROBIN JACOBS
Introduction; Literature Review; Why TEAMSTART?; The Essex Study; Objectives; Method; Findings; Findings from the Telephone; Follow-up; Discussion; Cost Benefit Analysis; Models for Implementation; Conclusion

14. From Entrepreneurship to Professional Management: An Examination of the Personal Factors that Stunt Growth   206
ANITA MACNABB
Background; The Study; Why Choose ISA?; Stage One: Group Study Findings; Stage Two: The Case Studies; Discussion; Conclusion

15. Habitual Owners of Small Businesses   217
PETER J HALL
Introduction; Current State of Knowledge; Relationships Found; Empirical Critique; The Key Decisions; Habitual Decisions; Factors Affecting Decisions; Factors Affecting Owner Outcomes; Conclusion

Foreword

Small businesses are possibly the most important sector in the UK PLC. Dynamic, entrepreneurial, energetic, innovative are just some of the words synonymous with this marketplace. Over the last few years, the rate of new business creation for this sector has dramatically increased, although so too has the rate of business failures, and their survival is one of the major issues.

As a major provider of external finance to small businesses, we recognise that support and services have to be delivered at the local level where they operate. Furthermore, the business support network is a vital link in the continued success of this sector and therefore it is important that effective working partnerships are in place.

In an increasingly global market, companies are finding that innovation – the successful exploitation of new ideas – will enable them to sustain their competitiveness. For small businesses to meet these challenges, it is important that we continue to research those areas which will help decision makers choose wisely for the future.

NatWest is delighted at again being given the opportunity to sponsor publication of papers from the 1993 ISBA conference. The annual conference is an established event making a pratical contribution towards the understanding of this sector, and is very relevant to organisations which support and save small businesses.

Ian Peters
Head of Small Business Services
National Westminster Bank

Contributors

SARAH AUSTIN, CENTRIM, University of Brighton, Brighton BN1 9PH.
AIDAN BERRY, Department of Finance and Accountancy, University of Brighton, Brighton BN2 4GJ.
ROBERT BLACKBURN, Small Business Research Centre, Kingston University, Surrey KT2 7LB.
GRAHAME BOOCOCK, Loughborough University Business School, Loughborough, Leics LE11 3TU.
KEVIN CALEY, East Midlands Venture Fund Managers Limited, GPT Business Park, Technology Drive, Beeston, Nottingham. NG9 2ND.
FRANCIS CHITTENDEN, Business Development Centre, Manchester Business School, University of Manchester, Booth Street West, Manchester M15 6PB.
MARC COWLING, Centre for Small and Medium Sized Enterprises, Warwick Business School, The University of Warwick, Coventry, CV4 7AL .
JAMES CURRAN, Small Business Research Centre, Kingston University, Surrey KT2 7LB.
SUE FAULKNER, Department of Finance and Accountancy, University of Brighton, Brighton BN2 4GJ.
ALAN FELSTEAD, Centre for Labour Market Studies, University of Leicester, Leicester LE1 7LA.
J MARK FORD, Just For Starters Ltd, 264A Washwood Heath Road, Birmingham.
MICHAEL GODWIN, Manchester Business School, Booth Street West, Manchester M15 6PB.
PETER J HALL, Centre for Small and Medium Sized Enterprises, Warwick Business School, The University of Warwick, Coventry, CV4 7AL.
MARK HUGHES, Department of Finance and Accountancy, University of Brighton, Brighton BN2 4GJ.
ROBIN JACOBS, Enterprise Research and Development, St John's Innovation Centre, Cowley Road, Cambridge CB4 4WS.
JO JOHNSON, Department of Finance and Accountancy, University of Brighton , Brighton BN2 4GJ.
ANITA MACNABB, NISBI-The Small Business Institute, Ulster Business School, University of Ulster, Shore Road, Newtownabbey, BT37 OQB, Northern Ireland.
IAN MARSHALL, Nottingam Business School, Nottingham Trent University, Burton Street, Nottingham, NG1 4BU.
DAVID NORTH, Centre for Enterprise and Economic Development Research, Middlesex University, Queensway, Enfield, Middlesex EN3 4SF.
JULIAN NORTH, Small Business Research Centre, Kingston University, Surrey KT2 7LB.
MONDER RAM, University of Central England Business School, Perry Barr, Birmingham, B42 2SU.
MARTYN ROBERTSON, Leeds Business School, Leeds Metropolitan University, 80 Woodhouse Lane, Leeds LS2 8AB .

DAVID SMALLBONE, Centre for Enterprise and Economic Development Research, Middlesex University, Queensway, Enfield, Middlesex EN3 4SF.

DAVID. J. STOREY, Centre for Small and Medium Sized Enterprises, Warwick Business School, The University of Warwick, Coventry, CV4 7AL.

IVAN TUROK, Centre for Planning, University of Strathclyde, Glasgow Gl lXN.

SHAILENDRA VYAKARNAM, Enterprise Research and Development, St John's Innovation Centre, Cowley Road, Cambridge CB4 4WS.

PAUL WESTHEAD, Centre for Small and Medium Sized Enterprises, Warwick Business School, The University of Warwick, Coventry, CV4 7AL.

HELEN WINNIFRITH, 40 Newbold Terrace East, Leamington Spa, Warwickshire, CV32 4EY.

ADRIAN WOODS, Small Business Research Centre, Kingston University, Surrey KT2 7LB

MARGARET WOODS, Loughborough University Business School, Loughborough, Leics LE11 3TU.

CHAPTER 1

Small Firms: Public Policy Issues in Partnerships for Growth

FRANCIS CHITTENDEN, MARTYN ROBERTSON AND
IAN MARSHALL

INTRODUCTION

The 16th Institute for Small Business Affairs policy and research conference was hosted by Nottingham Trent University. As has become customary a wide range of papers was presented based upon both academic and action research which contributed to the body of knowledge of small and medium enterprises (SMEs) and offered implications for policy towards this sector. This book contains a selection of these papers chosen for their contribution and relevance to the present policy environment.

When seeking to summarise last year's contributions it was possible to draw on the Department of Employment's report 'Small Business in Britain' (DoE 1992) to provide a research policy framework within which to position the findings. However with the transfer of responsibility for small businesses to the Department of Trade and Industry (DTI) this publication has been withdrawn. As a result this chapter is primarily driven by the content of the papers comprising this volume, without reference to the extent to which research output may be seen to contribute to the rational search for information required to formulate policy towards this sector.

Discussion in this chapter adopts the following progression. Firstly, issues relating to the financing of small firms are presented. One specific genre of business facing particular financing challenges is technology-based firms; and so discussion migrates to this area which may re-emerge as an issue of some importance (Oakey 1994).

Some high technology firms choose to locate on science parks. This introduces the observation that firms adapt behaviour patterns to their local environs. The extent to which this process of adaptation to, and impact upon, the locale influences the behaviour and employment characteristics of firms is considered in the context of both large and small firms.

The topography of firms includes the physical, human and commercial infrastructure with which they interact. Nowhere is the importance of these links more closely defined than in the case of a franchise. Exploration of the reality of large firm/small firm linkages continues in the context of one such network.

From here the discussion turns to issues central to public policy relating to SMEs. Topics considered include the dependence of service sector employment growth on the performance of a small number of firms; the relevance of quality assurance and standards for business support organisations and small firms; and the response of inner city firms to targeted interventions.

If policy towards the small firms sector is to offer realistic prospects for positive outcomes an appropriate understanding of the management challenges facing SME owners is essential. The analysis concludes with a review of three management issues which are important in the context of public policy:

- the prospects for team managed new firms
- some of the personality traits influencing owners' ability to develop a management style appropriate for an expanding firm
- factors influencing the propensity for ownership of more than one business.

Finally the chapter concludes with a review of government policy towards small firms and offers suggestions for the emerging agenda.

FINANCE AND THE SMALL FIRM

One of the most topical issues of 1993 has been the adequacy of financial resources available to small firms, particularly from third parties such as the banks. Sadly much of the debate has arisen from a relatively small number of specific examples which have attracted media attention. Whilst the substance of these cases has, on enquiry, largely been found to be unrepresentative they do highlight the importance of adequate financial resources to the well being of the small firms sector; especially when balance sheets have been weakened by prolonged recession and recovery begins (Schumpeter 1934).

Bank lending to small firms is more important to the prospects of the sector than is the case for large firms (see, for example, the review in Ch 3, Stanworth and Gray 1991). In Chapter 2, Michael Godwin presents an analysis of trends in bank lending to unincorporated firms during the 1980s. This study, which is conducted at the macro level, identifies the significant increase in facilities extended to the sector over the past decade and, using regression analysis, the author explores the factors determining aggregate demand for bank lending by unincorporated firms.

The significant growth in facilities extended provides further evidence of the debtor/customer paradox which has attracted so much media attention. Relatively young and very small (usually unincorporated) firms have tended to be the most vociferous critics of the UK banks during the 1980s. In contrast, this research shows that they exhibited considerable enthusiasm for bank finance. Demand was also largely insensitive to the cost of those funds, as measured by interest rates.

Some will interpret these observations as evidence of the oligopolistic structure of the institutional finance markets accessible to SMEs. Others (for example Bannock 1994), cognisant of similarities in the behaviour of banks and small businesses in countries where there is a lower level of concentration amongst the suppliers of debt finance, regard this behaviour as evidence of the inherent problems of lending to small and young firms. These difficulties result from the relatively high levels of information asymmetry and agency costs.

Many accept the inherent uncertainties associated with lending to smaller businesses. Such firms are under the direct and immediate control of one or a few highly independent individuals whose interests may, in times of commercial difficulty, conflict with those of the financier. Often the business has a short or even non-existent track record on which lenders can make judgements about the innate abilities of the owners and the attractiveness of the niche within which they operate. One rational response to these factors would be for banks to avoid the regressive cost of credit decision for young small businesses by openly insisting on full security. Such a policy would enable lenders to drive down the cost curve. Market forces should ensure that the resultant savings would be shared with customers.

Another response to the operational uncertainties associated with young businesses is to seek to minimise the reliance on bank finance by increasing the level of equity funding available, at least to the more ambitious of such firms. In Chapter 3 Grahame Boocock, Margaret Woods and Kevin Caley report on the establishment of the Midland Enterprise Fund located in the East Midlands. This analysis of the first nine months of the fund incorporates the characteristics of potential investees, the nature and quality of information provided and the evaluation criteria adopted by the fund. This is a fascinating action research project which provides valuable insights into the difficulties associated with providing small sums of equity capital to businesses on a local basis.

Sarah Austin and colleagues pursue the topic of financing small firms in Chapter 4 where they present a comparative analysis of research into thirty firms in the UK and France. The chapter starts with a useful literature review of patterns of external finance available to SMEs in the two countries, before considering the sources of finance for technology-based firms. There is no evidence that the French have identified private sector solutions to the additional challenges of coping with technological risk in an environment already characterised by high levels of uncertainty. Perhaps, in this area too, the behaviour of UK financial institutions reflects the economic rationality of their managers and shareholders.

SPATIAL INFLUENCES

Pursuing the theme of technology firms, in Chapter 5 Paul Westhead, David Storey and Marc Cowling present the early results from a longitudinal study of hi-tech firms located on and off science parks, compared with a sample of low technology businesses. Using a Logit model they seek to determine factors associated with survival and failure. As yet the work is incomplete, but the study appears to confirm earlier results that technology-based firms have a lower rate of failure than other classifications of business (Storey and Strange 1992). Evidence that location on a science park has a significant impact on prospects for survival or growth are, however, equivocal (Oakey 1985).

Chapter 6 continues to explore the impact of business location upon performance. In this chapter David North and David Smallbone, who received the Institute for Small Business Affairs award for the best research paper, extend their analysis of a panel of established manufacturing firms by examining differences in performance between businesses based in inner city, outer metropolitan and rural districts. Location does not appear to affect the growth rates achieved by these spatially diverse samples. However, the Inner London firms required higher increments of turnover for each new job and the most rapidly growing urban firms were those that identified new methods to enable expansion, for example through sub-contracting elements of production. Inner city firms paid higher wages and achieved higher productivity improvements. They also faced the greatest skill shortages and some migrated to other regions during the period of study. This paper has clear implications for TEC, Business Link, local authority and central government policies.

EMPLOYMENT CREATION

Chapter 7 reports the findings of continued research into a panel of service sector firms conducted by Adrian Woods, Robert Blackburn and Jim Curran. This analysis identifies relatively high survival rates (50–90%) over the recessionary period between 1990 and 1993. However these aggregate figures mask wide diversity between geographical locations and sector of operations. Overall the sample has exhibited employment growth but this is concentrated in just 20% of the firms. Whilst there is early evidence that the business owners interviewed were more optimistic about the end of the recession than in 1992, most remained cautious.

This paper also examined the level of interaction of the sample firms with their local TECs. In 1991/2 just over 10% of the firms had used their TEC for help or advice. In 1992/3 this rose to just under 12%; indicating perhaps that TEC difficulties in engaging the small business community remain.

Chapter 8 continues the debate regarding the role of government in providing support and advice to the SME sector. This chapter by Helen Winnifrith discusses the activity measurement criteria adopted by the Department of Employment and their practical application within TECs. The author argues that there is little consistency in the use of these performance criteria. In addition it is important that the current yardsticks are recognised as short-term, restricted outputs. They do not indicate whether businesses have performed better as a result of the interventions. The paper appeals for concentration on the real goals and acceptance that it will take many years to draw valid conclusions.

During the 1980s the adoption of performance standards has not only been the penchant of government, however. This period has seen a considerable increase in enthusiasm amongst businesses for the quality standard BS5750. The word quality presents an enticing notion implying the possession of desirable attributes. BS5750 is, however, a quality assurance system based upon the consistent application of a procedure to ensure that all outputs are of equivalent standard. The standard implies consistency of product or service rather than any elemental characteristic associated with 'excellence or customer delight'.

Chapter 9 explores the adoption of BS5750 amongst a sample of small manufacturing and service firms. It is found that, whilst 95% of firms interviewed were aware of the standard, its use is concentrated in particular sectors such as electronics manufacture and employment agencies. Larger firms are also more likely to apply the standard.

Adoption also tends to be more attractive to small firm suppliers of larger companies who are themselves registered. In some instances registration is a necessary condition of the supply contract. BS5750 may also be adopted as a means of differentiating the business from its competitors; this is especially likely in markets where competitive pressure is increasing. However, in some sectors customer pressure for registration is declining as experience of the impact of BS5750 builds up.

PARTNERSHIPS: SMALL FIRMS AND LARGE FIRMS

The introduction of BS5750 in order to meet the requirements of one or a few large customers is an example of the dependency of small firms on their environment, including the markets on which they rely. Two further chapters explore this theme. In Chapter 10, Ivan Turok considers the extent to which multi-national electronics companies in Scotland have developed supplier linkages within the local economy.

Turok finds that just 12% of components are purchased locally and that the relationship between small firm supplier and multi-national customer is more frequently characterised by cost minimisation and short-term convenience for the multi-national. This contrasts with a more idealised scenario in which the high level of interaction possible with proximate suppliers results in accelerated product development and increased responsiveness to market conditions.

The relatively low level of localised purchasing reflects weaknesses both in the industrial base of the region and in the existing trading links of multi-nationals. The author praises Scottish Enterprise's capacity building initiatives and argues for their extension. The UK government's non-interventionist stance is contrasted with the more constructive approach of the European Commission. This paper is of particular relevance to the role of Foreign Direct Investment in regional development. The skills and capacities of local indigenous supplier networks must be sufficiently strong for local economies to maximise the benefits of inward investment.

Chapter 11 examines the reality of relationships between large and small firms and is based upon a case study of the Coca-Cola company and its franchised bottlers in Germany during the 1980s. The analysis concludes that the independence of franchisees is heavily bounded by the requirements of the franchiser. Originally many bottlers were family businesses whose objectives encompassed the well-being of the 'family' and its position in the local community. In contrast the objectives of the franchisor were overtly sales and profit maximisation.

As a result, increasing concentration in the market for bottled drinks resulted in the franchisor adopting a more strident policy towards its franchisees. The Coca Cola company introduced an arrangement to control prices and manage key accounts through a franchisor/ee controlled joint operation. In addition mandatory sales and investment targets were established for franchisees. In the drive for efficient scale the number of franchisee bottlers has been reduced by almost 90%.

PARTNERSHIPS: PUBLIC AND PRIVATE SECTOR

Close trading relations are not the exclusive province of the private sector. It may be argued that partnerships exist between the public and private sector whenever there is a developmental or dependent relationship between the parties. Chapters 12 and 13 examine forms of partnership between business support agencies and their clients.

Chapter 12 explores the manifestation of one such partnership, where a local TEC develops relationships with a number of inner city firms mainly employing fewer than 10 staff. It might be anticipated that the objectives of all parties to this initiative would be to increase opportunities for business development. Superficially this would be the case.

However, in this action-research study Mark Ford and Monder Ram identify an important conflict in the expectations of the two parties. The small business advisers conducted a health check on the client firms which largely resulted in recommendations about the management of the business. However, the owners' expectations were more focused upon the external constraints facing the firm – such as how to obtain grants or cope with skill shortages. They were less convinced that the consultants could tell them how to run their businesses. The paper concludes that a process consulting model is much more likely to meet the substantive expectations of the client firm. It seems that in developing working partnerships the importance of recognising the implicit objectives of the parties is critical. Often these are not articulated; and even if they are, semantics may defeat the efficacy of the communication.

It has been argued, since 1992, that public policy towards small firms suffered from a lack of objective clarity (Chittenden and Caley 1992). Progress has been made since then, in a number of areas including a clearer definition of the objectives of the business start-up scheme (formerly the Enterprise Allowance Scheme). TECs have now been given much greater flexibility in the way this is operated and the funding mechanism is such that the establishment of survivor businesses is more important than temporarily reducing the numbers of unemployed.

This topic is addressed in more detail in Chapter 13 which received the Forum of Private Business Award for the best policy orientated conference paper. The authors, Shailendra Vyakarnam and Robin Jacobs, report the results of an action research study conducted for Essex TEC on the potential impact of encouraging team managed start-ups with opportunities for sustained growth.

The research reviews experience of new businesses and reports on the results of focus groups which examined the possibility of establishing an entrepreneurial team creation network. Comparing the costs of jobs created under the business start-up scheme the paper concludes that focusing the nucleus of support towards team managed new ventures offers a potentially attractive cost/benefit.

The attractiveness of team managed ventures centres around the depth and complementarity of skills; the need to rationalise and communicate the basis of decisions which would otherwise be taken intuitively; and embedding of the delegation paradigm which often represents a barrier to growth in single or dominant owner businesses.[1] These issues are further considered in Chapter 14.

PATTERNS OF GROWTH

In this chapter Anita MacNabb continues her study of the core values of business owners (MacNabb and McCoy 1992) using identity structure analysis (Weinrich 1980). Through a number of case studies the author discerns the characteristics exhibited by small business owners which may inhibit the continued growth of their firms. These include the heavy reliance on family support, lack of aspirations to change and an autocratic management style, especially when combined with very high levels of personal confidence.

The theme of examining the behavioural characteristics of small business owners continues in Chapter 15. Peter Hall explores the issue of multiple business ownership, which has received relatively little attention to date. Drawing on European research this chapter concludes that as many as 40% of business proprietors may be classified as 'multiple owners' either through the sequential operation of one business followed by another, or through a portfolio approach where more than one enterprise is operated simultaneously.

Hall argues that the factors which influence choices of multiple ownership include: the owners' intrinsic ability; personality traits and motivation; and situational context – which is a function of industry structure and chosen business strategy. Many small business researchers are familiar with examples of multiple ownership and this category of small business owner offers both challenges and opportunities for those providing services to the small business sector and government officials responsible for policy.

CONCLUSIONS

When writing the introductory chapter to this book three years ago the most important policy recommendation centred around the separation of social policies which focus on the objectives of reducing unemployment from economic policy which is concerned with the creation of wealth.

Since then responsibility for small firms has transferred to the DTI and a number of steps have been taken to differentiate the encouragement of start-ups from support for employment generation through growing firms. The major element of support for micro-firms which has emerged relates to removal of the regressive burden of compliance costs, for example through raising the VAT threshold and reducing the administration of PAYE. There are other initiatives in the pipeline, such as the withdrawal of the statutory audit for micro-companies. These are to be generally welcomed as consistent with encouraging enterprise through maximising business owners' opportunity to concentrate on the commercial operation of their businesses. However, considerable further scope for improvement remains, especially amalgamating the PAYE and National Insurance systems.

Major advances in the area of supporting wealth creation have been slower to emerge, although Business Links have been formed more quickly than originally anticipated. However some of the 'partnership' issues considered in this volume have been amongst the most testing elements of the birth of these new organisations. A list of some of the factors influencing the formation and operation of such 'partnerships', based upon the observations of Chapters 10, 11, 12 and 13, might include the following:

1. The underlying objectives of the parties, both individual and corporate aspirations
2. The location and control of the financial resources
3. The capacity of the partners to meet each other's needs
4. Trends in the external (competitive) environment and the requirements of clients
5. The culture of each organisation
6. The intended nature of the partnership (dependence or developmental)
7. The timescales involved.

Reviewing the Business Link initiative under these headings might suggest the following conclusions.

Underlying Objectives

Whilst the TECs, local authorities, Chambers of Commerce and Higher Education sectors would each subscribe to the general view that it is in their interests for the local economy to flourish, their origins and the reality of their day to day operations, which shape their own and their public's perception of their roles, are widely disparate.

On an individual basis, however, the timing of the Business Link initiative to coincide with the public/private sector employment decision facing TEC-based civil servants could be seen as highly influential. The relative position of UK Chambers of Commerce, compared with the Public Law status enjoyed by such bodies in a number of EU states could also have been an important element in harnessing support from this sector.

Control of Financial Resources

Critical to this initiative is the location and control of additional resources within the DTI. Whilst the total sums of money are, in government programme terms somewhat limited, in the context of TEC enterprise budgets they do represent a useful increment. Perhaps the objectives of the DTI also relate to its relative positioning in the small business arena vis a vis the Department of Employment, which had spawned the TECs.

The Capacity of the Partners to Meet Each Other's Needs

This is a challenging area. Whilst it is possible to see what each of the parties can contribute to Business Links, budgets, staff, membership lists, premises etc. the reciprocal flows are harder to identify. In the short term some of the payback is of a psychological nature, being seen to be actively engaging the 'community'; working within government policy – and thereby being acknowledged or legitimised by government, as examples.

Other benefits flow to the parties as a result of increased aspirations for achieving objectives; for example TECs have on their own been demonstrably unsuccessful in engaging the small business community (as referred to in Chapter 7). As agents of the government their risk of 'failure' is reduced if their principals encourage adoption of a new initiative with ostensibly greater chances of success.

However, few of these psychological benefits are likely to stand the test of time. After initial enthusiasm wanes the supporting organisations are likely to consider the cost of their involvement and compare these with the revenue streams which result. The financially weaker are likely to embark upon the appraisal process first. The cost of participating in these activities, including the opportunity cost of management time, is likely to be quite high – and possibly regressive. Medium-term prospects for the initiative will, therefore, depend upon the generation of an adequate public or private sector cash flow stream.

Trends in the External Environment and the Requirements of Clients

At the macro level trends in the external environment may be characterised by gradual economic recovery and continued streamlining of the large corporate sector. These may result in continued growth of the SME sector, with the possibility of the emergence of more 'growth corridor firms', if the barriers to growth can be overcome. Certainly compared with other advanced economies the UK SME sector has accounted for a smaller proportion of GDP (Stanworth and Gray 1991, Ch 1) and is heavily concentrated towards the micro end of the size distribution (Storey 1993).

The requirements of small firms are more problematic as evidenced by Chapter 12. The poor penetration of TECs into this market has already been referred to (Chapter 7). In addition evidence of delivery of initiatives into more established small firms (Smallbone, North and Leigh 1993) identifies that in the Business Link target market (20 to 200 employees) no more than one firm in six used any public or semi-public assistance (approximately half to one-third of the number who used private sector consultancies).

Interestingly the more successful firms and those which had participated in management training were more likely to use both public and private sector sources of advice. There was also a sectoral bias with science-and-technology-based firms being more likely to use consultants than, for example, more traditional sectors such as printing, textiles etc.

The Cultural Environment of Each Organisation

Returning once again to the internal partnership issues of Business Links, the diversity of the organisations represented is indicative of the miscellany of cultures involved. For example the civil service paymasters, the large company managers, the small business consultants, representatives from higher education and officers from the local authority to name only some. If analysts of large company mergers can attribute sub-optimal performance to cultural differences between large corporates operating in the similar industry sectors the scope for contention in Business Links must be considerable.

The Nature of the Partnership (Dependence or Developmental)

Almost by definition the nature of this partnership is intended to be developmental. The objective being to bring together a wide range of sources of support and advice for SMEs and provide an integrated service. The results should be developmental for the partner organisations who will thereby be able to pool resources, share communication costs and serve a larger number of firms. However, the examples identified in Chapters 10 and 11 appear to indicate, at least in the private sector, that developmental relationships between organisations of vastly different size and influence are the exception rather than the rule.

The Timescales Involved

One of the particular problems facing all organisations relying upon public sector support for their resources is the reluctance of government to commit expenditure beyond the very limited time horizons associated with the fiscal year. Whilst introducing the Autumn budget represents a modest improvement, there is an undoubted conflict between the objectives of Business Links intervention in the small firms market and the budgeting and (as referred to in Chapter 8) performance monitoring standards applied by governments.

Prognosis

Based upon the above analysis it may be seen that there is little congruence between the ideal conditions for the emergence of Business Links as developmental partnerships and the dynamics likely to facilitate the achievement of this goal.

As a result it may be postulated that the performance of the Business Links, like the TECs, will be regionally diverse. Those organisations operating in more favourable geographic environments, usually rural or suburban areas enjoying inward migration, above average levels of educational achievement (Westhead and Birley 1994) and greater propensity for growth-led job creation (Chapter 6) should outperform those in inner city or old, urban industrial regions.

The level of market penetration of Business Links will, however, appear to be higher than the TECs. This will be achieved as a result of the narrower market definition adopted; targeting larger small firms which exhibit growth potential (possibly only 20% of the population – Chapter 7); whilst also collecting approaches from firms without this definition. The improving economic climate will also enable more SME managers to seek external advice, to undertake management training and to pay for external services; once again increasing the opportunities for Business Links.

However, unless the improved economic climate also results in additional revenue streams, for example from new government initiatives or at least continued funding at the present level, it may be postulated that the present 'partnership' arrangements will be subjected to tension. Three possibilities are apparent:

1. One dominant 'partner' will emerge, probably based upon financial resources either directly funding or (more likely) purchasing services from the Business Link. The other players will then either withdraw or minimise their commitment where departure is deemed politically unacceptable.
2. The Business Link management will identify additional revenue streams which will enable them to sustain the relationships by ensuring that each party is (just) sufficiently rewarded to remain involved. These revenue streams may be either public or private sector. In the public sector, for example European funds, competition with other partners (e.g. TECs) may result. In the private sector extension of the role of Personal Business Advisers into areas offering higher prospects for client satisfaction, such as the provision of highly specific advice (Smallbone, North and Leigh 1993), may result in conflict with other consultants and financial advisers. 'Turf wars' may be anticipated.
3. The Business Link may cease to be a focal activity for any of the partners. Continued operation in the short/medium term may be anticipated but the level of impact is likely to be minimal. Examples of such token organisations may be found in other areas, such as the less active Chambers of Commerce.

POLICY RECOMMENDATIONS

Whatever the outcome it will be difficult to know the impact of these organisations on the SME sector for a number of years, possibly the end of the next economic cycle. In the meantime it is almost impossible to discern any far reaching government strategy for the SME sector.

The barriers to growth remain. Chapters 1 to 4 discuss these issues. Although banks and venture capitalists have a surplus of funds some small business owners continue to complain about the terms on which these are available. It is known from statistics of the small business sector that small and especially young firms are substantially more risky than the overall population of business. In the absence of security the risk premiums banks need to charge make loans prohibitively expensive. It is not until firms have been established for about six years that their track record emerges and macro-statistics indicate that survival becomes more predictable (Ganguly 1985). Evidence also appears to be that external equity can only be appropriate for a minority of such firms. In addition present fiscal policy exacerbates the gearing position of small firms as owners are encouraged to withdraw profits in order to minimise taxation (Chittenden 1991).

These difficulties are increased in the context of technology businesses despite their exhibition of lower rates of failure (Chapter 5) than other small firms. In advanced economies this sector might be expected to offer opportunities for sustained growth. However, in the absence of any realistic government policy towards the encouragement of such businesses it may be argued that the past decade has been wasted (Oakey 1994). Without government support, such as that observed in France, enthusiasm for the sector has waned and most venture capitalists and many banks now see the technological dimension of such enterprises as another risk factor to be accounted for.

The first element in a comprehensive strategy towards the SME sector should relate to removing the financial barriers to growth. The Enterprise Investment Scheme,[2] informal investors' networks and Venture Capital Trusts are useful first steps, but are unlikely to have significant impact. Steps must be taken to encourage business owners to retain profits in their businesses. This can only be achieved through fiscal measures, making re-investment of profits in the firm as attractive as investment in pension schemes or Personal Equity Plans.

In addition research has shown that the late payment of suppliers' invoices has, paradoxically, resulted in significant reductions in liquidity of the private sector. This results in higher operating costs and, as the UK appears to have the worst record in Europe, a loss of international competitiveness (Chittenden, Kennon and Mahindru 1993). Whilst the recent White Paper offered some proposals in the area these are unlikely to be successful, by themselves. Legislation should be introduced to provide for an automatic right to interest on invoices paid late (Chittenden, Kennon and Bragg 1993).

The combination of fiscal reform and a statutory right to interest would do much to reduce the finance gap which presently exists for SMEs and would have little impact on government borrowing.

The second barrier to growth is the motivation of business owners. It is clear that many of the self-employed have no aspirations to grow (Curran, Blackburn and Woods 1991). However, Chapter 7 identifies that some 40% of service sector SMEs are now growing faster than inflation and this proportion is similar to the results of other studies such as the NatWest/Small Business Research Trust quarterly surveys. In addition research has shown that for businesses with aspirations to grow this objective is ranked highly as both a personal and business goal, suggesting that strong motivations for growth do exist (Chittenden 1994). This is a prerequisite of the 'picking winners strategy' which Business Links are, at least tacitly, pursuing.

The third barrier to growth is lack of management skills. Initiatives such as Investors in People and the potential mentoring role of Personal Business Advisers are directly relevant here. Chapter 12 identified the need for process consultancy skills in these situations. However it appears from the analysis by Smallbone and North (1993) referred to earlier, that the opportunities for revenue generation arising from this type of 'soft' consultancy could be limited. Ongoing public sector support for such activities may, therefore be required.

The continued release of management time in SMEs by reducing the regressive burden of compliance costs should remain a priority, especially rationalisation of the PAYE and National Insurance systems. Similar comments apply to initiatives such as BS5750. When businesses inappropriately adopt this standard, possibly as a result of external pressures, they subject themselves to the costs of maintaining quality assurance systems. These costs are almost certainly regressive; whereas the benefits of operating such systems appear to accrue progressively.

Initiatives such as BS5750 do have a role to play in improving the consistency of product and service quality, and in improving market efficiency by signalling information on the management systems of businesses. However, the formal systems they presently imply are not appropriate for all businesses of all sizes.

The final barrier to growth is the existence of skill shortages. National initiatives exist in this field, for example the NVQ movement which has the advantage of accrediting performance 'on the job', thus reflecting the circumstances in which much SME staff training takes place (Johnson and Gubbins 1992). The recent White Paper also re-affirms commitment to this field. Chapter 6 introduces some interesting questions relevant to this issue. The Inner London firms surveyed in this study had grown and exhibited higher productivity increases despite being relatively disadvantaged in terms of labour costs and skill shortages. Further study of the coping strategies adopted by these businesses should provide useful insights which could be of wider application, especially as the recovery gains momentum.

NOTES

1. There are, of course, costs associated with a team managed new venture, apart from the expenses of rewarding a team (as opposed to an individual) for their executive or non-executive involvement. Possibly the greatest of these is the effort required to sustain the commonality of objectives of a number of people working in the frenetic, resources indigent environment of a new small business (Welsh and White 1981).
2. The Enterprise Investment Scheme is a revised version of the Business Expansion Scheme, announced in the November 1993 budget.

REFERENCES

BANNOCK G (1994) The future of small business banking, a report for National Westminster Bank PLC.

CHITTENDEN F (1991) Taxation, Ch 5 in Stanworth J and Gray C (eds), Bolton 20 Years On: The Small Firm in the 1990s, Paul Chapman, London.

CHITTENDEN F AND CALEY K (1992) Current policy issues and recommendations, in Caley K, Chell E, Chittenden F and Mason C (eds), Small Enterprise Development: Policy and Practice in Action, Paul Chapman, London.

CHITTENDEN F, KENNON A AND MAHINDRU S (1993) Payment practices and cash flow in the UK, Germany and France, in Chittenden F, Robertson M and Watkins D (eds), Small Firms: Recession and Recovery, Paul Chapman, London.

CHITTENDEN F, KENNON A AND BRAGG R (1993) Payment Practices and Legislation in the European Community: a Comparative Study, National Westminster Bank, London.

CHITTENDEN F (1994) Tax Planning in SMEs, paper presented to the Institute for Small Business Affairs Research Conference, European Research Press, Manchester.

CURRAN J, BLACKBURN R AND WOODS A (1991) Profiles of the small enterprise in the service sector, Kingston University, May.

DEPARTMENT OF EMPLOYMENT (1992) Small Business in Britain, HMSO, London.

GANGULY P (1985) UK Small Business Statistics and International Comparisons, Ch 19, Bannock G (ed), Paul Chapman, London.

JOHNSON S AND GUBBINS A (1992) Training in small and medium-sized enterprises: lessons from North Yorkshire in Caley K, Chell E, Chittenden F and Mason C (eds) Small Enterprise Development: Policy and Practice in Action, Paul Chapman, London.

MACNABB A AND McCOY J (1992) Growth orientation and control issues from the small firm owner's perspective, paper presented to the 15th National Small Firms Policy and Research Conference, Southampton, November.

MENDHAM S, CHITTENDEN F AND POUTZIOURIS P (1994) Small Businesses and BS5750, report to the DTI, Small Business Research Trust, London.

OAKEY R (1985) British University Science Parks and High Technology Small Firms: a comment on the potential for sustained industrial growth, International Small Business Journal, 4, pp58–67.

OAKEY R (1994) (ed) New Technology-Based Firms in the 1990s, Paul Chapman, London.

SCHUMPETER J (1934) The theory of economic development, Harvard University Press, Cambridge, Massachusets.

SMALLBONE D, NORTH D AND LEIGH R (1993) Support for mature SMEs: developing a policy agenda in Chittenden F, Robertson M and Watkins D (eds) Small Firms: Recession and Recovery, Paul Chapman, London.

STANWORTH J AND GRAY C (1991) Bolton 20 Years On: The Small Firm in the 1990s, Paul Chapman, London.

STOREY D AND STRANGE A (1992) Where are they now? Some Changes in Firms Located on UK Science Parks in 1986, New Technology Work and Employment, 7, pp 15–28.

STOREY D (1993) Should we abandon support for start-up businesses?, in Chittenden F, Robertson M and Watkins D, Small Firms: Recession and Recovery, Paul Chapman, London.

WEINRICH P (1980) A manual for identity exploration using personal constructs, Social Science Research Council.

WELSH JA AND WHITE JF (1981) A small business is not a little big business, Harvard Business Review, July/August.

WESTHEAD P AND BIRLEY S (1994) Environments for business deregistrations in the UK 1987–1990, Entrepreneurship and Regional Development, forthcoming.

CHAPTER 2

Bank Lending to Unincorporated Firms in the UK, 1976–92

MICHAEL GODWIN

INTRODUCTION: THE SUPPLY OF, AND DEMAND FOR, BANK FINANCE

It would appear from existing research that, in the UK, the demand by businesses for bank finance is likely to be primarily related to short-term macro-economic conditions in the economy, rather than to long-term economic trends (1); the working capital needs of the firm are likely to be particularly important(2). In the longer term, changes in the number and profitability of small firms will also affect the demand for loans. While the attractiveness of bank finance in comparison with other sources of finance might be expected to vary over time as margins change, commercial banks provide the vast bulk of UK industrial and commercial finance.

The supply of bank loans will be limited by the availability of loanable funds and by the banks' views on prospects for the economy as a whole. The distribution of those loans between businesses of different sizes and sectors will depend partly on the banks' strategic assessment of their preferred loan portfolio and partly on their assessment of the relative quality of individual loan applications from businesses in different sector and size groups. Except for the smallest loans, banks require personal or business collateral to secure their position (3). The establishment and growth of small firms will often be constrained by whether such assets are available: in many cases, the proprietor's house will be the only pledgeable asset. Consequently, the supply of loans to finance the start-up and expansion of new small firms is likely to be influenced by the price of houses (Black et al 1992, 4). In some sectors, substantial business assets will often be available as collateral: for example, plant is often available in manufacturing and construction; in others, such as business services, this is less likely.

This paper focuses on analysing the bank borrowing behaviour of unincorporated firms, the smallest businesses in the economy. The basic econometric technique of ordinary least squares analysis is used to track borrowing over a 16-year period. The analysis provides a basis for forecasting the overall amount of bank lending to small firms. However, it does not attempt to examine the distribution of bank loans by size and sector. It is intended that size and sector issues will be examined during future work.

Chapter 2
DEFINING THE VARIABLES

The definition of 'small firms' is always problematic (Hertz, 1982, has written a whole book on the subject, 5). In this paper, it has been taken to mean 'unincorporated firms', that is to say, sole proprietor firms and partnerships. The dependent variable (BLSS) consists primarily of bank loans to unincorporated firms (i.e. sole proprietors and partnerships). It also includes lending to trades unions, universities, clubs and charities, so in theory it should be downrated to exclude loans to these non-profit bodies: but the overwhelming majority of BLSS is believed to be small business lending (6). More importantly, this definition excludes loans to small companies. A chart of VAT-registered traders by legal form and turnover (Figure 1) shows that unincorporated businesses form the majority of the smallest firms. However, there are a substantial number of small companies as well, and there is a case for uprating small firm lending to include small company loans. Unfortunately, data to do this were not available.

Unincorporated firms are thus typically small, but in aggregate they make a substantial contribution to employment. In a 1990 survey of 146 unincorporated firms advertising in the Yellow Pages (7), it was found that nearly 75% of respondent unincorporated firms employed staff: the average unincorporated firm provided 7 jobs (including owners), and the largest employed 40 people. Admittedly a sample out of the Yellow Pages will exclude the smallest 'word-of-mouth' self-employed, but it is likely that this survey identified businesses which were typical of those with substantial financing requirements. While many were in services (30%), a high proportion were in construction (25%) and distribution (25%), and as many as 1 in 8 were in manufacturing. Manufacturing and construction firms are likely to have more substantial financing requirements than service businesses, and firms in the distribution sector will often incur high financing costs in holding stocks (8).

FIGURE 1
Companies and Unincorporated Firms Registered for VAT, 1990

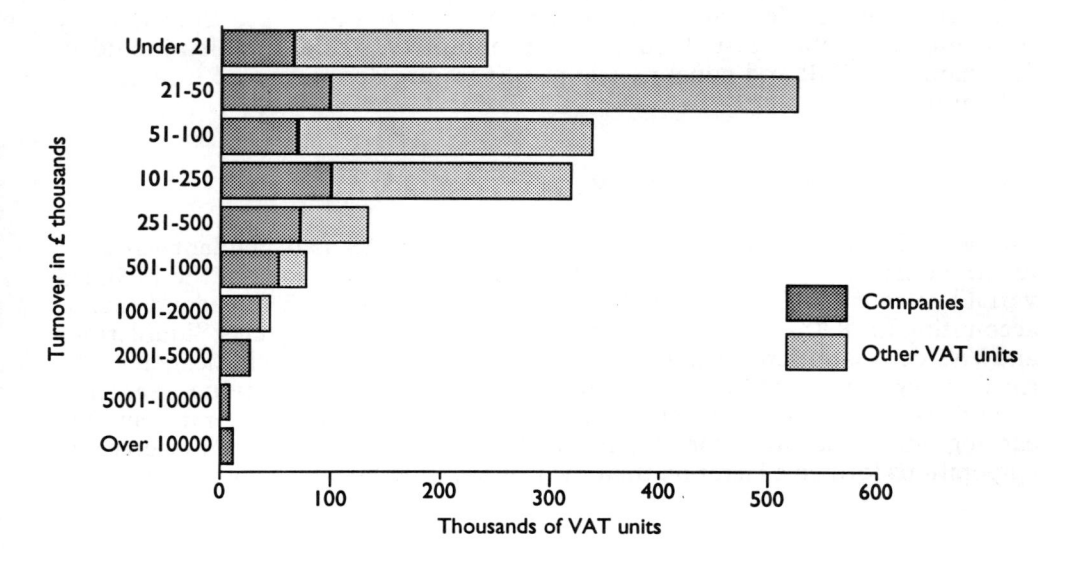

FIGURE 2
The Rise in Average Size of Loans to Unincorporated Firms

**Bank Lending to Unincorporated Firms
Average Loan Size, 1980–1990**

◇ Current prices
□ Constant prices

Analysis of the average loan per unincorporated firm 1980–90 is set out in Figure 2 (9); current price data and adjusted data in 1985 constant are shown. Both of these series show a strongly rising trend over time (£7,769 to £36,112 in current prices, £11,021 to £27,111 in 1985 prices). This increase, taken in conjunction with the growth in the number of small firms during this period, has resulted in bank lending to small firms rising from 2% to 7% of GDP.

In the list of the variables analysed, the dependent variable, bank lending to small firms, is denominated in current prices, and so are the majority of financial variables tested. Some real economic variables are also included: for example, GDP and consumer expenditure are denominated in constant 1985 prices.

EXPLORATORY FACTOR ANALYSIS

Factor analysis of these main variables, omitting BLSS as dependent variable, identified five factors: the first accounted for 69.0% of variance in the included variables: most variables loaded strongly on this factor. The second factor, accounting for 8.8% of variance, consisted mainly of bankruptcies, liquidations and VAT deregistrations; it was also negatively correlated with job vacancies. The third factor accounted for 7.7% of variance, and consisted of savings, earnings and prices variables. The fourth factor, consisting primarily of base rates and the earnings yield, accounted for a further 4.8%. Finally, credit given and received by corporations formed a factor on their own, accounting for 4.0% of variance.

It may be seen from factor analysis that GDP, Fixed Capital Formation, Real Consumer Expenditure and the various bank and building society loans variables (BLIC, BLPSH and BSTL) all load strongly on Factor 1; in other words, Factor 1 apparently links various indicators of overall economic activity (including consumption). It may thus be interpreted as representing overall economic performance. It was, however, notable that bank base rates, unemployment, and corporate credit given and received did not load significantly on this factor. The second factor is associated with business failure; and the third factor may be seen as reflecting behaviour associated specifically with changing prices. Base rates virtually form a factor of their own (although they are linked with earnings yields), as do industrial and commercial credit given and received.

Perhaps the most interesting conclusions from this analysis were that while many economic variables tended to move together over the 16-year analysis period, business failures, unemployment and, particularly, bank base rates were to some extent outside this mainstream. From the point of view of the analysis of small firm lending, this preliminary analysis gave warning that many of the independent variables would be correlated, giving rise to difficulties with multicollinearity. However, in view of the fact that nearly 70% of the variance in the independent variable dataset could be interpreted as relating to a single explanatory factor, it was essential to surmount the difficulty.

REGRESSION ANALYSIS: THE FIRST SERIES OF REGRESSIONS

A number of regression analyses were performed taking BLSS as the dependent variable. Initial attempts at regression revealed problems of non-normality using this dependent variable (9). This non-normality was caused by one unexplained peak in 1986 Quarter 2: this was assumed to be a data collection glitch, and was smoothed into the two adjacent quarters (£350m into each).

The initial analyses revealed a problem of autocorrelation. Durbin-Watson statistics were low, and residuals plots showed clear evidence of serial correlation. Attempts to use the factor scores in regression analysis foundered on these difficulties and it was decided that the main contribution that the factor scores could make was to demonstrate that many macro-economic variables were highly correlated with the dependent variable, but that this was not true of bank base rates (10). The weak correlation of small firm lending and base rates, which was repeatedly confirmed during the analysis, suggests that the banks have very little scope for influencing lending to small firms by minor interest rate adjustments.

Problems of multicollinearity and autocorrelation appeared frequently during subsequent analyses. These were tackled in a number of ways. Bankruptcies, compulsory liquidations and creditors' voluntary liquidations were found to be highly correlated with each other (Figure 3), and it was decided in view of the strong links, in both conceptual and statistical terms, between these variables, to compute one 'failure' variable which was simply the sum of bankruptcies and liquidations.

FIGURE 3
Correlations of Bankruptcies, Compulsory Liquidations and Voluntary Liquidations

Correlations:	B	CLC	CLV
B	1.0000	.8237**	.7764**
CLC	.8237**	1.0000	.9425**
CLV	.7764**	.9425**	1.0000

N of cases: 70   1-tailed Signif: * - .01   ** - .001

In order to explore the contributions of each individual variable, all variables were used in the next few analyses (except that FAILURE was used instead of B, CLC and CLV). Some equations which yielded reasonable r^2 and Durbin-Watson statistics turned out to be problematic on tests for heteroscedasticity and functional form. For example, in Equation A, the r^2 was very good at 0.998, but there were problems with heteroscedasticity. Not all of the t-statistics were significant: notably, the t-statistics for AIIZ, FAAM, GDP, BLPSH, RCE and BSTL. This is interesting because many of the less significant variables — the savings ratio, retail sales volume, bank lending to households, building society lending and consumer expenditure — relate to the consumption sector, and are thus less likely to be related to small firm credit requirements than variables such as Business Failures, Fixed Capital Formation and Bank Lending to the Industrial and Commercial Sector, which relate to the supply side of the economy (11).

Thus the primary conclusion of this first series of analyses was that small firm financing requirements do not appear to be driven by consumer behaviour. Attempts to refine the model by excluding unpromising variables encountered further problems with serial correlation. An early attempt to solve this problem was by use of an autoregressive error technique. Subsequently, lagged independent variables were also introduced into the analysis because the object was to predict bank lending, not simply to correlate it: it was therefore necessary to track the behaviour of variables over time. While this approach yielded reasonably good results, when all independent variables were lagged once to examine predictive potential in the next quarter, it was not found to be sufficiently accurate to predict quarter to quarter changes in BLSS. The general upward trend in stocks of the dependent variables caused forecasts to point continuously upwards, failing to predict the major downturn at the beginning of the 1990s.

USING DIFFERENCES IN BLSS AS THE DEPENDENT VARIABLE (CBLPSS)

To find a way round these difficulties, a differenced dependent variable was created, namely the quarterly change in BLSS, {$BLSS_t - BLSS_{t-1}$}. A second series of analyses concentrated on quarter to quarter changes, using this variable, CBLPSS, as the dependent variable, and examining it in relation to recent changes in the independent variables. In general, use of this dependent variable solved the autocorrelation problem and thus permitted the use of straightforward OLS analysis. R^2s are lower using this approach, but results seem to be more robust.

In this second batch of analyses, many variables were examined for 1, 2 and 3 preceding quarters. The most promising variables examined proved to be bank lending for previous quarters to corporations and small firms, and gross domestic fixed capital formation. A typical equation was Equation B. One factor which shows up consistently is $CGDFCF_{t-2}$. If the significance of $IBLIC_{t-1}$ is also accepted, the story is that Fixed Capital Formation went up 2 quarters ago: this in turn led to an increase in the financing requirement of large firms last quarter (12).

There was still, however, concern about serial correlation and normality with this equation. Another problem with this second batch of analyses involved multicollinearity between changes in lending to the corporate sector and in lending to small firms. All the regressions on small firm loans and loans to companies seem to show that loans to companies 'drive', or at any rate precede loans to small firms: using only the previous 3 lags of differenced lending to companies IBLIC to predict CBLPSS yields an r^2 of 0.552, whereas using the previous 3 lags of CBLPSS to predict IBLIC yields an r^2 of only 0.395. If both variables are included in regressing CBLPSS, lagged IBLIC appears significant and lagged CBLPSS does not; but if $IBLIC_{t-1}$ is omitted, $CBLPSS_{t-1}$ becomes significant. This would indicate strong multicollinearity between the two variables, although the correlation coefficient is not outstandingly high (0.74). The story is blurred by this difficulty of distinguishing between IBLIC and CBLPSS.

In any case, using lagged values of the dependent variable causes difficulties with interpreting the DW statistic, and in view of the problems of multicollinearity discovered between CBLPSS and IBLIC, it was decided to omit lagged values of the independent variable from further equations. Indeed, on further reflection, the influence of the banks' own policies on lending gave rise to concern. It seems likely that bank lending to small firms is not fully independent of other bank lending: banks will probably operate broadly similar commercial lending strategies across the board at any given time, depending on the prevailing economic conditions: all lending will tend to rise during a boom and fall during a slump. Although the time direction was right, there was some doubt about whether bank lending to industrial and commercial companies and bank lending to households were causally related to small firm bank lending – it seemed probable that they were all driven by the economic cycle. Consequently, a third series of regressions was run on bank lending to small firms omitting other bank lending altogether.

A 'TRICKLE-DOWN' INTERPRETATION OF THE DATA

It was not immediately apparent why some 'long' lags of 2 or 3 quarters should show up well on the t-statistics, while shorter lags, such as differenced gross fixed capital formation $CGDFCF_{t-1}$, do not. It was hypothesised that increased fixed capital formation 2–3 quarters ago leads quickly to an increase in bank lending to the corporate sector, which has to finance its increased investment rate. With increased fixed capital formation, corporations place more orders with small firms. Thus the investment effect 'trickles down' into small firms a quarter or two later. However, these orders are placed on credit: thus orders from corporate firms initially impose larger working capital financing requirements on unincorporated firms. Purchasing on credit is normal practice, and large firms are often in a strong position to negotiate long periods of credit for themselves; but it is worth noting that small firm working capital requirements would also be accentuated by bad paying on the part of large companies.

Conditions in the unincorporated sector may thus be seen as largely dependent on the performance of the corporate economy, from which smaller firms obtain most of their orders (either directly, or indirectly through intermediate firms). It had already been established that small firm financing requirements were not related strongly to consumer behaviour. The unincorporated sector may be seen as a reactive, price-taking sector which uses bank loans primarily to fund working capital. Thus, an upswing in investment in the corporate sector is assumed to generate more orders to smaller, ancillary firms. Small firms frequently have to agree to grant long periods of credit to their customers: and even then, they frequently encounter late payment. So, for the small firm sector at least, an increase in output is likely to increase outlay on variable costs such as wages and materials. Thus an increase in orders to small firms will initially generate a demand for increased working capital, and hence increase bank borrowing by small firms.

Further analysis investigated the introduction of bank base rates and earnings yields into an equation in addition to bank lending to large firms and fixed capital formation, using lags 1, 2 and 3 for all variables (Equation C). Results were not particularly striking, although r^2 was slightly improved from the preceding equation at 0.62, and the Durbin-Watson statistic was also improved at 1.55.

OMITTING BANK LENDING FROM THE INDEPENDENT VARIABLES

At this point in the analysis, in order to further develop the 'trickle-down' approach, attention was concentrated on the behaviour of the corporate sector, in particular, corporate gross trading profits and corporate (rather than overall) gross fixed capital formation. While the basic perspective that the main reason for small firms seeking bank finance was for working capital, it was intended that other aspects of the demand for bank lending from small firms would also be explored. However, the perspective developed in analysis series 2, that the unincorporated sector demand for bank loans was primarily to fund working capital, and that this demand was not price-sensitive, continued to be the backbone of these analyses.

It had been suggested in discussions that the main financial dimensions of small firm behaviour are profitability, liquidity and solvency. Variables were added to the database with the aim of exploring these dimensions. In particular, it was intended that the influences of startup borrowing, expansion borrowing and distress borrowing could be identified and distinguished from day-to-day working capital borrowing. There are two very distinct elements in growth of demand for credit by small firms: (a) the growth in the number of small firms, and (b) the growth of demand per firm. These two elements should be examined separately. Consequently, an attempt was made to incorporate births and deaths of firms explicitly into the model. Changes in the size of the small firm population, and to business profitability and confidence, were therefore introduced into the analysis.

Chapter 2

Business formation rates were included: the number of new VAT registrations per quarter were estimated from Customs and Excise annual data, as were deregistrations (14). House prices (considered by Black et al (1992, 15) to be the primary source of small firm collateral) were again included with the use of an average house price variable. Other variables considered for inclusion at this time included unemployment, job vacancies, the savings ratio, RPI, the raw materials index, credit given and received by corporations and real personal disposable income. It had been hoped that data on the size of bankruptcies could be found, but following the Insolvency Act changes in 1986/7, DTI no longer collect these data.

For this series of analyses, AAAS, fixed capital formation by industrial and commercial companies, was substituted for GDFCF, gross domestic fixed capital formation, on the argument that if the 'trickle-down' interpretation was correct, corporate investment would be more relevant to the small firm sector than the overall investment level. It was also felt that EY, the earnings yield, could be usefully broken down into profitability and share prices: accordingly, a gross trade profits variable (AIAO) and the FT All-share Index (AJMA) were used instead of EY (for some analyses, the 30-share index AJMT was used instead).

The number of new VAT registrations was used as an indicator of small firm formations (16). The aggregated numbers of bankruptcies and liquidations (voluntary and compulsory) were taken to proxy small firm deaths. Gross trading profits of the corporate sector and gross corporate fixed capital formation were used as indicators of corporate sector performance. The unemployment rate was assumed to influence the relative attractiveness of self-employment in comparison with job search in the employment market (17), as unemployed individuals setting up in business are especially likely to require substantial bank finance. The Financial Times All-share Index was taken as a proxy for business confidence in general. Credit received by the corporate sector was assumed to proxy credit given by the small firm sector. As before, independent variables were lagged; analysis was by ordinary least squares (OLS), and in the case of financial variables, the quarterly difference was compared, rather than the absolute stock.

Equation D uses most of these variables, selecting one time-lag only except for variables where earlier testing showed clearly that other lags were preferable. R^2, at 0.80, is considerably improved in comparison with the second set of analyses. Further analysis omitted the variables with the least promising t-statistics and concentrated on the variables set out in Figure 4.

Using only these eight variables (plus an intercept term), an r^2 of 0.79 can be obtained (Equation E). Other variables and lag periods have been tried. Most equations pass the tests for serial correlation and heteroscedasticity.

Equation E seems to be both intuitively and analytically a reliable model. However, the fact that the constant remains significant is an indication of an omitted variable. It is reasonable to argue that the All-Share index, being composed of corporate share prices, is an indicator of corporate sector confidence rather than small firm confidence, and a more representative indicator of small firm confidence was sought and added in at a late stage in the analysis. The government's longer and shorter cyclical indicators were both tested, and a two-year lag on the shorter cyclical indicator was found to perform well (Equation F), reducing the constant to insignificance. The fact that the shorter

FIGURE 4
Key Variables in the Analyses

DEPENDENT VARIABLES

CBLPSS — The quarterly difference in bank lending (£m) to the non-household personal sector, which consists mainly of unincorporated businesses.

INDEPENDENT VARIABLES

CAAAS — The quarterly change in fixed capital formation by industrial and commercial companies: positive relationship expected.

CAIAO — The quarterly change in gross trading profit (seasonally adjusted and after deduction of stock appreciation) of industrial and commercial companies in £m: positive relationship expected.

CAJMA — The quarterly change in the *Financial Times* All-share Index (1962=100): positive relationship (wrongly) expected.

CFCAX — The quarterly change in average house prices: positive relationship expected.

BCJE — The unemployment rate: positive relationship expected.

FAILURE — The sum of liquidations (compulsory and voluntary) plus bankruptcies: negative relationship expected.

NEWREGQR — New VAT registrations per quarter (estimated from Customs and Excise annual data): positive relationship expected.

SHORTER — The CSO shorter leading indicator: negative relationship expected.

INPT — A constant term.

FIGURE 5
Quarterly Changes in Bank Lending to Unincorporated Firms: Fitted Values (dotted line) and Actual Values (continuous line)

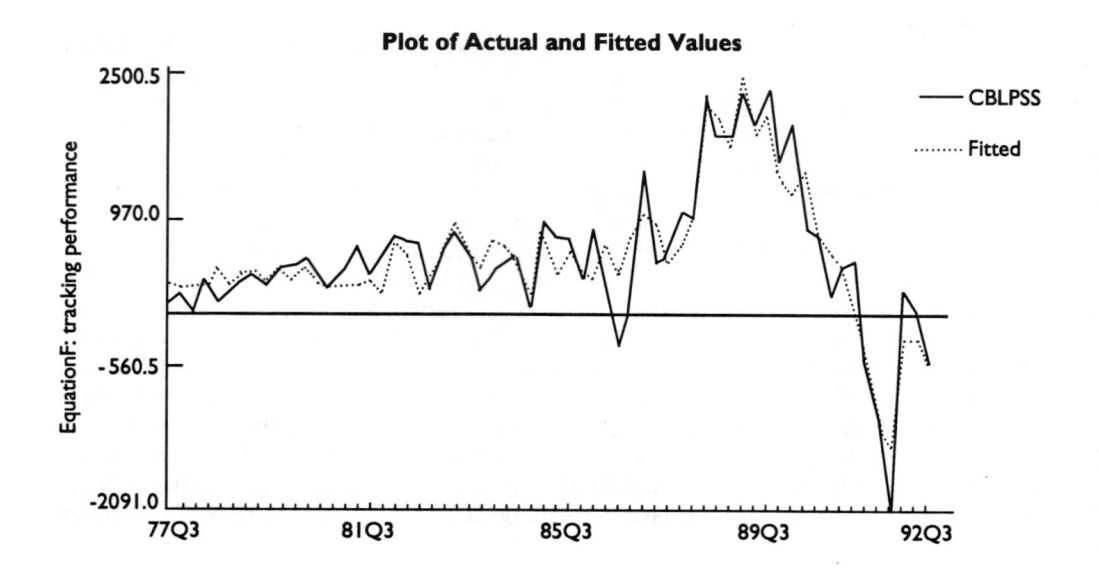

Plot of Actual and Fitted Values

FIGURE 6
Forecast Testing Four Quarters in 1992: Comparison of Forecast (dotted line) with Actual (continuous line)

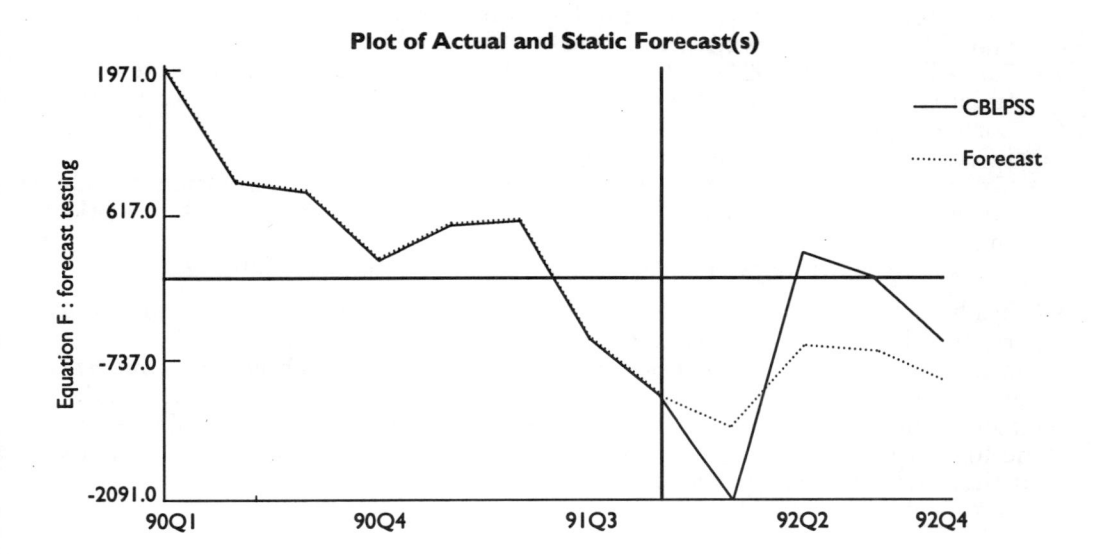

leading indicator had more influence on small firm borrowing than did the longer leading indicator again reinforces the idea that the sector is very sensitive to short-term factors (18). The strong negative coefficient on the shorter leading indicator suggests that, as with the share indices, what is being picked up here is the 'precautionary' motive for borrowing. As confidence rises, the need for 'rainy-day' balances is felt less strongly: precautionary borrowing is inversely related to cyclical expectations.

The tracking performance of Equation F is illustrated in Figure 5. Subsequently, this equation was tested for forecasting performance over the four most recent quarters (Equation G), by excluding 1992 from the analysis and then testing the predictions of changes in bank lending to unincorporated firms against actual 1992 observations. The forecast test is illustrated in Figure 6. Although the forecast fails to capture the full magnitude of the fairly violent swings in 1992, it does pick up the turning points, which is a reasonable achievement (19).

CONCLUSION

It is considered that the achievement of accounting for four-fifths of the variance in the quarterly changes in bank lending to unincorporated firms, a highly volatile series, is respectable. The model derived from the conclusions is illustrated in Figure 7. Judging by the t-statistics on Equations E and F, we may conclude that the main influences on the demand by unincorporated firms for bank credit are:

- New firm registrations, which may reflect not only optimism among new start-ups, but may also be picking up expansion plans of existing firms (20);
- Failures: the strong negative coefficient suggests that this variable is simply reflecting firm deaths rather than picking up any increase in distress borrowing;
- The unemployment rate, which reflects the increase in borrowing needs generated by redundant worker start-ups;
- The All-share index (21) and the Shorter Leading Indicator: the negative coefficients on these variables suggest that as optimism rises, precautionary borrowing falls. They may also relate to the firm's ability to generate finance internally, rather than by borrowing;
- Gross corporate trading profits, and corporate fixed capital formation, which are assumed to influence orders to small firms, and thus increase their working capital requirements;
- House prices, which will affect the amount of collateral available (22).

It has been found that for some variables, the lag structure appears strongly at a particular level (e.g. 1–2 quarters for unemployment); whereas in other cases, the lag structure is much less apparent. On failures, high correlations are obtained for 1, 2, 3 and 4 lags. These variable lag structures suggest a 'halo' effect, rather than an influence at one time-point. This could be explained by the formal failure rate being merely the focal point of a larger wave of firms cutting back on activity over several quarters.

FIGURE 7
Demand by Unincorporated Firms for Banks Credit: The Model

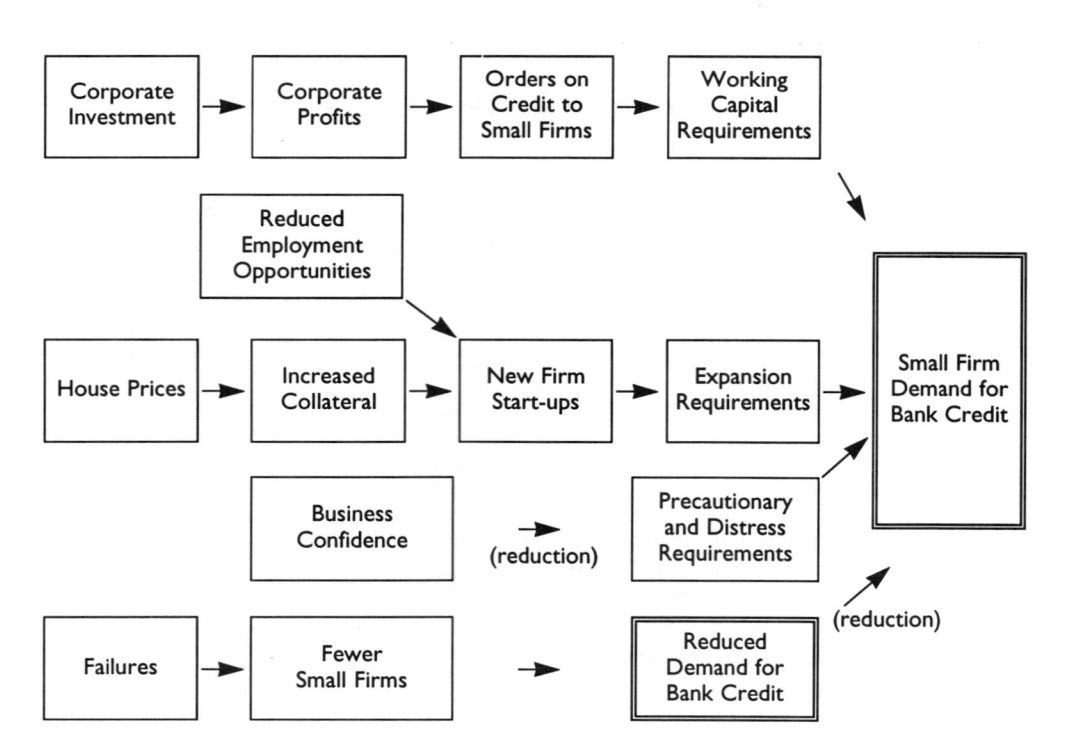

It is interesting that when the variables affecting start-ups are brought into the analysis, their contribution tends to overpower the 'trickle-down' effects found in the second series of analyses. This may be because of the unambiguous relationship between start-up and an immediate requirement for short-term finance. Nevertheless, the influence of corporate behaviour may still be observed in the presence of corporate profits and investment in the analysis: the results of the third series of analyses may be seen as amplifying, rather than negating, the results of series 2.

In conclusion, it is worth emphasising that this strong third series of explanatory analyses of quarterly changes in the level of bank borrowing by small firms was developed using macroeconomic independent variables. Variables such as bank lending to other sectors, and bank base rates, which might be expected to influence small firm bank borrowing strongly, were seldom included. Bank borrowing by the corporate sector was omitted because there were doubts about its independence from the dependent variable. However, it was perhaps surprising that the interest rate appeared to have little effect on borrowing. A further attempt to bring interest rates into the analysis was made at this late stage, using the real interest rate (i.e. bank base rate minus RPI) rather than the base rate. However, it made no improvement in the performance of the model.

It may therefore be stated with some confidence that changes in the level of borrowing by small firms are determined largely by macroeconomic conditions rather than by interest rate policy. It is possible that the level of new firm formation, which is assumed in this analysis to be influenced by house prices and unemployment, may also be affected by interest rates, and thus exert an indirect influence on bank borrowing. Similarly, the interest rate may well be among the factors which influence the level of business failures.

The findings of this analysis are consistent with the idea that small firms' demand for bank finance is driven by corporate economic performance, but is constrained by the availability of collateral. Base rates and real interest rates have little effect. New firms in particular have significant financing requirements. Small firms appear to be borrowing largely to finance working capital when they obtain orders; they require this finance regardless of current interest rates. They are also sensitive to business confidence, and tend to reduce precautionary borrowing when confidence is rising.

RECOMMENDATIONS FOR POLICY

Many small firms are dependent on large firm orders which they are obliged to accept if they want to remain in business. Both banks and large firms are more likely to be able to protect their own interests more effectively than small firms. If small firms are unable to cut back on borrowing when interest rates rise, it is to be expected (although this analysis does not confirm it) that the effect of a rise in bank interest rates will be a squeeze on their margins, since they are unlikely to be able to pass on cost increases to large customers.

Competition between banks is not sufficiently keen in the UK for small firms to find much scope for 'shopping around', and small firm business is not sufficiently valuable and risk free for them to worry about losing some small firm accounts (23). Evidence of this lack of competition is provided by Bannock and Morgan (1988, 24), who found that small firms pay up to 2.8% over 'prime rate', compared with only 2.02% for firms with 100+ employees. A number of researchers comment on the banks' lack of knowledge of small business borrowers, emphasising the 'information asymmetry' between the owner, who has detailed knowledge of the business, and the bank, which does not (25). However, it is important to note that Wynant and Hatch (1991), in an important Canadian study (26), found that owners were over-optimistic, so that asymmetric information may not necessarily imply more realistic risk assessment by owners. Binks et al (1988) (27) also criticize banks' knowledge of individual industries, banks' knowledge of client firms' markets, provision of business advice, cost of bank services and the general availability of credit. The 'hands-off' tradition appears to have resulted in a poor, low-information relationship between small business borrowers and banks.

It would appear that commercial banks do not seem to be particularly interested in the unincorporated firm sector (28). They finance it because a small percentage of these firms will grow and become valued customers; they compensate for their lack of understanding of the market by insisting on collateral for any substantial loan. Many researchers have asked why these very small firms do not seek finance elsewhere, notably through bringing in additional partners (29). Part of the explanation is that very small firms tend to be close-knit family units where independence and family control are strong business motivations. They are thus unlikely to welcome outside participation, and, in general, the returns being made are not substantial enough to attract business angels (there are exceptions). They tend to be smaller than the firms identified as being clearly in the 'equity gap' situation (30).

One of the keys to the relationship is the availability of collateral to be pledged. Typically, small-firm owners have only one major asset: the family house. Banks have also traditionally preferred collateral in the form of real property. Consequently, the price of houses is highly important to this sector. The property crash has had a substantial impact on the banks, who have been caught both by lending too heavily to such a volatile sector, and by losses on collateral for failed loans, and very small firms have been particularly hard hit by this shrinkage in the value of their main collateral asset.

So an endemic problem in the unincorporated sector is that creditworthiness is constrained by the behaviour of the domestic property market: when house prices take a tumble, banks are unwilling to extend credit. The model shows that house prices have a significant impact on borrowing: as house prices fall, so does bank borrowing by small firms. The most probable explanation of this relationship is that firms are having real problems keeping lines of credit open at a time when banks are seeking to cut back or refuse loan applications solely because of the weakness of the housing market. It is important to emphasise that this is taking place at exactly the time in the business cycle when any business expansion would be most welcome.

Small firms cannot dictate to the economy; they only expand when they see opportunities. If a loan is turned down at the particular moment when an opportunity arises, the firm either forfeits an order, or accepts it without adequate working capital and then risks getting into liquidity difficulties. Might there be a case for government intervention to offer the banks some incentive to re-schedule loans to small firms during recession years when their income is falling? One of the main losses to the economy in a recession is that all the expertise and goodwill – the human capital – which have gone into a business which fails due to a temporary cash crisis are lost. If a proportion of these firms could be tided over, the economy would benefit in the longer term, and the losses on those businesses which never returned to viability might well be outweighed by the economic gains from saving others. A system of credit guarantees could be introduced for those who, because of falling house prices, find their collateral eroded. While few would want to see extensive government interference in the working of the market, it is desirable that the government should promote a stable, secure macroeconomic environment. When firms suffer because of government failure to damp down the volatility of the property market, it seems reasonable that the government should take some action to mitigate the consequences.

NOTES

1. Burns et al (1992) found in a study of 5 major European countries that UK firms were unusually dependent on short-term finance, especially overdrafts. Smaller firms generally preferred overdraft and short-term finance: long-term loans and especially equity were thought to be relatively difficult to obtain. Binks (1991), in a critical paper on bank lending to small firms in the UK, argues that this is because the UK's 'deposit protection service' is inferior to the 'industrial banking' tradition which prevails in Germany and Japan. The lack of such a tradition in the UK results in more stringent evaluation criteria for long-term loans.
2. Moore and Threadgold (1985) argue that bank credit is needed to cover working capital: they use OLS analysis to examine the corporate sector. However, there seems no reason why Moore and Threadgold's view that the working capital needs of the firm are the main influence on its bank credit requirements should not apply to the small firm sector as much as to the corporate sector.
3. In Canada Wynant and Hatch (1991) found that 87% of small business loans involved a personal guarantee by a key principal, and 63% involved a guarantee by the principal's spouse; about one third of personal guarantees involved pledging assets. Security was not seen by the bank as a substitute for low risk, and personal guarantees were sought to prevent owners from siphoning off assets.
4. Black J, de Meza D and Jeffreys (1992) argue that because of the importance of collateral for small firms, new firm registrations are strongly influenced by the price of houses, which represent a principal source of collateral. Wynant and Hatch (1991) provide Canadian evidence which also emphasises the significance of collateral as a key factor in small firm loans, including business plant and premises as well as houses.
5. Hertz, L (1982) In Search of Small Business Definition, Washington, DC. University Press of America.
6. Financial Statistics Explanatory Handbook (1991) December.
7. Freedman J and Godwin M (1992) Legal form, tax and the micro business in Caley K, Chittenden F, Chell E and Mason C (eds) Small Enterprise Development: Policy and Practice in Action, London, Paul Chapman.
8. Chant and Walker (1988) emphasise the substitutability of trade credit for bank credit. No attempt is made in the present paper to examine trade credit, but its availability is likely to vary widely by size and sector.
9. Data on number of unincorporated businesses are derived from Department of Employment (Daly 1991). These data exclude firms which are not registered for VAT, so they will overstate loans to some extent.
10. Non-normality disrupts the t-statistics; 'this assumption is fundamental to hypothesis testing' (Ramanathan, p 87). Because a and b depend on the Ys, which in turn depend on the random Us, they are also random variables with associated distribu-

tions. Estimates of a and b are obtained by way of linear combinations of the residuals (Us): if the Us are non-normal, a and b are non-normal: hence the t-tests are disrupted. OLS is still the most consistent and efficient (best) unbiased linear estimator 'BLUE' without this property; however, it is not also the Maximum Likelihood Estimator (MLE) when U is non-normal.
11. More extensive analysis, including the details of the intermediate equations, is contained in an earlier report. However, this report only analyses data to the end of 1991.
12. It is believed that the non-significant t-statistic for house prices in Equation A results from the 'masking' effect of the presence of these less relevant variables.
13. A criticism of this interpretation is that the strong relationship between fixed capital formation (GDFCF) and bank lending to industrial and commercial companies (BLIC) (r=0.955) makes it confusing to interpret analysis which involves both of these variables. However, the temporal order seems clear, with fixed capital formation tending to rise before corporate bank borrowing.
14. Data specifically on unincorporated VAT registrations are not available for the whole period of the analysis, but they form the majority of VAT registered firms. Between 1980 and 1990, unincorporated firms constituted 69.2% of the register on average. Data on VAT registrations and company registrations are only available on an annual basis. In consequence, the quarterly figures have been interpolated.
15. op. cit.
16. In fact many small firms operate below the VAT threshold, but little data are available on these micro-firms. Quarterly VAT registration estimates were interpolated from annual data. The overwhelming majority of new registrations are small firms. The VAT threshold is uprated regularly but during the period under analysis was kept roughly constant in real terms. A large hike in the threshold in 1991-2 has subsequently resulted in a significant fall-off in registrations and an increase in deregistrations.
17. As argued by Schumpeter (1939).
18. The shorter leading indicator is composed of five factors: change in real consumer credit (£m, 1985 prices); real gross trading profits of companies (£m, deflated); new car registrations (thousands); change in new industrial orders during the past four months (% balance); and expected change in stocks of materials (% balance).
19. Unfortunately the analysis does not pass Chow's second test for predictive failure. Earlier forecast testing on 1991 data had been more successful, presumably because the data were more stable than those for 1992.
20. It should again be emphasised that the use of VAT registration data in this model was based on annual data: so the use of these equations in actual forecasting would necessitate the use of quarterly VAT registration data, which exist but are not generally available.
21. In all instances of unexpected signs, several different lags were tested, and the negative signs appeared consistently.
22. An attempt was made to use the value of housing equity instead, taking the total value of residential buildings minus housing loans from building societies and banks: but the resulting variable was only available up to the end of 1990, and correlated so closely with FCAX that it was not used.
23. Binks et al (1989) found that the similarity in the responses for each bank is dramatic, and that this is more easily explained as cartel-like behaviour than as competitive behaviour. Although Competition and Credit Control nominally abolished the bank cartel in 1971, corporate inertia has actually left the cartel mentality intact.
24. Bannock G and Morgan EV (1988) Banks and Small Business: An International Perspective, Forum of Private Business, Knutsford.
25. Burns et al (1992) found that companies' relationships with lenders were good, although in Britain lenders were not seen as having a good knowledge of the industries and markets in which borrowers operated. They point out that this information asymmetry could be a cause of the small firm finance gap, as argued by Stiglitz and Weiss (1981).

26. Wynant and Hatch (1991) found that owners were unable to view their own prospects objectively; interviews with owners and their accountants discovered that the vast majority of owners were 'overly optimistic', despite not having adequate business plans or financial management; this was particularly true of the value of business assets pledged as security. Nominally, security usually exceeds the value of the loan, but asset values are often subject to 'shrinkage' on the failure of a business. Many assets realised far below stated values, and in combination with legal and other wind-up costs, meant that the recovery rate on failed loans was as low as 64% of outstanding loans and interest.
27. Binks et al (1988) argue that a closer relationship, with more information flowing between borrower and bank, would enable banks to offer better advice, which in turn would facilitate 'income-prospects' based lending, making loan conditions more flexible.
28. 'Past experience with problem accounts has caused some account managers to view small businesses as high-risk customers that require considerable effort to monitor and manage, but generate little profit for the bank', Wynant and Hatch (1991).
29. Equity finance is not available to unincorporated firms.
30. Wynant and Hatch (1991) found that many small businesses were reluctant to seek outside equity, expecting it to be prohibitively expensive and restrictive on their independence. 'It was clear that most small business managers have a very limited familiarity with the potential sources of equity funds and would be unable to fully evaluate the costs and benefits of an equity capital proposal.'

ACKNOWLEDGEMENTS

Acknowledgements are due to NatWest, who awarded the fellowship under which this research was carried out; to Dr Premchander of Bangalore Institute of Management, who carried out the initial groundwork for the project; and to Professor Doug Wood at MBS, who provided much stimulating guidance and discussion on project issues. All analysis in this paper is based on published data from Economic Trends, Financial Statistics, and the VAT register. The data were analysed on the regression package Microfit. Remaining omissions, errors and misinterpretations are all the responsibility of the author.

REFERENCES

BANK OF ENGLAND (1993) Bank lending to small businesses, Bank of England Quarterly Bulletin, February.

BANNOCK G AND MORGAN EV (1988) Banks and Small Business: An International Perspective, London: Forum of Private Business.

BINKS MR (1991) Small businesses and their banks in the year 2000, in Paths of Enterprise, Curran J and Blackburn R, (eds) London: Routledge.

BINKS MR, ENNEW CT AND REED GV (1988) Survey by the Forum of Private Business of Banks and Small Firms, London: Forum of Private Business.

BINKS MR, ENNEW CT AND REED GV (1989) Small Businesses and Banks: an Interbank Comparison, London: Forum of Private Business.

BLACK J, DE MEZA D AND JEFFREYS D (1992) House prices, the supply of collateral and the enterprise economy, unpublished paper.

BURNS P, BURNETT A, MYERS A AND CAIN D (1992) Attitudes of smaller firms towards financing and financial institutions in Europe, Cranfield.

CHANT EM AND WALKER DA (1988) Small business demand for trade credit, Applied Economics, 20, 861–876.

DALY M (1991) VAT registrations and deregistrations in 1990, Employment Gazette, November, revised in Bannock G and Daly M (1994) (eds) Small Business Statistics, London: Paul Chapman.

DAVIES E P (1994) Bank credit risk, forthcoming Bank of England Working Paper.

DEWHURST J AND BURNS P (1983) Small business finance and control, London: Macmillan.

FREEDMAN J AND GODWIN M (1992) Legal Form, Tax and the Micro Business, in Caley K, Chittenden F, Chell E and Mason C (eds) Small Enterprise Development: Policy and Practice in Action, Paul Chapman.

HARRISON R AND HART M (1983) Factors influencing new business formation: a case study of Northern Ireland, Environment and Planning, A, vol 15, pp 1395–1412.

HERTZ L (1982) In Search of a Small Business Definition, Washington DC: University Press of America.

HUDSON J (1989) The birth and death of firms, Quarterly Review of Economics and Business, 29, 2, Summer, pp 68–86.

HUDSON J (1987) Company births in Great Britain and the institutional environment, International Small Business Journal, 6, 1, Autumn, pp 57–69.

HUTCHINSON RW AND MCKILLOP DG (1992) Banks and Small to Medium Sized Business Financing in the UK, NatWest Bank Quarterly Review, Feb.

JOHNSON P (1986) New firms – an economic perspective, London: Allen & Unwin.

LOVELL R (1983) Review of Economics and Statistics, February, p1 ff.

MOORE BJ AND THREADGOLD A R (1985) Corporate Bank Borrowing in the UK, 1965–81, Economica, 52, 65–78.

NEDC REPORT Lending to Small Firms (1986) Committee of Finance for Industry, London.

ROBSON MT (1991) Self-employment and new firm formation, Scottish Journal of Political Economy, vol 38, no 4, November, pp 352–368.

SCHUMPETER JA (1939) in Business Cycles, New York: McGraw Hill.

STIGLITZ J AND WEISS A (1981) Credit rationing in markets with imperfect information, American Economic Review, vol 71, pp 393–410.

WYNANT L AND HATCH J (1991) Banks and small business borrowers, London, Ontario: Western Business School, University of Ontario.

YAO-SU HU (1984) Industrial Banking and Special Credit Institutions, London: Policy Studies Institute.

CHAPTER 3

The Equity Gap in the East Midlands: An Initial Assessment of the Operation of a New Venture Capital Fund

GRAHAME BOOCOCK, MARGARET WOODS
AND KEVIN CALEY

INTRODUCTION

This paper revisits a long-standing debate relating to the workings of the financial sector and the alleged lack of long-term external funds for small and medium sized enterprises (SMEs), the 'equity gap'. The setting up and initial operation of a new venture capital fund, the Midland Enterprise Fund for the East Midlands, provides the focus for a discussion of key issues affecting SMEs, the financial community and policy makers alike.

The analysis is based on research undertaken by staff from Loughborough University. The team were given the opportunity to monitor the operation of a new, independently managed venture capital fund, and this paper presents the findings of the first stage of the research. The findings are based on the enquiries and applications to the Midland Enterprise Fund for the East Midlands (MEF) during the first nine months of its life.

METHODOLOGY

The researchers were given free access to study and record information on both general enquiries and formal applications to the venture capital fund. In addition, details of the investment appraisal process used by the fund manager were made available.

Information relating to all parties making enquiries, and those submitting formal applications for funding was collected in two different ways:

1. A questionnaire was distributed, as an insert in the fund brochure, to all telephone enquirers requesting further information on the fund.
2. Summary data was prepared on all business plans received by the fund, together with the progress of the application through the MEF appraisal process.

The paper which follows summarises our findings from this base data (1).

Analysis of the types of companies requesting further information on the MEF, and those businesses applying for finance reveals a number of issues of importance to the financial community and government policy makers.

Firstly, the number of general enquiries suggests that small businesses are anxious to tap into any new sources of funds available. Furthermore, there is a general level of dissatisfaction with the current funding options available to SMEs. There are indications that there is a high level of pent-up demand for small scale equity finance. The number of investment opportunities that such demand represents indicates that there is potentially a real, as well as a perceived, equity gap. This can only be confirmed by a longitudinal study of both successful and unsuccessful applicant companies.

Secondly, the quality of the business plans submitted was generally quite low. This is not necessarily indicative of the quality of the underlying business, as we discuss later, but does suggest a lack of management training, and a need for assistance in preparation of key data. There is a potentially very important role to be played by the TECs in this regard.

Finally, in seeking to make small investments which offer commercial rates of return, a fund manager faces problems of potentially high costs in appraising funding applications, and a risk that normal due diligence processes are excessively time consuming. The time scale for decision making in SMEs is often much shorter than that in larger concerns, so that 'excessive' due diligence work could lead to the loss of potentially good investment opportunities. This risk has to be traded against that of unsuccessful investments. The implication of such problems is that there is a potential role to be played by public bodies in subsidising the costs of commercial funds, because there is a beneficial pay-off to the economy from the employment and income generating effects of SMEs.

BACKGROUND

For over 60 years successive governments have commissioned reports which, either explicitly or as part of a wider study of a related area, have addressed the question of whether small and medium sized enterprises (SMEs) suffer inequalities in the market for finance [inter alia: MacMillan, 1931; Radcliffe, 1959; Bolton, 1971; Wilson, 1979; DTI/Aston Business School, 1991]. There have also been numerous contributions on this issue from academics, practitioners, quasi-government bodies and powerful SME lobby groups.

These reports and articles have almost invariably concluded that inequalities in funding do exist, inequalities which essentially stem from two factors: SMEs have a greater risk of failure compared to larger, well-established companies; and the appraisal costs of providing smaller amounts of finance are relatively high. However, the scale of the problem arising from these inequalities, particularly the size and impact of any equity gap, remains the subject of debate.

The equity gap could exist in perceived or real terms. Previous research in this field has acknowledged the perception that SMEs are being denied access to equity finance which is more generally available to larger concerns. However, it has proved difficult to isolate any real gap, in the form of the explicit denial of funding to commercially viable companies – confirmed by the recent authoritative study by the University of Cambridge (1992).

The one area of agreement amongst researchers is that high technology firms suffer more than conventional SMEs in the market for funds (ACOST, 1990; DTI/Aston Business School, op cit).

This paper describes the initial stages of a research project which seeks to measure more precisely the extent of any equity gap in the East Midlands, in both perceived and real terms.

THE UK MARKETS FOR RISK CAPITAL

Since the early 1980s, the nature of the financial support available to SMEs, from both private and public sources, has been subject to considerable change.

In the private sector, the major clearing banks have significantly increased the amount of funds channelled to SMEs. The banks' emphasis on the provision of short-term facilities had been criticised by Wilson (op cit); since then, much of the borrowing has been granted on more flexible repayment terms. The recent controversies over the treatment of SMEs by the UK clearers have been well documented, but the basic proposition that traditional bank facilities should not be classed as risk capital has never been in dispute.

Alongside the growth in conventional bank finance, the supply of venture capital expanded at a tremendous rate over the decade to 1990. Statistics produced by the British Venture Capital Association (BVCA) reveal that investment in the UK peaked at £1.4bn in 1989, declined to £1.1bn in 1990 and £1.0bn in 1991, but recovered to £1.25bn (2) in 1992.

The BVCA, in its latest annual report (BVCA, 1993), stated that:

'Notwithstanding the recession, venture capitalists have successfully identified many investment opportunities, and the industry remains well placed to provide significant support to UK businesses as the economic situation improves.'

However, critics consider that the UK venture capital industry has moved away from its original ethos of providing patient money to high risk enterprises.

The average financing received by investee companies over recent years has been in excess of £0.7m; for 1992, the figure was £0.95m. Whilst start-up and other early-stage deals showed the lowest average size of financing, at £0.33m and £0.43m respectively, these categories accounted for only 6% of the total amount invested by BVCA members. Furthermore, investments generally tend to be in 'safe' industrial sectors; only 4% of the amount invested went into the computer and electronics-related sectors, and a substantial proportion of the industry's funds are committed to management buy-outs.

In the public sector, government initiatives since 1979 have attempted to remove or compensate for market imperfections. The government is determined to intervene only when the private sector markets fail to meet the legitimate funding needs of SMEs. For example, the Business Expansion Scheme (BES) has been scrapped, on the grounds that the venture capital sector now meets the equity needs of SMEs (a proposition disputed in this paper); by contrast, the Loan Guarantee Scheme (LGS) was relaunched in the 1993 Finance Act – the government clearly feels that high risk, yet viable, propositions are being turned away from the banks (3).

Despite the evolving nature of both private and public support measures for SMEs outlined above, it is still widely claimed that a shortage of long-term finance (equity and/or loans) exists at the lower end of the financing spectrum, especially for amounts of below £250,000.

THE EAST MIDLANDS

The five counties comprising the East Midlands are: Leicestershire (Leics); Derbyshire; Nottinghamshire (Notts); Lincolnshire; and Northamptonshire.

The industrial base of the region as a whole is strongly diversified. Its key industrial sectors include metals, minerals, chemicals, engineering, textiles, footwear, food processing and printing. There is also a considerable amount of agriculture, as well as a growing services sector, particularly firms connected with the leisure/tourist field. The region is not noted for expertise in the high tech sphere, although some pockets of activity are emerging.

Whilst there are some very large home-grown concerns, such as Boots and Rolls Royce, they do not dominate the local economy. Investment by overseas-based multinationals has been minimal, until the arrival of Toyota at Derby. The economic performance of the region is thus heavily dependent upon activity in the SME sector, typically firms operating in the more traditional manufacturing industries.

For external funding, SMEs in the region tend to rely upon the major clearing bank groups, not just for overdrafts and loans, but also for hire purchase, leasing and factoring. There is also close co-operation between the banks and suppliers of risk finance; funding packages are often syndicated.

With regard to venture capital, of the £1.25bn invested by BVCA members in 1992, only £88m (7% of the total) was invested in businesses located within the East Midlands. If the level of investment is compared to the number of VAT registered businesses in the region, investment activity in the East Midlands is below average (BVCA, 1993, op cit). There is no major independent fund based in the region and the existing supply of venture capital is dominated by the 3i Group, in the shape of its Leicester and Nottingham offices.

Compared to the venture capital industry as a whole, 3i has traditionally been more active at the lower end of the financing spectrum and it is prepared to invest in a greater number of early-stage deals; around 40% of its investments in 1992/3 were for amounts below £150,000, although these accounted for only 5.5% of the total sum invested by the group (3i, 1993). In practice, the fixed costs associated with the appraisal of applications seeking below, say, £100,000 deter many potential investee companies.

In an effort to counter the latter problem, 3i's 'Core Capital' scheme was launched during 1991. Aimed at potentially high growth firms, the scheme provides equity capital in amounts of up to £250,000. The use of standardised application forms keeps appraisal costs to a minimum and external investigation of the company's business plan is not required. Only a modest number of transactions had taken place in the East Midlands under this initiative by the summer of 1993.

Although the broad thrust of government policy has been to reject the direct funding of SMEs, firms in the East Midlands can still find direct funding from (quasi) public sector bodies within the region. British Coal (Enterprises) Ltd

(BCE) invests alongside conventional lenders to create jobs in the former coal mining areas; similarly, Nottinghamshire County Council provides loan facilities where job creation/preservation forms part of the investment criteria used.

Indirect government measures available to SMEs in the region include the LGS and the BES. For many years, the former was little used in the East Midlands; bankers were wary of using a facility which had seen a high rate of failure of LGS-assisted companies in the early 1980s. Over the past three years, utilisation of the scheme in the region has revived, contrary to national trends. Even so, only 315 guarantees, totalling £6.3m, were issued for the whole of the East Midlands and Eastern Region in the twelve months to March 1993 (figures supplied by the Department of Trade and Industry).

Likewise, the amount raised under the BES is minimal. For the 1991/2 tax year, a total of £15m was invested in the region (Inland Revenue, 1993); however, this figure was almost entirely committed to investments in assured tenancies, rather than high risk enterprises.

From our discussions with representatives of the local financial community, government bodies and SMEs, the consensus of opinion is that the funding avenues for small businesses in the East Midlands have undoubtedly improved and that the local financial markets function reasonably efficiently. The perception remains, however, that some genuine requests for external finance are being denied.

THE NEW VENTURE CAPITAL FUND

As President of Business in the Community, HRH The Prince of Wales set up a working party to devise a suitable means of delivering expansion capital in a cost effective manner. In 1991, as a result of this initiative, Midland Bank plc announced its intention to invest in, and to co-ordinate, a network of 11 regional enterprise funds (see McMeekin, 1991).

The Midland Enterprise Fund for the East Midlands (MEF) was one of the first of these funds seeking to demonstrate that it is possible to make small investments (less than £125,000) and produce the level of returns required to attract institutional investors. To do this it is necessary to establish a low cost way of identifying, vetting, completing and monitoring suitable investments to ensure that such investments can be commercially viable. MEF is managed by a new, independent company, Midland Venture Fund Managers Limited, and the investors include Midland Bank, Lincolnshire TEC and a number of individuals. Investors have no say in the investment policy of MEF or of individual investments.

The initial objective was to establish a network of regional funds each with £3m to £5m of capital but severe difficulties were experienced with fund raising due to:

1. The lack of a successful track record in managing a fund of this type for profit and the general belief amongst institutional investors that it could not be done.
2. The small size of the individual funds compared with the minimum investments that large institutional investors were prepared to bother with.
3. The effect of the Maxwell affair on the willingness of smaller pension fund trustees to make relatively high risk investments.

The outcome of the initial fund-raising efforts by the 11 funds starting in November 1991 was that only two funds were able to attract any significant funding (Yorkshire and Humberside and the East Midlands) and they were launched in October 1992 with around £1.5m each.

Subsequently Midland Bank have promoted the establishment of the remaining funds during 1993 and seven regions have raised sufficient monies to ensure that there is adequate finance available for all viable projects. The remaining two funds are still awaiting confirmation of adequate levels of financial support from their local communities.

The East Midlands Fund makes investments of up to £125,000 in businesses located in the five counties of the East Midlands. It is structured as a limited partnership with a life of ten years, with the capital being drawn down from investors in four equal annual instalments. It is planned to make the investments in the first five years.

Investee companies must be capable of rapid growth and because the investment is in the form of a shareholding, with no security, MEF shares the risks (and the rewards) with the other shareholders. This has a significant effect upon the relationship between MEF and the investee company since MEF cannot call in its investment if difficulties arise and the potential to share in the profits means that MEF is committed to maximising the success of the business.

INITIAL ENQUIRIES TO THE FUND

A short questionnaire was distributed to those contacting the MEF, by telephone or letter, in the first five months of its operation (4). These enquiries were therefore mainly 'off the street' rather than via bankers, accountants or other intermediaries. Of 190 questionnaires distributed, 59 were completed and returned, a response rate of 31%. The responses allowed us to build a profile of the types of businesses making enquiries. This profile is detailed below.

The vast majority of enquiries (75%) came from limited companies, and the products or services supplied covered many categories. The main category was the provision of services, which accounted for 37% of respondents. This category included firms engaged in property maintenance, training, various forms of consultancy, project management and security. Consumer related manufacturing was the second most important area of business (19%). It was no surprise that there were no enquiries from SMEs operating in the traditional manufacturing industries of the region, such as textiles and clothing.

Young businesses accounted for the bulk of enquiries, with 36% being start ups or firms with less than twelve months trading record. A further 35% were less than five years old, and of these many were between twelve and twenty-four months of age. This age profile suggests that the propositions tend to be high risk, and largely outside the remit of established businesses required by the fund managers, who have limited start-up investments to 15% of their portfolio.

Turnover levels were on average low, as was to be expected given the age profile of applicants. A summary is shown in Table 1.

With the majority of the figures being concentrated in the lower turnover bands, the implication is that modest profit levels are currently being achieved.

TABLE 1
Turnover Levels of Questionnaire Respondents

TURNOVER £000 LAST FINANCIAL YEAR	NO.	%
New company	11	19
Not yet produced audited a/c	12	20
0–99	8	14
100–249	9	15
250–499	7	12
500–999	4	7
1m–5m	8	13
5m–plus	0	0

The return available to a venture fund depends to some extent on the uses to which an investment will be put. We asked respondents to identify and rank the three main areas to which the funding would be applied. Table 2 shows a summary of the responses given.

The need for increased investment in working capital to support growth in sales is evident. The emphasis on service sector companies, as mentioned earlier, suggests that for the sample as a whole, the tangible assets to secure external funding would be of limited value. Hence venture capital is more appropriate than bank finance.

Expansion almost invariably requires investment in fixed assets, but there is also a need for funds to support marketing, employing additional sales staff, market research and R & D.

TABLE 2
Proposed Uses of Venture Funding

	TOTAL	1ST	2ND	3RD
Premises	23	6	9	8
Plant and m/c	35	13	11	11
Other assets	2	2		
Research/dev't	13	5	4	4
Marketing	30	7	14	9
Working capital	51	24	12	15
Repayment of existing borrowing	15	3	5	7
Other (both MBOs)	2	1		1

The repayment of other borrowing lines will rarely find favour with investors – can sufficient growth be generated by replacing one source of funding with another?

Funding requirements from the venture capital fund varied widely. Comments such as 'not assessed as yet' and 'the maximum possible' were also noted. In fact 14% of respondents had not quantified their requirements, suggesting that firms are casting around for funds with no clear idea of how future operations will be financed.

There was a predominance of requests in the £50,000–75,000 range. For investments of this size, especially where MEF is asked to provide 100% of the finance required, an investee company will fail to generate the growth required to yield a satisfactory return unless there are exceptional circumstances. However, if MEF could attract other funding bodies to a proposition, then a modest investment might enable syndication of a more substantial investment programme.

The need to involve other suppliers of funds also applies to those firms seeking to raise the maximum investment level (£125,000) from the fund.

COMMENTS ON EXISTING SOURCES OF FINANCE

Of the 59 firms in the sample, 45 had sought funds from other sources, as indicated in Table 3.

TABLE 3
Other Sources of SME Finance Approached by Applicants

SOURCES APPROACHED	NUMBER
Bank loan	22
Hire purchase/leasing	4
Finance co.	2
Venture capital	27
Other	13
Total	68

The total of 68 approaches from the 45 firms gives an average of approximately 1.5 per respondent. The other 14 firms in the sample had not (yet) sought funds from other sources. A number of firms took the opportunity to comment on their experiences with other financial institutions.

The banks were seen as generally supportive, without being risk takers. Specific criticisms centred on the banks' insistence upon tangible security cover, a problem exacerbated by the heavy discounting of assets held under a standard bank debenture.

The difficulty of raising small amount of venture capital was frequently mentioned; the 27 attempts to raise venture capital had almost invariably failed. In addition, three firms had approached private investors for assistance.

The funding sources in the 'other' category included all of the direct and indirect government sources identified in this paper.

The modest investment limit of MEF meant that a large number of firms sought 100% finance for the proposed expansion programme. Three firms were actually seeking more than the cost of their proposed investment programme, presumably to bolster a weak balance sheet and/or to repay other lenders. Both approaches suggest a degree of naivety in the enquiry.

The overall picture of businesses making enquiries to the fund is one of small, high risk ventures (frequently start ups). Such companies lack the security backing required by the banks, and management is to some extent unsure of the total funding needs. A scenario such as this might be said to indicate that there is no equity gap, because it suggests a lack of high quality investment opportunities. To analyse this issue further, summary information was prepared with respect to applications for funding, ie business plans.

THE BUSINESS PLANS

The rapid expansion that can be generated by a one-off large injection of equity is attractive to managers of SMEs who are otherwise faced with a choice of growth funded by debt – a potentially risky strategy – or re-invested profits, which is a relatively slow route to growth.

This means that it is to be expected that small companies will quickly seize on any opportunities to obtain equity finance. This is exactly what we found in our observations of the establishment of a new venture fund. What we also saw, however, was that opportunities were rapidly lost by poor preparation of the funding application.

In order to attract investors, MEF must ensure that the overall return on investments is at a commercial rate. Commercial viability of a business is thus the starting point for appraisal, but another key requirement is growth potential. Funds must be released and reinvested elsewhere on a regular basis, and a five-year time scale for realisation of an investment is not unrealistic. High rates of growth are also required to compensate for the losses on less successful investments. When these requirements are combined, the business plan is used as the starting point for assessing the commercial future of an enterprise.

The reasons for rejection of applications are useful indicators of the investment criteria being used by the fund managers and also reveal issues which need to be addressed in the training of entrepreneurs. We can look at each of the grounds for rejection in a little more detail (Table 4).

TABLE 4
Applications for Venture Capital Funds First Six Months of Fund Life

GROUNDS FOR REJECTION OF APPLICANTS	NUMBER
Incomplete Plan	30
Insufficient Growth Potential	18
Limited Market Size	15
Inappropriate Project Size (for fund)	14
Start up Business	12
Lack of Unique Selling Point	12
Management Skills/Commitment	12
Excessively High Risk	12
Applications Withdrawn	9
Level of Competition	8
Weak B/Sheet or Poor Margins	11
History of Failure	6
Other	11
Total Reasons for Rejection	170
Total Number of Applications	97
Average Number of Reasons Per Applicant	1.75

INCOMPLETE PLANS

The single most important reason for rejection of an application was submission of an 'incomplete plan'. This is somewhat surprising as all telephone enquirers were sent a leaflet which stated that 'applications can only be accepted in the form of a comprehensive business plan'. The term comprehensive was then defined as a plan demonstrating:

good market opportunities for growth, management skills to exploit such opportunities and a financial structure adequate to fund the required resources.

This implies a need for a plan which drafts a clear and full picture of the business and illustrates the potential investment opportunities available.

The common types of omissions that generated the description 'incomplete plan' included:

- lack of market data
- poor information on competitors
- directors' CVs.

One example was a plan describing the market for its products as 'all shops'.

The problem that such plans represent for the fund manager is that he/she is unable to identify the real potential of a business due to lack of information. For fear of the worst, and because of the volume of plans to be considered, the plan is rejected on the grounds of excessive risk.

In an attempt to improve the overall quality of the plans received, MEF have now compiled a set of guidance notes on preparing a business plan, and a copy of these notes is sent out to all enquirers.

An important discovery from our appraisal of plans was that those submitted via intermediaries were usually of a higher quality than those coming direct from applicants. This suggests that intermediaries are fulfilling two useful functions: firstly, in selecting out the companies suitable for venture funding, and secondly, in monitoring the plan preparation process to ensure the application is of a high quality. The TECs could play a very valuable role here, in offering advice and training to companies assembling a business plan for a funding application, and a number of TECs are beginning to become increasingly involved in this area viz the sponsorship by Walsall TEC of the notes on preparing a business plan circulated by MEF.

MARKETING

Market potential is of prime significance to the equity investor, as it forms the basis for the accumulation of capital gain on the investment. The value of the equity will rise by reinvestment of profit and, using traditional finance theory, the present value of the future earnings stream will be the key determinant of corporate worth.

A target rate of return of 25–30% compound is not unusual for a venture capital fund. Successful investee companies must exhibit very high growth potential to compensate for the inevitable failed investments. This means that an emphasis on outstanding market potential is largely a consequence of the investment returns required by the fund.

The importance of market and market related issues to a successful application can be extrapolated from Table 4 (Table 5).

In other words, 67% of all applications were rejected on the grounds of market limitations. The rejection was not simply on the grounds of a lack of ABSOLUTE potential, but poor market research and strategic thinking which might facilitate an increase in potential. The fund management made comments on the inadequacies of background market research in support of business plans. Comments as simple as 'the market is vast' were not particularly unusual.

TABLE 5
Market Related Factors as a Basis for Rejection of Applications for Venture Capital

REASON FOR REJECTION	NUMBER OF APPLICANTS
Limited Growth Potential	18
Inadequate Market Size	15
Start up Business (unproven market)	12
Lack of Unique Selling Point	12
Level of Competition	8
Total	65

RISK

Reformulating the data from Table 4 in terms of elimination of obvious risk to the fund, we get the results shown in Table 6.

TABLE 6
The Influence of Non-Market Risk Factors on the Decision to Reject Funding Applications

REASONS FOR REJECTION	NUMBER OF APPLICANTS
Excessively High Risk	12
Weak B/sheet or Poor Margins	11
History of Failure (management)	6
Total	29

Note that this excludes start ups as a risk factor, but still means that 30% of rejections are risk related. If start ups are included in the definition of risk, the rejection rate rises to 40%.

The risk is primarily financial, with applicant businesses earning very low net margins, or overtrading. Both such difficulties imply bad management. At the extreme, the accounts submitted by two companies showed them to be insolvent.

THE MANAGEMENT TEAM

Quality of management helps to alleviate investor risk, and ensure the fulfilment of a business' true potential. Measures of management quality used by the MEF fund manager included skill mix, team spirit, market understanding and commitment to the company. Twelve applications (12%) were rejected on the grounds of inadequate management, and so on the basis of the data we have analysed, this factor is significantly less important than the market potential.

To summarise: the single most important cause of rejection in applying to MEF for venture capital was the submission of an 'incomplete' or 'inadequate' business plan. Further analysis shows three key requirements in applicant businesses: market potential, financial resources and management skills. If the plans rejected are ranked by frequency of occurrence of these rejection criteria the resulting order is:

- Marketing
- Financial Risk
- Management.

Study of the business plans, and an analysis of the potential investment opportunities they presented to MEF allowed us to second check the characteristics of applicant businesses. The questionnaire suggested that the typical profile for an applicant revealed small high risk businesses, with low security backing and a management uncertain of funding needs.

The business plan data reveals many companies unable to draw up high quality business plans, and trading in markets with inadequate growth potential. Knowledge of these characteristics is useful as a pointer to the need for better entrepreneurial training. Nonetheless, all such features are typical of SMEs in any region of the UK, and on their own are insufficient to generate any conclusions in relation to the presence of a real equity gap.

IS THERE AN EQUITY GAP IN THE EAST MIDLANDS?

In using the applications to MEF as a base against which to measure the existence of an equity gap in the East Midlands we devised a framework for appraisal of the commercial viability and suitability of funding applications. The first element in the framework was the appraisal procedure adopted by MEF managers.

The need was to assess how many (if any) SMEs that offered good investment opportunities were being denied access to equity finance. The MEF applications offered an ideal sample on which to base any such judgement because it represented the primary source of such funds for SMEs in the East Midlands area.

One problem posed by such an analysis is the potential subjectivity involved in judging the commercial prospects of a business. Nevertheless, standardised procedures and measures can be used in the appraisal process. Table 6a indicates the procedure followed by MEF management, together with the expected levels of rejection at each stage in the process.

In other words, the expectation is that only 2.5% of applications are likely to result in an investment which is finalised. Viewed in terms of points of highest rejection or fall-out, once a business plan has been received, there are three critical points in the appraisal process: the business plan, the first visit and the final documentation stage. The actual rate of rejection at each stage is shown on the Table 7.

TABLE 6A
MEF Investment Appraisal Procedure

ESTIMATED REJECTION RATE % OF TOTAL APPLICATIONS	STAGE OF APPLICATION
15.0	Initial enquiry
68.0	Receipt of plan
8.5	1st company visit
2.5 withdraw because of terms proposed	Meeting re terms of initial offer
0.5	MEF detailed review of proposal Credit searches & bank references
0.5	Investment decision by MEF board Due diligence report on critical factors Take up personal references
2.5 fall out	Draw up final documentation and complete

The stages shown in Table 7 do not correspond exactly with those in Table 6a, but the fallout rates at the three critical stages can be compared. The historical trend is also of interest. The actual rejection rate for business plans is above the expected for just the first time periods: the rejection rate is falling over time. Rejection implies a plan which is very obviously inadequate, or a situation in which the fund requirements in terms of the underlying business are clearly not met. In other words, it is not possible to make a clear judgement on the basis of the information available.

TABLE 7
Rejection Rates En Route Through MEF Appraisal

	% APPLICATIONS	
	FIRST 6 MONTHS	FIRST 9 MONTHS
Applications withdrawn	5.0	3.5
Business plan rejected	70.0	65.0
1st meeting	6.0	9.5
2nd meeting	9.0	11.5
Offers	2.0	1.0
This leaves a balance of:		
Investigations still under way	8.0	9.5
Investments	0	0

As indicated earlier, many business plans were found to be of low quality, and frequently incomplete. To form a truer picture of the underlying business requires additional information, and further investigation, ie not immediate rejection. In other words the fund management are not necessarily immediately turning down all weak applications: they are taking a positive view and investigating options where information is perhaps lacking but they sense some good potential.

The trend towards lower rejection rates in the later months of the fund is indicative of the observed rise in the quality of applications over time. In the early months, many businesses crawled out of the woodwork, attracted by the potential new source of funds. The more 'serious' applicants tended to come later, after the launch publicity had died down. Many of these later applicants were directed to MEF by the banks and other intermediaries.

The expected percentage of firms to be rejected after a first visit was 8.5; the actual levels were 6.0 and 9.5 respectively. These figures, however, are expressed in relation to initial applications. In terms of the companies actually being visited, the percentages are much higher. The expectation is to reject 50% of all firms visited. The actual figure for the first nine months indicates that 33% of companies visited were rejected. This confirms the trend identified in respect of lower than expected rejection rates. Again, the MEF management is positively seeking out the good features of companies via close and detailed investigation. This is the alternative to the negative view of getting rid as quickly as possible. To a large extent it is also a reflection of the type of businesses applying for small scale equity funding. The need is for some hand-holding and encouragement.

The next stage is a closer look which includes a number of elements, including requests for further information, market research, visits to the applicant's business site(s), meetings with management, and MEF Board discussions re the type of business, level of competition etc. The level of co-operation and speed of responsiveness of applicants to these initiatives was viewed as a useful indicator of the quality of the management. Repeated delays in delivering new data requested by the fund manager, or turning up late for appointments without explanation were seen as bad omens.

In one instance, where initial consideration was being given to making an investment offer, the partners of the business in question twice turned up late for meetings with fund directors, and on both occasions smelt heavily of alcohol: not a strategy designed to woo the hearts of venture fund managers!

The first visit is used to get a feel for the business and its management, thus aiding a judgement on the business plan. It is also an ideal opportunity to ask pertinent questions. If general impressions are favourable, the investigations can proceed to the next stage.

At the final critical stage between an offer being made, and the investment being placed, the expectation is that half of the remaining firms will withdraw. In practice, the fall-out rate proved to be 100% for the periods studied. In seeking an explanation for this, we looked at the length of time that applications were outstanding (Table 8).

The application outstanding for the longest period was made in November 1992 (ie five months previously). This was at the stage of having received a second visit, but since April, the application has lapsed.

TABLE 8
Analysis of 'Live' Applications in Month Six (April 93)

Under investigation	5
First visit completed	7
Second meeting completed	2
Applications lapsed	5
Offers made	2
Total	21
Applications	
<3 months old	20
3–6 months old	1

In contrast, the two offers made related to recent applications. One took the form of a small MEF stake as part of a much larger total package; the second has been put on hold until other finance is in place.

The oldest application dated back to January 1993, and had reached the stage of completion of a satisfactory second meeting.

TABLE 9
Analysis of 'Live' Applications in Month Eleven (Sept 93)

Under investigation	6
Second meeting completed	8
Applications lapsed	1
Offers made	14
Total	19
Applications <3 moths old	13
3–6 months old	2
6 months+	4

As with the April figures, two of the offers related to recent applications. Again, one was a small equity stake in a large and highly geared MBO. The second is on hold and subject to the resolution of certain problems relating to the business, in terms of negotiating property and mortgage finance.

Interpreting the statistics, there is an indication that many applications need three or more months of investigation before a clear decision can be reached. Much of this time is taken up with fund management waiting for information and revised plans, or other parts of the deal to come together. The peak time for final investment decisions is the three to six month period. Where more rapid offers are able to be made, certain conditions must be met: either a situation of low risk to the fund in a syndicated deal, or where offers are subject to compliance with specific preconditions.

Additional investigations inevitably take time, and there is always the risk that the delay leads to a good investment opportunity being forfeited, as applicants find an alternative source of finance. The appraisal procedures have therefore been modified to take account of this risk.

As an example, the decision to circulate enquirers with a business plan guide will serve to raise the quality of submissions, and so reduce the need for further information. Nonetheless, complexities in some applications are inevitable.

The introduction of a sharing of responsibility for investigation and due diligence work amongst MEF board members is a response to the perceived need for faster decision making. If good investment opportunities exist, the fund has a greater chance of implementing them if the speed of turn-round on investment decisions is increased.

CONCLUSION

The data obtained from our analysis of the questionnaire returns, business plans and MEFs appraisal procedure point to a number of possible conclusions:

1. The general quality of funding applications is low, but rising, and intermediaries have a potentially vital role to play here.
2. The investment appraisal procedures adopted by MEFs are standardised and so rejection criteria can be readily identified, as they are consistently applied.
3. There is a need for rapid follow up of applicants which warrant further investigation, in order to maintain company interest.

The long-term objective of this research programme is to test whether a perceived or real equity gap exists in the funding of SMEs in the East Midlands. On the face of it, the number of initial enquiries and applications to the fund would suggest that there is a pent-up demand for finance in the region, a demand which must contain (at least a few) genuine requests for assistance. The local economy is diversified and relatively buoyant, hence the fund is ideally placed to meet the needs of SMEs wishing to expand.

The perception of an equity gap is very strong, but does this extend to a real gap? The fact that the fund made no investments over the period studied to date would indicate that the answer to this question is negative, but this is not necessarily the case.

The fund managers had to adopt a cautious investment policy in the first few months of the fund's life; the track record and credibility of the fund could not be tarnished by early failures of its investee companies. At this stage, the fund has no means of diversifying risk within its portfolio – the ability to do this is a great strength of the 3i Group.

Despite its failure to make a single investment, the work of the fund managers has already had a beneficial impact on SMEs within the region. The fund managers make no profit whatsoever from their advisory (consultancy) activities and they have given impartial advice to many SMEs approaching the fund. Furthermore, a number of funding offers were made, which potential investee companies decided not to accept; others were directed to alternative sources of risk finance. Some firms which were initially rejected have returned with far more rigorous and realistic plans, which are being actively considered.

Whilst it is always possible that a potential high flier has been denied the chance to fly, our independent assessment of business plans submitted could not find any evidence of viable propositions being turned away. However, after the initial surge in applications, the standard of business plans being received is of much higher quality. A higher proportion of plans is being submitted via intermediaries, an important filtering mechanism.

We are convinced that the fund has a positive role to play in future, not only by making investments on its own account, but also by acting as a role model for the operation of other similar funds in future.

FUTURE RESEARCH AGENDA

We conclude by setting out a future research agenda – the objective of which is to test for the presence of a substantial real equity gap in the East Midlands region.

The critical question of whether the financial markets 'get it right' in assessing the funding requirements of SMEs remains unresolved. For example, a 1986 review of bank lending practices (NEDO, 1986a, p87) stated that 'the hypothesis that the allocation of finance to small firms by the clearing banks could be improved is likely to be true, although we have no idea of the misallocation'.

In past studies, the relationship between the two sides of the financial intermediation process has normally been dealt with in a somewhat static manner. Typically, the two sides are interviewed separately; the findings are then presented as an analysis of summary statistics (eg, 20% of companies had experienced problems with funding their investment plans) or as a series of case studies.

Our intention is to conduct a longitudinal study which will track the progress of those firms receiving funds from the fund, together with a sample of those that are rejected. Managers in a sample of rejected companies will be interviewed, to monitor their progress in finding alternative sources of finance or in amending their business plans to accommodate the lack of appropriate funding.

This interactive approach should introduce an element of dynamism into the project and, incidentally, ascertain whether the fund managers' decisions proved to be correct!

NOTES

(1) It should be noted that although Kevin Caley is named as a joint author, the research was conducted independently by the Loughborough staff, and his authorship is an acknowledgement of the great assistance received from Kevin in giving us access to the information, and without whom the research would not have been possible.

(2) The latest figures are not strictly comparable with previous years as, for the first time, the total includes debt finance where it is directly linked to an equity investment by the same institution.

(3) Previous attempts by the banks to provide risk/equity capital through their branch networks have faltered, notably the failure of the NatWest Growth Options venture in 1991. Nonetheless,there are signs of a growing willingness on the part of banks to consider providing equity; for example, over and above its involvement with the regional enterprise funds, Midland Bank has recently launched an ambitious programme to provide modest amounts of equity to unquoted companies through its branches.

(4) The distribution and analysis of the questionnaires, and the analysis of the applications submitted to the fund (referred to below) was conducted independently of the fund managers. Confidentiality was a paramount consideration.
(5) The supply of informal risk capital from private investors is thought to be a potentially valuable source of equity capital in the UK. However, there is no effective national mechanism to put potential investing firms in touch with willing investors. The government is hoping that the establishment of 'One Stop Shops' for business services will facilitate this process; it has also introduced capital gains tax relief for individuals who have sold their stake in established businesses but who wish to invest in another unquoted company. The fact that only three firms in the East Midlands had approached private investors confirms that a local network is also lacking.

REFERENCES

ACOST (1990) The Enterprise Challenge: Overcoming Barriers to Growth in Small Firms, HMSO, London.

BOLTON CMND 4811 (1971) 'Report of the Committee of Enquiry on Small Firms', HMSO, London.

BRITISH VENTURE CAPITAL ASSOCIATION (1993) (Graham Bannock & Partners) Investment Activity 1992, BVCA, London.

DEPARTMENT OF TRADE AND INDUSTRY/ASTON BUSINESS SCHOOL & COUSINS STEPHENS ASSOCIATES (1991) Constraints on the Growth of Small Firms, HMSO, London.

INLAND REVENUE (1993) Report for 1992, HMSO, London.

MACMILLAN CMND 3897, (1931) Report of the Committee on Finance and Industry, HMSO, London.

McMEEKIN D (1991) Midland Bank, Paper presented to the 14th National Small Firms' Policy and Research Conference, Blackpool.

NEDO: COMMITTEE ON FINANCE FOR INDUSTRY (1986) Lending to Small Firms: A study of appraisal and monitoring methods, National Economic Development Office, London.

RADCLIFFE CMND 827 (1959) Report of the Committee on the Working of the Monetary System, HMSO, London.

3I GROUP (1993) Annual Report and Accounts.

UNIVERSITY OF CAMBRIDGE, SMALL BUSINESS RESEARCH CENTRE (1992) The State of British Enterprise: Growth, innovation and competitive advantage in small and medium-sized firms' University of Cambridge.

WILSON CMND 7503 (1979) The Financing of Small Firms – Interim Report of the Committee to Review the Functioning of Financial Institutions, HMSO, London.

CHAPTER 4

Finance, New Technology and SMEs: A Comparative Study of the UK and France

SARAH AUSTIN, AIDAN BERRY, SUE FAULKNER,
JO JOHNSON AND MARK HUGHES

INTRODUCTION

This paper presents the findings of a comparative study, based on interviews with 30 SMEs in the UK and France. It investigates the financing practices of these firms, both generally and for new technology investments. It commences with a literature review of major differences of financing in the UK and France, including government assisted finance. This is followed by a summary of the methodology used and an overview of the key results of the research. Finally, the paper highlights areas of difference and their potential implications for UK policy and government initiatives relating to the growth of SMEs.

LITERATURE REVIEW: SMES AND EXTERNAL FINANCE

It is widely believed that UK SMEs experience greater difficulties in raising finance for growth than do larger organisations, a phenomenon generally referred to as a finance gap. Some evidence suggests that SMEs in France face similar problems (Watkins and Morton 1982). These problems are not just reflected in the ability of firms to obtain finance, but also in the terms on which the finance is offered. Thus it is argued that small firms are penalised by paying more for their finance than large firms, in the form of higher interest rates or more stringent security requirements. Interest premiums for SMEs in the UK have been shown to be around 2% (Wilson 1979, Bannock and Morgan 1988). Similarly, the French Ministry for Industry and Export reported that, in 1991, enterprises employing between 20 and 100 employees paid, on average, 2.6% over base rate for overdraft facilities, compared to average of 0.9% over base for firms employing over 500 employees (Ministere de L'Industrie et du Commerce Exterieur 1991).

In relation to security, banks in the UK have been particularly criticised for an over reliance on security. This is in line with a 'gone concern' approach where the emphasis is on the past and upon reliance on security. It can be contrasted with the 'going concern' approach which places more emphasis on future profitability and repayments of loans from future cash flows. Whilst there is some evidence to suggest that this approach is being used in the UK (Boocock 1989), there is also considerable doubt that it is being applied in the SME sector (Berry et al 1993a).

Although French SMEs may well face stricter security requirements than larger firms (Vickery 1986), a survey by Burns et al (1992) suggests that these requirements are less severe than those faced by UK SMEs. According to this survey, 74% of UK SMEs provided collateral against their loans, compared to only 41% of the French SMEs. For medium sized firms, research by Bossard (1991) indicates that personal guarantees and secured overdrafts were required in 47% of the UK firms, but only 32% of French firms. Binks et al (1992) suggest that such differences in the terms of finance may be partly determined by the prevailing economic conditions.

In defence of the premiums SMEs face, it has been argued that they may reflect higher than average debt to equity ratios in many small firms. For French SMEs, a study by the Credit d'Equipment des Petites et Moyennes Entreprise (CEPME 1988) indicates that they are, on average, more highly geared than larger firms.

Financing Patterns

The UK literature highlights a general aversion to external equity amongst SMEs. In the late 1970s the Wilson Committee suggested that about 75% of businesses would actively resist external participation (Wilson 1979). More recent evidence from Harrison and Mason (1990) suggests a similar figure. According to Bossard (1991), medium-sized French firms do not appear to share this aversion. However, this contrasts with the findings of Burns et al (1992), who indicate similar attitudes toward external equity in both UK and French SMEs. Table 1 shows that, in terms of the firms' priorities in raising finance, external equity is effectively last resort finance.

TABLE I
Priorities in raising finance

	BRITAIN	FRANCE
Overdraft	1	4
Short-term loan	3	1
Long-term loan	5	2
Subsidised loan	6	6
Lease/HP	4	3
Internal funds	2	5
Own equity	8	7
Institutional equity	7	8

SOURCE: Burns P, Burnett A, Myers A & Cain D, 1992, 'Attitudes of Smaller Firms towards Financing and Financial Institutions in Europe', Special Report 5, 3i/Cranfield European Enterprise Centre.

This suggests a shared reliance on debt finance across the two countries, although UK firms place greater reliance on the use of internal funds. There are, however, distinct differences in the type of debt used. Table 2 indicates that French SMEs are less reliant on short-term debt than UK SMEs (short-term sources represent 57% of total debt in France, compared to 76% in UK SMEs). In particular, UK SMEs are far more reliant on overdraft finance. This is confirmed by the Bossard survey (1991) which found that in the UK 60–75% of the medium-sized firms had overdraft facilities, compared to only 35% of the French firms.

TABLE 2
Percentage of total debt

TYPE OF FINANCE	PERCENTAGE OF TOTAL DEBT	
	BRITAIN	FRANCE
Overdraft	58	31
Short-term debt	18	26
Long-term loan	11	23
Subsidised loan	3	1
Lease & hire-purchase	10	19

SOURCE: Burns P, Burnett A, Myers A & Cain D, 1992, 'Attitudes of Smaller Firms towards Financing and Financial Institutions in Europe', Special Report 5, 3i/Cranfield European Enterprise Centre.

Consequently, French SMEs raise a greater proportion of their finance through medium and long-term sources of finance, including leasing and hire purchase. In both countries the popularity of leasing and hire purchase have been growing, despite the fact that these are perceived as expensive compared to other sources of debt finance.

These contrasting financing patterns of French and UK SMEs can be partly explained by investigating the different structures of the financial markets in each country. Binks et al (1992) suggest that there are unlikely to be significant differences between the basic financial products available to small businesses across Europe; instead differentiation is likely to occur in the way the products are delivered.

Financial Institutions and SMEs

Over the last 10 years the banking and finance system in France has undergone a transformation, characterised by significant modernisation, deregulation and innovation. The 1984 Banking Act played a key role in this transformation of the French banking system:

'In consequence of the new Banking Act promulgated in January 1984, the banking system has changed from an old-fashioned, rigid and compartmentalized system to a uniform and harmonised one'. (Boisseau 1990).

Short-term finance is principally provided by the commercial banks, although short-term loans are also available from cooperative banks, particularly for small businesses (e.g. Credit Agricole and Banques Populaires). These banks generally operate as a decentralised network of autonomous regional banks. However, in contrast to the UK, short-term finance tends to be used only to meet immediate working capital requirements. Overdrafts, as well as short-term loans, are available for this purpose but are expensive compared to other sources. Vickery (1986) suggested that, although interest premiums were higher for all types of finance, the difference was greatest for short-term finance, which may partly explain the lower usage of this form of finance by French SMEs.

Medium-term loans are the main form of lending and are largely provided by the commercial banks, for up to five years, or by specialist financial institutions. The main niche of specialist financial institutions is, however, in the provision of long-term loans (7–20 years). Firms will usually approach their deposit/commercial bank who will approach the specialist institutions on their behalf. Credit National is the main provider of long-term loans to private business, particularly for producers of industrial goods. CEPME specialises in extending medium- and long-term loans to SMEs. It was created in 1980 by the government to help firms with less than 500 employees and with turnover less than 200 million francs.

In contrast, SMEs in the UK are largely reliant on the commercial banks to meet their external financing needs. Although UK banks provide some medium- and long-term loans, they see their main role as the provision of short-term finance. Longer term loans are generally provided against freehold property (Berry et al 1993b). Unlike the French banks, UK banks view other institutions, such as leasing companies and venture capitalists, as more appropriate for providing longer term finance (Austin et al 1993).

Although the above discussion indicates that French SMEs have access to a broader range of finance and financial institutions, UK SMEs appear to be more content with their banks' advisory service. According to Burns et al (1992) levels of dissatisfaction were particularly high amongst French manufacturing firms (whereas UK manufacturing firms were surprisingly positive about the role of the their banks in providing advice). Care needs to be taken in interpreting these results as attitudes are tied to expectations as to the level of service they should receive.

Government Assisted Finance

In the UK, since the report of the Bolton Committee in 1971, SMEs have been given credit for the important role they play in the UK economy. In contrast, it was not until the 1980s that French industrial policy began to shift away from the creation and promotion of large firms (Szarka 1992). However, despite these changes and the introduction of policies, such as tax reductions and incentives, to encourage the unemployed to start their own business, Szarka argues that policy in favour of small firms remains underdeveloped. For example, many small businesses are in the tertiary sector and are therefore unaffected by policies aimed essentially at manufacturing industry.

In the UK, the emphasis of state support for SMEs has moved away from direct financial assistance, toward 'softer' forms of aid:

'through the 1980s there has been something of a shift in small firm policy, with less emphasis being given to the provision of 'hard' assistance in the form, for example, of financial support and more emphasis being placed in the 'software' elements of business assistance such as information, advice and training.' (Stanworth and Gray 1993).

Although UK SMEs can still obtain financial assistance through schemes such as the Small Business Loan Guarantee Scheme and the Business Expansion Scheme, the main thrust of government support is through the Consultancy Initiative, which was launched by the DTI in 1988 to provide half the cost of independent consultants in a number of designated areas.

In contrast, the French government has placed a greater focus on direct financial assistance, at both national and regional level. Thus the 1980s have witnessed a growth in the development of business support programmes, covering grants for building new premises, for automation of production and for start-ups which guarantee job creation (Batchelor 1991). The French government also directly intervenes in the financial markets by granting licences for specialist financial institutions:

'Specialist financial institutions are credit institutions carrying out a permanent public interest task assigned to them by the state.' (Boisseau 1990, p58).

Often finance provided by these institutions benefits from privileged terms or a guarantee (Boisseau 1990).

This contrast in the respective roles of the UK and French governments is highlighted by the Bossard survey (1991), which found that 50% of French medium-sized firms had received some form of subsidised finance compared to only 15% in the UK.

FINANCING NEW TECHNOLOGY

The UK literature highlights the problems that lenders and firms face in relation to new technology propositions. A number of studies have highlighted the problems bank managers experience in lending to high technology businesses (Oakey 1984, NEDC 1986). For example, Oakey concluded that bank managers were not competent to value the output of R&D. NEDC (1986) found banks to be excessively conservative in their attitudes to risk, frequently requiring personal guarantees as security. The study suggested that the capital market does not fully appreciate problems faced by firms in the electronics sector, although it argued that the firms themselves were not entirely blameless in their understanding of the needs of financial institutions. Another study, by Vyakarnam and Jacobs (1991), found that bank managers have problems distinguishing between 'good' and 'bad' businesses in the high technology sector. Problems may not be confined to 'high technology sectors' but are likely to arise in any proposition involving investment in new technology. For example, in relation to information technology, Deakins and Hussain (1991) found that the terminology and concepts of information technology were outside the comprehension of most bank managers in their sample. Many of these problems stem from the risk averse nature of bank lending:

'for bankers trained to prefer certainty to hope the financing of new technology presents a major challenge to the prudential lending instinct and the judgement of risk.' (Boardman 1984).

However, problems have also been attributed to the lack of technical understanding and experience of bank managers due to their generalist backgrounds. Vyakarnam and Jacobs (1991) suggest that banks can improve communication in this area by recruiting more science and technology graduates, which would enable initial learning barriers to be overcome.

There is evidence that new technology is problematic for other lenders. For example, the distribution of venture capital funds has shifted away from sectors which are likely to be involved in new technology, toward 'safer' service sectors. Also, the 'maturity' of the technology has been identified as one of the factors which attracts a risk premium in the venture capital appraisal process (Dixon 1989). Austin et al (1993) suggest problems for leasing managers in financing more specialised process technologies, particularly computer systems. Although the literature review revealed little specific information relating to financing new technology in France, there is evidence to suggest that lack of finance presents less of a problem for French SMEs than for UK SMEs when adopting microelectronics-based process and product technologies (Northcott et al 1985).

Government Support for New Technology

There is a contrast between France and the UK in their respective roles in supporting new technology and innovation. In France, there is stronger direct government intervention in 'the strategic planning, support and implementation of selected technologies', whilst the UK government places greater reliance on creating the 'right' market conditions for innovation and technology transfer (Caird 1992).

Despite these differences, both the UK and France offer some financial support for R&D, as well as incentives to promote the recruitment of staff for R&D activities (De Koning and Snijders 1992). The French government also provides a number of fiscal measures available to promote corporate R&D and technological developments.

UK financial support is offered to small firms through schemes such as the Small Firm's Merit Award for Research and Technology (SMART). This is a national competition which aims to help small innovative firms (with under 50 employees) by overcoming problems in obtaining funds from financial institutions.

In France, technology related support is offered via the Agence Nationale pour la Valorisation de la Recherche (ANVAR), which is a public agency, set up in 1980, with the aim of promoting and financing innovation across all sectors, particularly within SMEs. As well as providing consultancy services, it provides financial support for innovation and technology transfer in the form of an interest free loan or a grant.

METHODOLOGY

The research methodology involved 30 in-depth interviews with manufacturing-based SMEs in the UK and France. This qualitative approach sought to highlight the experiences of SMEs in financing new technology investments. The following section discusses the problematic nature of international SME research, the gathering of data, the analysis of data and reflections upon the research process.

The diversity of the UK SME sector was acknowledged through different definitions dependent upon the industry type i.e. manufacturing, 200 employees or less, road transport, 5 vehicles or less and retailing, £50,000 p.a. turnover or less, used within the Bolton Report (1971). The diversity amongst SMEs is still evident (Felstead and Leighton 1992) and when making international comparisons matters are further complicated. Meager (1992) offers the following explanations for differential self-employment trends across Europe; changing cultural aspirations, employment opportunities, employer strategies, legislative and policy environments and changing traditional patterns of inheritance of small businesses within families. It is suggested that 'disentangling the effects of these factors is a complex task which researchers are only beginning to tackle' (Meager 1992). In the current research our consideration of specific events, with each interview generating case studies in their own context seeks to acknowledge the diversity amongst SMEs.

In both countries, interviews were conducted with senior personnel in 15 SMEs who were involved in the appraisal process. Interviews followed the general interview guide approach (Patton 1980). Whilst the interviews began with a discussion of background information, the main focus was upon 'talking through' a specific example of the appraisal of a new technology investment. Interviews typically lasted an hour and were recorded to allow transcripts to be prepared. The interviews with French SMEs were conducted by the Junior Enterprise organisation of the Ecole Superieure de Commerce de Compiegne (l'ESCC) under the supervision and instruction of members of the UK research team. This follows the second model of international research identified by Heller (1993).

Data analysis was based upon the five stage model developed by Miles and Huberman (1984). At an early stage in the analysis coding was used to identify emergent themes and to reduce the large amounts of data gathered. The use of matrices and case studies proved particularly fruitful forms of data display, allowing conclusions to be drawn.

In conducting international comparative research, the complexity suggested by Meager (1992) was evident. Through collaborating with the ESCC a major problem of gaining access to French SMEs was removed. Also, some of the language difficulties involved in international research were addressed, although communications proved to be problematic. The research team was left with an impression that to completely match the UK and French samples was an illusory goal. However, as the conclusions discussed later demonstrate, the experiences of the French SMEs offer considerable 'food for thought' for UK policy makers.

KEY FINDINGS

This section summarises the key findings of the comparative study, focusing on areas of difference between the French and UK firms. The results of the UK study are reported more fully in Austin (1993).

Sample Characteristics

Tables 3, 4 and 5 give an overview of the characteristics of the French and UK firms. Table 3 indicates that, in the French sample, there was a greater concentration of very small firms (under 50 employees) than in the UK sample. However, in relation to firm turnover (Table 4), the samples were more similar.

TABLE 3
Size of sample firms

NO. OF EMPLOYEES	UK FIRMS	FRENCH FIRMS
0–49	8	10
50–99	3	3
100–149	4	1
150–199	0	1
200–249	0	0

TABLE 4
Turnover of sample firms

TURNOVER (£ MILLION)	UK FIRMS	FRENCH FIRMS(*)
0–0.5	3	2
0.5–2	5	7
2–5	4	3
5–8	3	3

(* converted at exchange rate 8.665)

Table 5 indicates that there were a higher proportion of subsidiaries among the French firms.

TABLE 5
Ownership status

OWNERSHIP STATUS	UK FIRMS	FRENCH FIRMS
Independent	10	8
Subsidiary	5	7

There were also some differences between the French and UK samples in terms of the types of activity in which they were engaged. More firms in the French sample were involved in more innovative work and were working in 'high-technology sectors'. In contrast, there was more of a balance in the UK sample between firms working in more 'low technology' sectors, where new technology was applied purely in their processes, and firms working with more sophisticated products. The key difference between the firms operating in 'low' and 'high' technology sectors was the importance of new product/process development and the need for high levels of R&D expenditure. It is acknowledged that the differences between the UK and French samples described above may have implications for sample bias.

Chapter 4

GENERAL FINANCING

Financing Problems

Overall, the French firms identified fewer financing problems than the UK firms. This in part relates to the low levels of debt in most of the French firms. Other reasons for the lack of financing problems in the French firms are explored below.

Use of Bank Finance

Although most of the French firms had used internal funds to finance investments, they were more willing (and more able) to use bank loans than was the case with the UK firms. Whilst the majority of the UK firms were reliant on their banks for overdraft facilities, few made any regular use of bank loans and saw these as difficult to obtain. The process of obtaining a bank loan was seen as rigorous and demanding by the UK firms. Consequently, the majority of UK firms expressed a preference for the use of internal funds. In contrast, most of the French firms used bank loans to finance investments and did not identify any particular problems in obtaining this form of finance. In fact, medium-term bank loans (approximately five years) appeared to be the main source of external finance for the French firms since very few referred to the use of overdraft facilities. The higher priority given to internal funds by UK firms and the greater usage of longer-term finance by the French are consistent with the survey by Burns et al (Tables 1 and 2).

Bank Appraisal

In terms of the bank appraisal process, the evidence indicated a greater emphasis on the 'going concern' approach in the French banks. In seeking bank finance, most firms were required to produce three years projected figures and a business plan. In contrast, the 'gone concern' approach of the UK banks has been highlighted by Berry et al (1993a). These differences between the UK and French banks may be related to the different types of finance they provide, with the longer term nature of the lending by French banks making it more appropriate to focus on future rather than past performance.

Use of Leasing

The French firms demonstrated less reliance on leasing than the UK firms. However, unlike the UK firms, the French firms were able to finance investments in capital equipment through the banks as well as the leasing companies, which may explain the greater reliance by the UK firms on leasing. The UK firms found the banks did not feel it was appropriate for them to provide investment for this purpose. It appears that the French banks are willing to use the equipment as collateral to secure the finance, which is similar to the leasing companies in the UK.

Relationships with Financial Institutions

The French firms were generally more positive than the UK firms about their relationship with the bank. As with the UK sample, it was largely the firms with low debt who were more positive about their banking relationship. The majority of the French firms saw the bank manager as a 'partner' in an advisory capacity (although in one firm the bank was a shareholder in the company). These firms valued the role of the bank in providing advice and stressed the importance of openness and trust in the relationship. As one SME manager commented:

'The secret of your success in a relationship with a banker is to tell him the truth.'

Another SME manager, however, argued that relations with financial institutions are changing as a result of current restructuring policies. He felt that the banks' reorganisation into business centres was making contact more impersonal and centralised.

The more positive responses from the French firms about their bank relationships may also stem from differences in the power relationships between the firms and their banks. The French firms appeared to be less dependent on their banks than the UK firms, which may partly relate to the different terms on which loan finance was offered, compared to overdraft finance. Since overdraft facilities can be called in at any time by the UK banks, this is likely to result in UK firms being more dependent on the goodwill of the bank. Another factor which may account for the lower dependency among French firms is the broader range of French financial institutions and the greater specialisation within the French banking system. Thus different institutions can be used for different purposes, for example the CEPME specialises in long-term finance. Consequently, the French firms were more likely to use more than one bank, which reduces the dependency, as experienced by the UK firms, on a single bank. One French firm used five different banks.

Although the majority of the French firms were positive about their bankers some firms expressed similar attitudes to those found amongst the UK firms. From this viewpoint, bankers were seen as 'louts and thieves'. Criticisms put forward were:

- banks are only interested in their payback and the short term – they are not willing to take risks
- they lack businesses understanding and industrial competence
- they do not understand small businesses
- they require too many guarantees/security to cover risks.

The strongest criticism came from smaller firms, which may suggest that there is room for the French banks to further develop their approaches to the small business sector.

Awareness of Financial Products

There was a higher level of awareness amongst the French independent firms about financial products and appropriate sources of finance than was the case with the firms in the UK sample. This may be related to the fact that the French SMEs tend to use a wider range of banks to meet their needs. This argument, however, becomes circular; use creates awareness and vice versa.

Chapter 4
FINANCING OF NEW TECHNOLOGY

Financing New Process Technology

New process technologies (which are bought in rather than developed by the firm) could be financed in both countries using the usual sources of finance; namely banks and leasing companies in France and leasing companies in the UK. French firms did not identify any problems in obtaining finance for this purpose although UK firms found it difficult to finance specialised or customised technologies.

Financing Innovation

For investment projects involving process or product development, French firms were able to obtain funds from ANVAR. ANVAR provides an interest free loan of 50% of the total project costs, to be paid back over three years. If a project is unsuccessful, then the loan does not have to be paid back. Two firms referred to the fact that some companies will pretend a project is unsuccessful so that it does not make repayments.

Nearly all the French firms had used ANVAR to finance technology-based projects, usually for developing new products. In contrast, few of the UK firms had used government supported schemes to finance technology related products. Although this may be partly explained by the lower technology bias amongst these firms, it also reflects clear differences in the levels of support for new technology across the two countries.

Because of the financial support offered by ANVAR, most firms did not experience any problems financing high-technology projects. The remainder of this section focuses on the role of ANVAR.

ANVAR Appraisal Process

In contrast to financial institutions in the UK, ANVAR puts the onus on the companies to provide the information in the appropriate format for the appraisal. Thus the requirements of ANVAR drive the companies to produce the information required. In the UK, lenders place little external pressure on firms to provide this type of information, particularly in relation to forecasts (Berry et al 1993b).

The format for the appraisal is set out in a standard form, which requests all the information required for ANVAR to conduct a technical and commercial appraisal of the project. The project will then be assessed by an 'expert' within ANVAR.

Raising Additional Finance

Since ANVAR provides only 50% of the total project costs, firms will have to finance the remaining half, either internally or externally. If the firm seeks external finance from the bank, the ANVAR report provides the basis of the bank appraisal. In fact, a number of firms found that it is easy to raise the additional finance in this way since the ANVAR report acts as proof of reliability. This also reduces the risk to the bank as they do not have to carry out a technical evaluation themselves.

However, not all firms were able to raise additional finance from the bank. The availability of external finance to supplement the ANVAR loan seemed to be a function of size which is, of course, often related to maturity of the business and, therefore, the risk profile. Thus the smaller firms experienced greater problems and were more likely to use internal resources.

The firms which had experienced such problems felt that the banks did not understand this type of investment and were not sensitive to the needs of the companies, consequently, they were not willing to take the risk.

CONCLUSIONS

Although this paper has been largely exploratory in its nature, it raises important issues which merit further consideration by UK policy makers. In relation to the general financing of SMEs, the paper highlights key differences in the availability of various financial products, with lending in France characterised by the predominance of medium-term finance, which is more suited to new technology investment. For new technology, the French government plays a key role as an intermediary, decreasing the risk to both the SME and the financial institution.

The widespread use of medium-term loans in France raises questions on the role of the banks in the respective countries. There appear to be no tangible barriers preventing UK banks from making medium-term loans more widely available without imposing excessive security requirements on SMEs. Differences in the nature of lending between UK and France may be attributed to cultural factors and the historical development of financial institutions.

However, given the current 'gone concern' focus of the UK banks, the reluctance to finance over the medium term is hardly surprising. Past profits are unlikely to be an accurate indicator of future performance since they ignore the impact of an investment on a firm. In contrast, the 'going concern' approach of the French banks allows investment plans to be financed on the basis of future potential and growth. The current structure of the UK banking system offers little incentive to change since, unlike French commercial banks, the UK banks face little competition from alternative sources of finance.

Although French banks take a longer-term view than UK banks, the French government acknowledges the failings of the market in providing long-term finance, particularly for SMEs. Unlike the UK, external equity finance is not viewed as the sole answer to meeting long-term financing needs.

In relation to new technology, the key problem for UK SMEs and financial institutions is the additional level of risk inherent in such investments. Although consultancy and advisory services offered to SMEs in the UK may assist firms in understanding and justifying new technology investment, it does little to help these firms to finance such technology. Consultants do not get involved in a proposition beyond expressing an opinion and therefore have no stake in the success of an investment. In contrast, the French government agency, ANVAR, acts as an intermediary between the banks and the firms. By offering financial support as well as technical expertise, it is able to reduce the risk for both parties. Thus for the banks it effectively provides a comfort level in the form of a financial guarantee.

This suggests that the way forward for the UK policy support for new technology lies not in viewing advice or financial support as alternatives, but in combining these elements and offering both technical and commercial expertise. Banks alone cannot be expected to take on the additional risk.

REFERENCES

Austin S, Berry A, Hughes M and Johnson J (1993) A Comparison of Bank and Leasing Appraisals for SME Investments in Capital Equipment, paper presented at the British Accounting Association South Eastern Area Group Regional Conference.

Austin S (1993) Barriers to Investment: the Appraisal and Financing of New Manufacturing Technologies in SMEs, paper presented at the Small Businesses and Enterprise Development Conference.

Batchelor C (1991) A Favourable Climate for Talking Turkey, Financial Times, Tues 11th June.

Bannock G and Morgan EV (1988) Banks and Small Businesses: An International Perspective, The Forum of Private Business, London.

Berry A, Faulkner S, Hughes M and Jarvis R (1993a) Financial Information, the Banker and the Small Business, British Accounting Review, Vol 25, No. 2.

Berry A, Faulkner S, Hughes M and Jarvis R (1993b) Bank Lending Beyond the Theory, Chapman and Hall, London.

Binks MR, Ennew CT and Reed GV (1992) Small Businesses and their Banks: An International Perspective, Commissioned by National Westminster Bank through Nottingham University Consultants.

Lord Boardman (1984) How Can Banks Help?, in Financing New Technology, Cambridge Seminar.

Boisseau C (Ed) (1990) Banking in France, Routledge, London.

Bolton J (1971) Report of the Committee of Inquiry on Small Firms, Cmnd 4811, HMSO, London.

Boocock G (1989) The Role of the UK Clearing Bank Groups in Providing Longer Term Finance to Small and Medium Businesses, The Association of Banking Teachers Bulletin No. 28, May.

Bossard Consultants (1991) Attitudes to Banking Services for Small Firms in Great Britain, Germany and France, Report for the National Credit Council in France.

Burns P, Burnett A, Myers A and Cain D (1992) Attitudes of Smaller Firms towards Financing and Financial Institutions in Europe, Special Report 5, 3i/Cranfield European Enterprise Centre.

Caird S (1992) What Support is Needed by Innovative Small Businesses?, Journal of General Management, Vol 18, No. 2, Winter.

Credit d'Equipment des Petites et Moyennes Entreprises (1988) Les Fondes Propres Des PME.

Deakins D and Hussain G (1991) Risk Assessment by Bank Managers, Department of Financial Services, Birmingham Polytechnic Business School.

De Koning A and Snijders J (1992) Policy on Small and Medium Sized Enterprises in Countries of the European Community, International Small Business Journal, Vol 10, No. 3.

Dixon R (1989) Venture Capitalists and Investment Appraisal, NatWest Quarterly Review, November.

Felstead A and Leighton P (1992) Issues, Themes and Reflections on the Enterprise Culture, in Leighton and Felstead (Eds), The New Enterpreneurs: Self Employment and Business in Europe, Kogan Page, London.

Harrison RT and Mason CM (1990) The Role of the Business Expansion Scheme in the UK, OMEGA, Vol 17, No. 2, p147.

Heller F (1993) Presentation at British Academy of Management Conference 1993, UK.

Meager N (1992) The Characteristics of the Self Employed: Some Anglo-German Comparisons, in Leighton and Felstead (Eds), The New Enterpreneurs: Self Employment and Business in Europe, Kogan Page, London.

Miles MB and Huberman AM (1984) Qualitative Data Analysis, Sage, London.

Ministere de L'Industrie et du Commerce Exterieur (1991) Les Chiffres Cles, Les PMI, SESSI.

NEDC (1986) Finance for Growth: A Study of Small and Medium-Sized Companies in the Electronics Sector, based on a study carried out for the Committee on Finance for Industry and Electronics EDC's by Coopers and Lybrand Associates, NEDO, London.

NORTHCOTT J, ROGERS P, KNETSCH W AND DE LESTAPIS B (1985) Microelectronics in Industry, An International Comparison of Britain, Germany, and France, PSI/Anglo German Foundation, London.

OAKEY R P (1984) Finance and Innovation in British Small Independent Firms, OMEGA Vol 12, No. 2.

PATTON MQ (1980) Qualitative Evaluation Methods, Sage, London.

STANWORTH J AND GRAY C (Eds) (1993) Bolton 20 Years On: the Small Firms in the 1990s, Paul Chapman, London.

SZARKA J (1992) Business in France: An introduction to the Economic and Social Context, Pitman, London.

VICKERY L (1986) France, in Burns P and Dewhurst J (Eds), Small Business in Europe, Macmillan, London.

VYAKARNAM S AND JACOBS R (1991) How Bank Managers Construe High Technology Entrepreneurs, paper presented at the 14th Small Firms Policy and Research Conference, Blackpool.

WATKINS D AND MORTON T (1982) Small Firms in Britain and Europe: the Perceived Environment, in Watkins et al (Eds), Stimulating Small Firms, Gower, Aldershot.

WILSON COMMITTEE (1979) The Financing of Small Firms, Interim Report to the Committee to Review the Functioning of the Financial Institutions, Cmnd 7503, HMSO, London.

CHAPTER 5

An Exploratory Analysis of the Factors Associated with the Survival of Independent High-Technology Firms in Great Britain

PAUL WESTHEAD, DAVID. J. STOREY AND
MARC COWLING

INTRODUCTION

During the past few decades it has been appreciated by national and local governments, universities and private industry that technological innovation has a key role to play in revitalising economically deprived localities. As a result policymakers throughout Europe and North America have been increasingly concerned with the creation of new technology based small firms (Oakey, 1984, 1985; Breheny and McQuaid, 1987; Aydalot and Keeble, 1988; Donckels and Segers, 1990; Roberts 1991). This effort has been particularly notable in the United Kingdom with the promotion of new technology-based firm start-ups in a variety of property led 'incubator' environment clusters (for a detailed summary see Grayson, 1993).

In order to gain an informed view of the benefits of a Science Park location detailed empirical evidence was collected through a questionnaire survey of firms located in 1986 on Science Parks in Great Britain. In 1986, it was also appreciated that a survey of all firms located on Science Parks 'alone would not provide a clear indication of the added value of a park, since there would be nothing with which to compare the responses. Hence it was decided that similar questions should be asked of a group of otherwise similar firms not located on a park' (Monck et al., 1988, pp. 101–102).

In total, 284 direct face-to-face interviews were conducted in 1986 (most frequently with the owner-managers of surveyed independent and subsidiary businesses), of which 183 were on a Science Park and 101 were not on a Park. This constituted 53% of all tenants on United Kingdom Science Parks at that time, with Heriot Watt the only significant location omitted. Monck et al., (1988, pp. 110–111) argued, 'that the firms in this survey do provide an adequate sample of Britain's new high technology industries, providing adequate geographical, technological, sectoral and ownership coverage'. During the 1986 survey data was collected about the personal characteristics of the founders of these businesses, the technological characteristics of the firms, aspects relating to the property management of Science Parks, their financing and management and finally their performance and economic contribution.

In 1990 a follow up pilot study of thirty-five firms from the original 183 Science Park tenants was conducted by Storey and Strange (1992) together with a review, using United Kingdom Science Park Association (UKSPA) data bases, of the other 148 firms. This pilot longitudinal study did not attempt any contact with the off park 'control' group sample of high technology firms. Storey and Strange (1992. p.18) found, 'that of the 183 firms located on a Science Park, and which were interviewed in 1986, 63% continued in 1990 to occupy some premises within the same Science Park. Of those 68 firms which have moved off, just over half (37 firms) continue to operate in some form, although possibly under a different owner. Of the remainder it is probably justifiable to regard the vast bulk as not trading in any identifiable form, and hence as failures'. Based on this empirical evidence Storey and Strange (1992, p.18) tentatively concluded that, 'the failure rate of firms on Science Parks is below that of UK businesses in general'.

It has been argued that, 'Recent research on entrepreneurship, management, and organisations has underscored the importance of understanding better the conditions that promote business survival and success' (Kalleberg and Leicht, 1991, p.136). The survival of new firms is of particular interest to prospective entrepreneurs as well as advisers and investors. Cooper (1993, p.242) for example, has particularly recognised the need to identify factors associated with business survival in order that, 'entrepreneurs can appraise their ventures accordingly, possibly modifying their plans or deciding not to start at that time'. Recently, it has been asserted by Keeble et al., (1993, p.204) that, 'Policy should perhaps rather aim at enabling existing small firms to survive'. Reynolds et al., (1993a) have also argued that government should invest more time and resources to encourage the survival and growth of established firms rather than encouraging the formation of even more new firms many of which are born to die.

A number of previous studies have analysed the closure of businesses at a regional level (Gudgin, 1978; Beesley and Hamilton, 1984; Keeble et al., 1993; Reynolds et al., 1993b; Westhead and Birley, 1994), an industry level (O'Farrell and Crouchley, 1983, 1987; Flynn, 1991; North et al., 1992), at an organisational population level (Freeman et al., 1983; Hannan and Carroll, 1992) as well as with regard to business (O'Farrell, 1976; Mountfield et al., 1985; Cooper et al., 1988; Westhead, 1988; Romanelli, 1989; Reynolds and Miller, 1989) and founder characteristics (Cooper et al., 1988; Reynolds and Miller, 1989; Bates, 1990; Cooper et al., 1991; Kalleberg and Leicht, 1991; Miner et al., 1992). Surprisingly, relatively few longitudinal studies have focused specifically on the survival of high-technology based firms (for notable exceptions see Cooper and Bruno, 1977; Bruno et al., 1992; Mahmood, 1992; Garnsey and Cannon-Brookes, 1993). Supporting the view held by Keasey and Watson (1991, p.15) that there is a need to develop specific models for different types of firm 'failure' this paper will make a contribution to the debate surrounding the survival of independent high technology firms.

From the outset it is acknowledged that, 'Survival and success are distinct aspects of performance that are determined by different processes...[but]... Organizational survival is a fundamental aspect of performance and a necessary condition for sustained business success' (Kalleberg and Leicht, 1991, p.137 and p.144). We also appreciate that, 'There are many paths to survival and many roads to failure for an entrepreneurial venture....[and]...it is important to point out that survival is a process rather a state' (Bruno et al., 1992, p.300 and p.301). A range of factors 'internal' as well as 'external' to the independent high-technology based firm need to be explored when trying to understand why certain ventures are more likely to survive than others. Following Cooper et al., (1991, p.68) we will explore the resource profiles of high-technology firms. We will identify whether variables collected in 1986 covering the resource bases of surveyed firms can be used to predict venture survival. With regard to public policy we appreciate that, 'It would be particularly desirable if we can identify performance determinants which are discernible prior to or at the point of start-up, rather than after significant capital has been committed' (Cooper et al., 1991, p.68).

The paper begins with a review of existing theoretical and empirical studies of the factors influencing the survival of independent firms. In the second section we provide a brief review of resource exchange and the population ecology theories. These are compared with conventional economic theories. Using these theoretical constructs the third section derives eleven separate factors likely to be influencing business survival/non-survival. The fourth section then turns to the current research looking at survival/non-survival of high-technology firms in Great Britain, with the fifth section providing a clear statement of the assumptions and limitations of the research. The sixth section then presents the results, beginning with a univariate framework linking each of the eleven factors to business survival/non-survival and then placing these into a multivariate model. Finally, some conclusions are presented.

PREVIOUS RESEARCH

Theoretical Issues: Explaining Business Survival

It has been argued by Cooper (1993, p.242 and p.244) that, 'Theoretical frameworks for analyzing influences upon new firm performance are not well developed...[and the]...central problem has been the lack of well-developed theories of causal relationships'. Nevertheless, numerous studies have explored the factors associated with the formation, survival and growth of new firms from theoretical standpoints such as the resource exchange and the population ecology perspectives as well as from the viewpoint of economic theory. Each of these are discussed below. Like Kalleberg and Leicht (1991, p.138) we believe that these, 'Macro and micro perspectives on survival and success are complementary'.

Resource Exchange Theory

Resource exchange theory views organisations (for example, new firms) as entering into transactional relationships with environmental factors because they cannot generate all necessary resources internally (Child, 1974; Pfeffer and Salancik, 1978; Pennings, 1982). The formation, survival and growth of new firms is therefore directly related to each firm's ability to gain access to predictable uninterrupted supply of critical resources. The environment (or the locality) is seen to contain a pool of resources (such as customers, suppliers, finance, land, property, machinery, technical information, etc) and the degree of resource abundance has been termed by researchers 'munificence'. Consequently, if firms do not secure through proactive and/or reactive strategies essential resources they are more likely to close than those ventures who have gained access to an uninterrupted supply of critical resources. This theory emphasises that survival in organisations is encouraged by differentiation and diversification. However, 'The focus of the resource dependence approach is different than population ecology in that the organisation is looked upon as more active in attempting to adapt to the environment' (Flynn, 1993, p.133).

Population Ecology Theory

The reasons for the closure of new firms are numerous (Flynn, 1991; Westhead and Birley, 1994) but new firms particularly suffer from a 'liability of newness' (Stinchcombe, 1965; Evans, 1987; Phillips and Kirchhoff, 1989; Audretsch, 1991) because they have a greater tendency to depend on the cooperation of strangers and have low levels of legitimacy (a view supported by Aldrich and Auster, 1986; Romanelli, 1989, p.386). Moreover, adherents of the population ecology perspective suggest that the processes of density (and 'carrying capacity'), legitimation and competition all play a role in the size of organisational populations.

Building upon resource exchange theories it has been suggested within the population ecology theory that the number of new firms in a particular niche (or a resource space) is influenced by the carrying capacity of the environment. Specht (1993, p.79) argues that, 'Carrying capacity is related to the density or number of organisations competing for the same resources in a niche. Density is determined by prior births and deaths in an organization's population'.

New firm formation and survival is seen to be influenced by two opposing processes: legitimation (legitimacy processes dominate when the size of the population is small) and competition (the competition process dominates when the size of the population is large) (Hannan and Freeman, 1988; Hannan and Carroll, 1992, pp.14–17). 'Legitimation of an organizational population means that its organizational form acquires the status of a 'taken-for-granted' solution to given problems of collective action. Competition refers to constraints arising from the joint dependence of multiple organizations on the same set of finite resources for building and sustaining organizations' (Hannan and Carroll, 1992, pp.vii–viii).

Further, both legitimation and competition are affected by density, defined as the number of organisations in the population. 'This theory proposes that rates of organizational founding and mortality vary with the strength of legitimation and competition processes and the latter depend on the density in specific ways. More specifically, the theory assumes that the legitimation of an organizational population increases with its density at a decreasing rate and that competition within organizational populations increases with density at an increasing rate' (Hannan and Carroll, 1992, p.16).

Hannan and Carroll (1992, p.16) also argue that both relationships are nonlinear and they suggest, 'The symmetry of the argument implies that the relationship between density and mortality rates has a U shape....Such a pattern of density dependence can generate the common pattern of growth of organisational populations. If the theory is correct, initial growth in density will trigger processes of legitimation that elevate founding rates and lower mortality rates.

The result is rapid growth in density. However, eventually density grows high enough that competitive processes outweigh legitimation processes, depressing founding rates and elevating mortality rates. The result is that growth in density slows and density stabilizes' (Hannan and Carroll, 1992. p.16). Therefore, within this perspective, firms in order to survive not only have to adapt but they also have to change rapidly in order that an appropriate organisation–environment relationship is developed. Here it is assumed that business survival is not only related to the availability of critical resources but also the ability to gain legitimacy as well as the ability to compete in potentially saturated markets. Moreover, the ability to move into new market niches (or markets) with higher levels of munificence and/or less competition for available resources.

Economic Theory

Economists assume that, in the long run, firms which are loss makers will exit the industry, whereas profit makers are assumed to continue in business. In the short run, however, loss makers which are able to cover variable costs and make a contribution to fixed costs may also survive. Moreover, economists' empirical work has noted that not all loss makers cease to trade and that it is not necessarily the largest loss makers which exit first. The work by both Baden-Fuller (1989) and Reid (1991) argues that the decision to quit depends on the anticipated profit, the rate of interest and the use of the resources employed within the firm both currently and in the future.

FACTORS ASSOCIATED WITH BUSINESS SURVIVAL/CLOSURE

The above theoretical frameworks indicate that a wide variety of factors are likely to influence business survival. These factors are each discussed in detail below.

Factor 1: Personal Background of Key Founder

Human capital variables (for example, measuring human capabilities) can influence the survival of firms (Bates, 1990). For example, it has been argued that women entrepreneurs are more likely to fail because they may have had 'fewer opportunities to develop relevant experience, to have fewer contacts who can provide assistance, and to have greater difficulty in assembling resources' (Cooper et al., 1991, p.69). The empirical evidence supporting this hypothesis is limited and rather mixed. Cooper et al., (1988, p.232) in their study of entrepreneurs across the United States have presented empirical evidence which suggests that firms established by women were less likely to survive. Whilst Kalleberg and Leicht (1991, p.150) in their study of 411 organisations in South Central Indiana, USA found women were no more likely than men to go out of business.

Age of the founder at the time of the start-up of the business has been used as a surrogate measure of experience. It has been suggested that experience is a positive influence on business survival but older founders (55 years or older) are more likely to operate businesses that subsequently close (Bates, 1990, p.558).

Similarly, Cooper et al., (1988, p.232) found that more mature firm founders (when they started the surveyed business) were more likely to survive. Moreover, it has been argued that businesses owned by founders with high levels of education and an ability to cope with problems are less likely to close. For example, a number of studies have suggested that founders with college education (bachelor's degree or more) are more likely to establish businesses which survive (Hoad and Rosco, 1964,pp.10–11;Cooper et.al., 1988,p.232; Bates, 1990,p.558; Cooper et al., 1991, p.72). Reasons leading to business start-up have also been suggested to be related with subsequent business survival in a study of entrepreneurs in Norway (Jenssen and Kolvereid, 1992, p.130). Supporting this view in the United States Cooper et al., (1988, p.234) noted that surviving firms were less likely to have been established by founders who had left their previous jobs because of 'negative' pushes (such as job discontinued or fired).

Factor 2: Work Experience of Key Founder

It is argued that one of the most important influences on the subsequent success of a new venture is the previous work experience of the founder (Cooper, 1981) and his/her relevant knowledge base (Cooper et al., 1991, p.69). Vesper (1980, pp.32–33) has argued that higher survival rates are recorded by founders who have established firms engaged in activities which they knew well prior to start-up. Experience and capability have been measured in a variety of ways in previous studies.

It is often suggested that individuals with management experience can cope with change and it prepares them with skills to cope with problems that may confront them whilst running a venture. Cooper et al., (1988, p.232) and Bates (1990, p.555) have presented inconclusive evidence to support the view that owners with management experience prior to owning tracked business encouraged their subsequent survival. Whilst Kalleberg and Leicht (1991, p.153) found in their survival study in the United States that businesses run by entrepreneurs with greater experience in an industry were not more likely to survive. Moreover, it has been argued that individuals who have left non-profit organisations may have had fewer opportunities to observe or develop experience directly relevant to managing the survival of an independent profit making business (Cooper et al., 1991, p.68). Contrary to expectation, Cooper et al., (1988, p.232) noted in their empirical study that firm survivors were not less likely to have come from a non-business background (for example, a non-profit making organisation). This study also showed that founders last employed in medium and large organisations were not significantly more likely to establish a new business that discontinued (p.233).

Further, people who spread themselves over many businesses might be unable to devote enough attention to the survival of all businesses in their portfolio (Kalleberg and Leicht, 1991, p. 148). As a result a founder who is a director or an owner of another business may be more likely to close a venture than a founder who focuses his/her attention on a single venture. This view has been empirically supported. Kalleberg and Leicht (1991,p.153) found that businesses headed by men who were involved in other companies were more likely to fail, but outside involvement was unrelated to business survival of women operated ventures. Similarly, Cooper et al., (1988, p.232) recorded that firm survivors were not more likely to be headed by individuals who had previously owned a business.

Cooper et al., (1988, p.234) have presented empirical evidence which indicated surviving firms were less likely to be headed by individuals who during the start-up period continued to work outside the surveyed business. It, however, must be noted that Reynolds and Miller (1989, p.167) found that the characteristics (age, education, years of experience, nature of career change to new firm and number of new firms started) of the principal founder were unrelated to subsequent new firm survival.

Factor 3: Characteristics of the Business

It is consistently found in empirical studies that the vast majority of new firms are born to 'die young' (Gudgin, 1978; Henderson, 1980; Carroll, 1983; O'Farrell and Crouchley, 1983; Evans, 1987; Westhead, 1988; Phillips and Kirchhoff, 1989; Romanelli, 1989; Bates, 1990). North et al., (1992) in their study of manufacturing businesses noted that new firms are particularly prone to 'infant mortality' and 'that firms generally need up to 10 years to become firmly established and that the age of them after this period tends to become less significant' (p.15). Conversely, O'Farrell (1976, pp.435–436) in his study of grant-aided manufacturing establishments in Ireland found that the frequency of closure was independent of the number of years in operation. Also, in a more recent multivariate survival analysis of manufacturing plants in Ireland O'Farrell and Crouchley (1987, p.326) noted that, 'contrary to the misleading results obtained in many cross-sectional studies, the age of a new plant is not associated with closure probability when the effect of other variables is controlled' (for a similar conclusion see Kalleberg and Leicht, 1991, p.152). On a further cautionary note Freeman et al., (1983, p.692) have warned that, 'Apparent age dependence in any death rate can be due solely to heterogeneity in the population; that is, the rate declines with age simply because units with the highest death rates fail early'. Nevertheless, the current study hypothesises that more mature firms will be more likely to survive.

O'Farrell and Crouchley (1987, p.315) have suggested that small firms tend to experience greater difficulties than large businesses. For example, they may suffer from extremes of profitability, they are more likely to be dominated by major customers and over dependent on a single product or service and suffer from managerial weaknesses, especially financial control and marketing. A number of studies have supported the view that as a firm becomes smaller relative to the minimum efficient size for its main industry it will be more likely to close (Mansfield, 1962, p. 1028). This view has been supported by considerable empirical evidence (Wedervang, 1965; O'Farrell, 1976; Gudgin, 1978; O'Farrell and Crouchley, 1987; Cooper et al., 1988; Westhead, 1988; Bates and Nucci, 1989; North et al., 1992) which have shown that businesses with small numbers of employees are more likely to close (for a dissenting view refer to Freeman et al., 1983, p.693; Mountfield et al., 1985, p.784; Kalleberg and Leicht, 1991, p.152). Further, O'Farrell and Crouchley (1983) in their study of manufacturing closures in Ireland over the period 1973–1981 found that the log of employment size was inversely related to the probability of closure. Mahmood (1992, p.203) using a longitudinal data base of over 12,000 newly established manufacturing plants in low as well as high-technology industries in the United States has also argued exposure to risk can be reduced by increasing the initial start-up size of firms (for a similar conclusion see Mountfield et al., 1985, p.784 and p.788; and

Cooper et al., 1988, p.237) and that, 'Start-up size tends to be important in reducing the hazard rate in both low and hightech industries' (Mahmood, 1992, p.206). Therefore, it is posited that firms with small employment sizes in 1986 will be more likely to close.

In the United States Vesper (1980) has asserted that survival rates are in part explained by the line of business (product or service) selected by the founder. Similarly, Henderson (1980, p.154) in his study of closures in Scotland has argued that sectoral variations in profitability will lead to sectoral variations in establishment closure rates. Moreover, he suggested that firms engaged in labour – rather than capital-intensive industries – will be more prone to closure because average variable costs represent a larger percentage of the long-run equilibrium price level in labour-intensive industries. Henderson also warned firms engaged in higher value-added knowledge-industries would require considerable long-term investment – in research and development, converting a new technology into a product, management functions and systems to cope with change, etc – in order to stay competitive. Empirical evidence testing the neo-classical economic theory view that inter-industry variations in profitability and hence closure will exist is rather mixed. Whilst inter-industry variations in business closure have been noted by a number of commentators (Henderson, 1980, p.167; O'Farrell and Crouchley, 1984, p.418; O'Farrell and Crouchley, 1987, p.324) the presumed relationship has been dismissed elsewhere (Reynolds and Miller, 1989, p.167; Beesley and Hamilton, 1984, p.283). However, in a recent review of trends in business registration and deregistration for Value Added Tax (VAT) in the United Kingdom, Daly (1991, p.583) found that the highest rates of new business registration as well as deregistration were recorded by service firms. Consequently, we hypothesise that those firms whose main industrial activity was manufacturing will be less likely to close.

Recent empirical studies at a regional level of analysis have found that new firm formation and business closure rates are spatially related. Environments with high levels of new business entry also have correspondingly high levels of business 'failure' (Audretsch and Fritsch, 1992, p.9; Westhead and Moyes, 1992. p.37; Keeble et al., 1993, p.124; Westhead and Birley, 1994). For example, it has been suggested increased localised competition may result in the closure of new as well as more established small firms who are unable to adapt and change within the new competitive environment. Moreover, Westhead and Birley (1994) found high business deregistration rates for VAT were particularly recorded in urban areas traditionally associated with declining heavy industries. We, therefore, hypothesise that firms located in 1986 in government designated 'assisted' areas for regional development assistance (Martin, 1985, p.382; Damesick, 1987, p.58) will tentatively be more likely to close. Further, it can be suggested that economically depressed areas in the 'north' (the remainder of Great Britain excluding the standard regions of East Anglia, the South East and South West of England – Birley and Westhead, 1990; Massey et al., 1992, pp.15–16) may be associated with considerably less local market demand for the goods and services of high-technology ventures. Consequently, we hypothesise that firms located in 1986 in the 'north' will be less likely to survive.

In recent years sponsorship by government agencies, business firms and universities has attempted to create an environment conducive to the birth and survival of organisations. 'Sponsorship is a deliberate attempt to make available a significantly higher and more stable level of resources in selected firms...[and]...When organizations are sponsored, their environment is enriched, providing legitimacy (Stinchcombe, 1965) to their birth and early survival' (Flynn, 1993, p.129 and p.131). Associated with this trend has been the rapid growth in the number of Science Parks in the United Kingdom to encourage the formation, survival and growth of high-technology firms. Moreover, it has been suggested by UKSPA that a firm's survival chances are higher on a Science Park rather than off park (a view supported by Storey and Strange, 1992, p.18). UKSPA have asserted that many Science Parks firms 'would not have survived if they had located off-park' and the support for new businesses on Science Parks has been the 'salvation of the academic entrepreneur' (Grayson, 1993, p.120).

However, it has been argued by Smilor and Feeser (1991, p. 171) that 'picking winners' and targeting sponsorship to particular businesses is doomed to failure because of the chaotic process of formation and subsequent survival (for a dissenting view see Reynolds and Miller (1989) who argue that business survival can be predicted). Drawing upon the population ecology model Flynn (1993) has identified a number of potential problems with sponsored environments such as Science Park locations. First, 'in the later stages of the sponsored organization's life cycle, the ability to effectively compete for scarce resources is seriously undermined by the previously buoyant, sponsored environment' (p.131). Second, 'The process of intervention by public and private organizations into communities may actually create new organizational forms through alteration of the existing ecology of the community. These new forms may be quite different from the requisite form of the relevant population, thus contributing to a lower level of later stage survival' (p.132). Third, 'the new sponsored organization may in fact be, illegitimate, because its incubating environment was artificially inflated with resources. As the density of the population increases, these new, sponsored firms would have a higher mortality rate versus unsponsored organizations. Sponsored organizations may have difficulty understanding survival in a high density environment where firms compete for limited resources' (p.132). Fourth, due to sponsorship new organisations have a low probability for long term survival because after the period of sponsorship the organisation is no longer buffered from environmental and competitive shocks. 'Sponsorship, by reducing competitive disturbances and constraining organizational learning, may produce unintended consequences by aiding the survival of organizations with potential weaknesses' (p.134). As a result negative selection may occur with non-survival attributes being transferred to the generation of firms and thus leaving a narrower set of survival-enhancing attributes within the population (Aldrich et al., 1984). Finally, 'Organisations incubated in sponsored and stable environments may be inhibited in their ability to devise effective strategies for survival beyond the period of sponsorship because of their lack of experience in coping with more uncertain environments' (Flynn, 1993, p.134).

It has been suggested that businesses whose legal form is an incorporated company will be less likely to close. 'Incorporation is an indicator of the extent to which a business is institutionalized and has certain legal and financial protection that may inhibit dissolution' (Kalleberg and Leicht, 1991, p.148). For example, in the United States Kalleberg and Leicht (1991, p.152) found that incorporated businesses headed by men were less likely to go out of business. Whilst Reynolds and Miller (1989, p.167) noted that new firms initiated as sole proprietorship (with lower legitimacy) had a significantly lower propensity to survive.

Related to size and legitimacy Reynolds and Miller (1989, p.167) found that new firms with larger initial sales had a greater propensity to survive. Level of sales turnover was also used by Reid (1991) as a market variable in his study of the survival of 73 firms located in central Scotland. He noted businesses having larger levels of sales were more likely to survive (p.554).

North et al., (1992, pp.17-18) have found, 'that the ownership of freehold property can help determine whether or not a firm survives. It was certainly the opinion of managers of surviving businesses in freehold property that ownership of their premises had been a key factor contributing to their survival either by holding down fixed costs (especially in marginal businesses...or by providing collateral for borrowing....In contrast, firms in rented property sometimes had to withstand significant rent increases, and, in some instances, to suffer displacement to make way for redevelopment schemes'. We, therefore, hypothesise here that firms located in leased premises in 1986 will be more likely to close.

The survival of businesses can be influenced by the supply of pertinent resources (Hannan and Freeman, 1977). One important resource that needs to be met is the availability of industrial floorspace. This view is supported by Fothergill and Gudgin (1982, p.8) who found in their study of employment change in the United Kingdom that areas recording marked losses in employment were those generally associated with cramped sites which did not meet the requirements of modern industry. Conversely, in a study of the survival of footwear manufacturing establishments in the East Midlands of England Mountfield et al. (1985, p.784) noted that plants located in medium sized premises were more likely to close, especially if these premises were multi-storey. We, however, posit firms located in premises with large floorspaces in 1986 will be more likely to survive than their counterparts who were based in small premises.

Various studies have shown that businesses established by teams of partners are more likely to survive (Vesper, 1980, pp.40-42; Cooper et al., 1988, p.234). This is because, 'The presence of partners leads to a greater depth of expertise. Resource dependence theory suggests that partners can be viewed as means to add to the resource and skill base of the venture. Partners may also enhance the credibility of the venture to potential lenders and other constituents' (Cooper et al., 1991, p.69).

Factor 4: Customer Base

It is appreciated that the formation, survival and growth of any venture is dependent upon the availability of resources and the ability to gain access to them. In order to satisfy some untapped demand the independent firm needs to supply a product and/or service to satisfy this excess demand. Therefore, the survival of any business is ultimately dependent upon there being a demand for its products and/or services. Romanelli (1989, p.381) has presented empirical evidence to support her hypothesis that young firms had a higher likelihood of survival when demand was increasing. Moreover, Cooper (1993) has found in his research that new firms with strategies focused on particular markets and a small number of products or services in the short term have achieved superior performance. He, however, acknowledges that, 'the concentration of risk upon a narrow resource base and the dependence upon narrow markets means that performance often is not stable' (p.245). Interestingly, Kalleberg and Leicht (1991, p.154) in their study found that generalist firms moving away from a narrow customer base decreased the probability of business failure among female headed businesses. In marked contrast, Cooper et al., (1988, p.234) found that geographical background of customers served by surviving and closing firms were about the same.

Factor 5: Competitive Structure

There may be competition for scarce resources. Environments with excess demand can sustain larger numbers of competing firms than those with limited resources (or lower carrying capacities). The likelihood of a firm surviving in a selected market niche is in part determined dependent upon the strength and intensity of competition (Romanelli, 1989, p.371). For example, Romanelli (1989, p.381) found in her study of minicomputer producers in the United States that the likelihood of new firm survival increased when competitive concentration was declining. Similarly, Kalleberg and Leicht (1991, p.152) found that women headed businesses in highly competitive markets were more likely to have gone out of business.

It has been suggested that localised competition between like entities for finite resources eventually leads to differentiation (Hawley, 1950, pp.201–203). Moreover, over time competition may lead to selective pressures and less-fit competitors will be pushed out of the market. Supporting this hypothesis Baum and Mezias (1992, p.595) in their study of organisational failure rates in the Manhattan hotel industry found that failure rates were lower for organisations in competition with large competitors. Consequently, we hypothesise here that high-technology firms whose regular competitors are small firms are more likely to close.

Factor 6: Networking

Low and MacMillan (1988) have argued that ventures can shape their own survival by building networks. It can be suggested that founders with dense and varied personal and business networks of contacts can gain information to overcome business development problems. Those firms who have gained access to a wide and diverse relevant knowledge base through contacts with professional advisers may be more likely to survive. Cooper et al (1991, p.69) have appreciated that, 'In general, access to information networks provides specific data and encouragement, as well as helping to identify blind spots. The act of seeking information may also reflect more comprehensive planning, a higher degree of managerial sophistication and the startup of larger, more promising ventures'. Moreover, it has been suggested that universities are an important element of the local infrastructure and they can act as a vehicle for the sponsorship of high-technology firms through the use of grants and contracts and industry sponsored research (Flynn, 1993, p.146).

Factor 7: Financial Base

The survival of any business is in part a function of the management's ability to secure and gain access to finance and working capital. Reid (1991, p.550) has suggested that, 'A distinction needs to be made between financial inception and points further down the line when the owner manager may have established credibility for surviving'. Further, it has been hypothesised that the worst small firms projects are those launched using purely personal finance (De Meza and Webb, 1988). A recent longitudinal study of 4,429 firms established by males in the United States conducted by Bates (1990, p.551 and p.558) found that, 'Financial capital input levels, irrespective of owner education, are strong determinants of small business survival prospects ... [and] ...Financial capital endogeneity notwithstanding, firms with the larger financial capital inputs at start up are consistently over-represented in the survivor column'. This view is supported by Cooper et al., (1988, p.237) who noted during their longitudunal study of 2,858 firms across the United States covering a variety of manufacturing as well as service industries that firms with larger levels of initial capital had a greater propensity to survive (also see Vesper, 1980, pp.47–48). The authors of this study were surprised to note that there were no differences between surviving and closing firms with respect to sources of initial funds. Contrary to expectation, Cooper et al., (1988, p.234) found that closing firms had not over-relied upon personal savings as a source of funds. However, in a study of new firms in Scotland Reid (1991, p.552) noted that a firm entirely launched exclusively on personal finance was more likely to close. Reid (1991, p.552) also presented empirical evidence to support the hypothesis that the ability to acquire additional finance after the start-up period was the sign of a good project and was positively associated with business survival.

In North-East England Storey et al., (1987a, p.323) recorded during their study of manufacturing companies that business failure was associated with the presence of a secured bank loan. Conversely, Reynolds and Miller (1989, p.167) in their follow-up study of 550 new firms in Minnesota, USA found no difference in the initial financial support, informal or formal, between firms that survive and close. However, O'Farrell and Crouchley (1983, p.423; 1987, p.326) in their multivariate analysis of the closure of manufacturing firms in Ireland noted that, 'Grant-aid at start-up improves the liquidity of the plant and significantly reduces the chances of early closure' (O'Farrell und Crouchley, 1987, p.326).

It has been asserted by Flynn (1991, p.226) that, 'A firm's profitability is also likely to be an important factor in the exit decision. As a firm fails to maintain an acceptable level of profits, its likelihood of survival diminishes' (also see Schary, 1991, p.348). This view has been supported in a study of manufacturing companies in north-east England which emphasised the importance of gearing and profitability for survival prediction (Storey et al., 1987a).

Factor 8: Technology – Sophistication and Inputs

Wilkens (1987) has suggested that innovation is essential to small business growth and development. Interestingly, Kalleberg and Leicht (1991, pp.152–153) found during their study that businesses headed by men who frequently engaged in innovative behaviours were less likely to survive than other businesses. Within the economics literature it has been hypothesised (Gort and Klepper, 1982; Winter, 1984) that the technological and knowledge conditions determine the relative ease with which new firms are able to innovate and therefore survive. In a survival study across 295 four-digit SIC industries Audretsch (1991, pp.446–447) found, 'holding the total amount of innovative activity in the industry constant, an increase in the ability of small firms to innovate leads to a higher survival rate'. Moreover, Audretsch presented empirical evidence to support the hypothesis that new firm survival rates were positively related to the extent of small firm innovative activity.

Factor 9: Technology Diffusion – R and D Outputs

The survival of small firms is in part due to their flexibility in being able to meet the needs of rapidly changing market niches. It has, therefore, been hypothesised that small firms with large product and/or service ranges can readily exploit market niches and as a result they are more likely to survive (Reid, 1991, p.552).

Factor 10: Management Functions

It has been claimed that the success level attained by a young firm may depend upon whether or not competent managers are added and authority is shared in the business (Cooper, 1993, p.247). Supporting this view Hoad and Rosko (1964) noted during their study of manufacturing firms in the United States that venture success was influenced by the variety of experience in selected businesses. More recently, it has been suggested by Cooper et al., (1991, p.68) that new ventures often fail because they are generally associated with narrow skill bases which restrict and determine the strategy options available.

Factor 11: Start-up Problems

Results from a longitudinal study of 250 high-technology firms in Silicon Valley conducted by Bruno et al., (1992, p.291) found that, 'Among the factors predicting failure were product market problems such as product timing difficulties, problems of product design, or inappropriate distribution channels; financial difficulties such as initial undercapitalization or problems with the venture capital relationship; and managerial/key employee problems such as imbalance in the management team or succumbing to the trappings of success. Reid (1991, p.553) noted in his study that those owner managers who had suggested that their business had earlier experienced cash-flow problems were less likely to stay in business. However, Reynolds and Miller (1989) found no relationship between thirty-five cited start-up problems and business survival in essentially low-technology industries. They suggest, 'This may be because the firms with more problems are often those with higher growth rates and more initial sales' (p.167).

THIS RESEARCH

Research Objectives

There have been increasing calls for more longitudinal research that charts the survival and progress of businesses over time (Aldrich, 1992; Churchill, 1992; van de Ven, 1992). Consequently, this paper reports empirical evidence from a second and much more extensive longitudinal follow-on survey of independent firms located on and off Science Parks in 1986. Attempts have been made to contact all 135 independent firms located on Science Parks in 1986 as well as the 92 independent off park firms. The research discussed in this paper followed three levels of analysis:

1. To chart the survival from the ends of 1986 and 1992 of 227 independent essentially high-technology based firms originally surveyed by Monck et al., (1988) in 1986 engaged in 'hard' manufacturing activities as well as more 'soft' service sectors (Bullock, 1983, p.2).
2. To isolate the leading factors from those previously detailed in the research literature which have a significant association with business survival in the total sample (the Science Park and off park samples combined). Firm survival will be particularly explored with regard to resource exchange theory rather than the population ecology theory mainly due to the nature of the data available for analysis. The resource profiles of surveyed firms will be used to determine business survival. Moreover, we will explore whether the factors associated with the survival of high-technology based firms are similar to those previously reported in earlier studies which have overwhelmingly charted the survival of businesses in low-technology sectors.
3. Within a multivariate framework we will identify the web of factors most closely associated with high-technology business survival.

Definition of Independent Organisation Closure

Defining business closure or 'failure' is a major problem and a variety of definitions have been utilised (Scott and Lewis, 1984, pp.30–42; Goudie and Meeks, 1991, pp.445–446; Keasey and Watson, 1991, pp.14–15; Watson and Everett, 1993, pp.37–39). 'The reasons for closure are many and varied and are not solely associated with business failure' (O'Farrell and Crouchley, 1983, p.412). Consequently there is no universally accepted definition at the point in time when a business can be said to have closed (or 'failed') (Birley, 1986). Moreover, we appreciated from the outset that a definition of closure needs to be chosen which enables a valid and direct comparison to be made between firms located on as well as off Science Parks. It also needs to recognise the quality of information about the off park firms is weaker than that for Science Park firms. A definition therefore has to be employed which the researchers can be confident ensures that both groups of firms are being treated comparably. The following definition of independent organisation closure was utilised.

An independent business is regarded as a closure if in 1992 it is no longer identifiable as a trading business. An independent business which moves locations but continues as a trading business is not regarded as a closure.

Note that firms sold to new owners are counted as continuing firms as long as they remain in operation: departure of an owner is not equated to business discontinuance (Bates, 1990, p.553). A similar definition was utilised by Cambridgeshire County Council and by Garnsey and Cannon-Brookes (1992, p.8 and p.9) in their longitudinal study of high-technology businesses associated with the Cambridge Phenomenon (also see Kalleberg and Leicht, 1991, p.144). This is a more wide ranging definition than that which has been used by

UKSPA who have used the following definition. A business is defined as a closure where it goes into receivership or liquidation at the time at which it ceases to trade on or off the Science Park. (1)

METHODOLOGY

Analysis of assembled data was conducted in three stages:

Stage 1: The survival of independent firms surveyed in 1986 was ascertained by contacting Science Park managers and searches through telephone listings, telephone books and local trade directories. For untraced businesses additional evidence from direct fieldwork was gathered from individuals adjacent to the original location of the firm surrounding its current status and location (a similar method was used by Reid, 1991, p.547).

Stage 2: On the basis of a review of the business survival and closure literature preliminary hypotheses were constructed to identify those individual factors statistically associated with business survival. Moreover, based on the data collected during the survey in 1986 it was possible with reference to the research literature to identify 11 factors/themes associated with the theories stated above. The 11 factors listed in Table 1 have been inductively as well as deductively derived from the research literature and have been discussed elsewhere (Flynn, 1991; Westhead and Birley, 1994). They relate not only to the 'internal' characteristics of key founders and their businesses but also in part to their perception of the wider competitive 'external' environment where their firm was located. The assembled factors cover the themes identified by Cooper and Gimeno Gascon (1992, p.302) and Cooper (1993, p.242) bearing upon the performance of independent start-ups – characteristics of the entrepreneur, the process of starting, environmental characteristics and initial firm attributes. Following, Kalleberg and Leicht (1991, p.159) we appreciate that, 'survival and success are divergent aspects of performance determined by processes at several levels of analysis, including the industrial context of an organization, the organization itself, and the individual entrepreneur'. In relation to these 11 factors 69 variables derived from the original 1986 questionnaire survey returns were considered and explored here. Chi-square and Student's 't' tests are conducted to identify individual differences between founder and business characteristics and subsequent business survival.

Stage 3: The third stage of analysis explores the multivariate influences on business survival. A number of previous studies which have predicted business 'failure' using financial ratio data have utilised the discriminant analysis technique (Altman, 1968; Taffler, 1982; Bates and Nucci, 1989; Bates, 1990) in order to achieve their objectives. It is, however, increasingly being appreciated that an efficient use of discriminant analysis is not possible on many data sets and particularly the technique is inappropriate when many of the variables are not multivariate normal in their distribution (Keasey and Watson, 1987, p.345). To overcome this problem the multivariate web of factors associated with business survival will be identified by the widely used logit analysis technique (O'Farrell and Crouchley, 1983; Keasey and Watson, 1987; Storey et al., 1987a; Bates, 1990; Audretsch, 1991; Schary, 1991; Cooper et al., 1991; Cressy, 1992).

TABLE I
Chi-Square and 't' Test Differences Between Key Founder and Business Characteristics by Business Closure/Survival

SELECTED INDEPENDENT VARIABLES AND THEIR HYPOTHESISED DIRECTION OF ASSOCIATION WITH BUSINESS SURVIVAL	CLOSURES NO.	%	SURVIVORS NO.	%	SIGNIFICANCE LEVEL OF THE CHI-SQUARE STATISTIC	CLOSURES MEAN	SURVIVORS MEAN	SIGNIFICANCE LEVEL OF 'T' STATISTIC (TWO-TAILED TEST)	NUMBER OF VALID CASES
(a) Personal Background of Key Founder									
1. Gender of key founder – male (+/–)					n.a.				214
No	1	1.4	4	2.8					
Yes	69	98.6	140	97.2					
2. Age of key founder when business first started to trade (years) (+)						38.5	37.7	0.612	138
3. (Age of key founder when business first started to trade)^2 (years) (+)						1580.1	1493.7	0.547	138
4. Key founder has paper qualifications (+)					0.797				207
No	11	16.7	20	14.2					
Yes	55	83.3	121	85.8					
5. Key founder has a bachelor's degree or more(+)(DEGREE)					0.110				202
No	32	50.0	51	37.0					
Yes	32	50.0	87	63.0					
6. Key founder unemployed or likely to become unemployed immediately prior to establishing this business (–)					0.664				210
No	55	78.6	115	82.1					
Yes	15	21.4	25	17.9					
(b) Work Experience of Key Founder									
7. Key founder held a management position in last organisation (+)					0.082				198
No	11	16.2	37	28.5					
Yes	57	83.8	93	71.5					
8. Key founder was last employed in a Higher Education Institute (HEI) (–)					0.111				194
No	63	92.6	105	83.3					
Yes	5	7.4	21	16.7					
9. Key founder was last employed in a public sector organisation (–)					0.114				199
No	56	82.4	93	71.0					
Yes	12	17.6	38	29.0					
10. Employment size of last organisation worked in by key founder (+)						469.7	974.5	0.068	143
11. Key founder was last employed in a non-manufacturing industry organisation (+/–)					0.098				194
No	36	53.7	51	40.2					
Yes	31	46.3	76	59.8					
12. Key founder the director or owner of any business other than this one (–)					1.000				207
No	51	72.9	100	73.0					
Yes	19	27.1	37	27.0					

Chapter 5

SELECTED INDEPENDENT VARIABLES AND THEIR HYPOTHESISED DIRECTION OF ASSOCIATION WITH BUSINESS SURVIVAL	CLOSURES NO.	%	SURVIVORS NO.	%	SIGNIFICANCE LEVEL OF THE CHI-SQUARE STATISTIC	CLOSURES MEAN	SURVIVORS MEAN	SIGNIFICANCE LEVEL OF 'T' STATISTIC (TWO-TAILED TEST)	NUMBER OF VALID CASES
13. Business ever been a part time activity at any stage for key founder (−)									
No	55	77.5	99	71.7	0.469				209
Yes	16	22.5	39	28.3					
(c) Characteristics of the Business									
14. Age of business in 1986 (years) (+) (AGEBUS)						4.5	7.4	0.000	164
15. Total employment size of the business (September 1986) (log) (+)						0.8	1.0	0.006	187
16. Business main industrial activity is manufacturing (−)									
No	53	72.6	97	63.0	0.201				227
Yes	20	27.4	57	37.0					
17. Business located in a government designated 'assisted' area 1986 (−) (ASSIST)									
No	42	57.5	67	43.5	0.067				227
Yes	31	42.5	87	56.5					
18. Business located in the 'north' (1986) (−)									
No	26	35.6	51	33.1	0.825				227
Yes	47	64.4	103	66.9					
19. Business located on a science park (1986) (+/−)									
No	30	41.1	62	40.3	1.000				227
Yes	43	58.9	92	59.7					
20. Legal form of the business is a company (+)									
No	11	15.1	18	11.9	0.656				224
Yes	62	84.9	133	88.1					
21. Legal form of the business is a sole proprietorship (−)									
No	69	94.5	145	96.0	n.a.				224
Yes	4	5.5	6	4.0					
22. Absolute sales turnover of the business in the last financial year (1986) (log) (+)						5.2	5.3	0.156	192
23. Absolute sales turnover of the business in the last financial year (1986) as a proportion of the total employment size of the business (1986) (log) (+)						4.2	4.1	0.785	131
24. Business located in leased premises (−)									
No	20	28.6	48	31.8	0.745				221
Yes	50	71.4	103	68.2					
25. Size of unit occupied by the business (sq. ft.) (log) (+) (LOGSIZEU)						3.1	3.3	0.009	219
26. Business had more than one shareholder when it was set up (+) (SHARE)									
No	16	23.9	17	12.1	0.051				207
Yes	51	76.1	123	87.9					

SELECTED INDEPENDENT VARIABLES AND THEIR HYPOTHESISED DIRECTION OF ASSOCIATION WITH BUSINESS SURVIVAL	CLOSURES NO.	%	SURVIVORS NO.	%	SIGNIFICANCE LEVEL OF THE CHI-SQUARE STATISTIC	CLOSURES MEAN	SURVIVORS MEAN	SIGNIFICANCE LEVEL OF 'T' STATISTIC (TWO-TAILED TEST)	NUMBER OF VALID CASES
(d) Customer Base									
27. Number of customers sold to in the last twelve months (1986) (+)						139.8	104.8	0.488	217
28. Percentage of total output (by value) sold to three largest customers (−)						52.3	48.7	0.394	191
29. Proportion of customers that depend entirely, or almost entirely on the business for their supply of a particular product or service (+)						46.5	55.6	0.167	188
30. Percentage of businesses products/services (by value) sold to customers up to 10 miles away (−)						15.7	11.1	0.229	205
31. Proportion of businesses output (by value) subcontracted to external manufacturers/assemblers (+/−)						19.0	13.3	0.211	203
(e) Competitive Structure									
32. Number of firms the business directly competes with on a regular basis (−)						8.5	17.8	0.095	185
33. Regular competitors are small firms (−) (COMP)									
No	24	53.3	80	73.4	0.026				154
Yes	21	46.7	29	26.6					
(f) Networking									
34. Business established links with locally-based government research institutions or large corporations in the area (+)									
No	60	85.7	117	77.5	0.213				221
Yes	10	14.3	34	22.5					
35. Business established links with local Higher Education Institute (HEI) (+)									
No	17	24.6	19	12.7	0.043				219
Yes	52	75.4	131	87.3					
(g) Financial Base									
36. Number of sources of finance used during the start-up period (+)						2.3	2.4	0.609	219
37. Main source of finance used during the start-up of the business was personal savings (−)									
No	36	50.0	68	46.3	0.706				219
Yes	36	50.0	79	53.7					
38. Number of sources of finance used during the last financial year (1986) (+)						3.1	3.2	0.749	223
39. Main source of finance was personal savings during the last financial year (1986) (−)									
No	63	87.5	123	81.5	0.346				223
Yes	9	12.5	28	18.5					

SELECTED INDEPENDENT VARIABLES AND THEIR HYPOTHESISED DIRECTION OF ASSOCIATION WITH BUSINESS SURVIVAL	CLOSURES NO.	%	SURVIVORS NO.	%	SIGNIFICANCE LEVEL OF THE CHI-SQUARE STATISTIC	CLOSURES MEAN	SURVIVORS MEAN	SIGNIFICANCE LEVEL OF 'T' STATISTIC (TWO-TAILED TEST)	NUMBER OF VALID CASES
40. Loan/overdraft from clearing bank used as a source of finance during the last financial year (1986) (−) (BANK)					0.090				223
No	24	33.3	70	46.4					
Yes	48	66.7	81	53.6					
41. Grant from a local, national, or European government used as a source of finance during the last financial year (1986) (+)					0.197				223
No	55	76.4	101	66.9					
Yes	17	23.6	50	33.1					
42. Surveyed business had made a net profit before tax in the last financial year (1986) (+)					0.647				189
No	17	31.5	49	36.3					
Yes	37	68.5	86	63.7					
(h) Technology – Sophistication and Inputs									
43. Technical novelty of main product/service group (as perceived by respondents) is at least advanced technology for manufactured products and/or at least a service based on knowledge new to the UK (+/−)					0.236				213
No	24	36.9	41	27.7					
Yes	41	63.1	107	72.3					
44. Research and development work still continuing in the business (+)					n.a.				214
No	7	10.6	9	6.1					
Yes	59	89.4	139	93.9					
45. Total R & D expenditure as a percentage of turnover (1986) (+)						24.7	23.2	0.773	136
46. Number of qualified scientists and engineers engaged in R & D as a percentage of total employees (1986) (+)						26.3	27.9	0.809	81
(i) Technology Diffusion: R & D Outputs									
47. Number of new products/ services launched in the last two years (1986) to the existing customer base (+)						3.0	4.7	0.328	189
48. Number of new products/ services launched in the last two years (1986) in new markets (+)						1.9	2.4	0.481	189
49. Number of patents or applications taken out in the last twelve months (1986) (+)						0.5	0.6	0.878	203
(j) Management Functions									
50. Number of management functions covered by individuals in the management team (range from 1 to 7) (+)						3.7	4.1	**0.080**	225

SELECTED INDEPENDENT VARIABLES AND THEIR HYPOTHESISED DIRECTION OF ASSOCIATION WITH BUSINESS SURVIVAL	CLOSURES NO.	%	SURVIVORS NO.	%	SIGNIFICANCE LEVEL OF THE CHI-SQUARE STATISTIC	CLOSURES MEAN	SURVIVORS MEAN	SIGNIFICANCE LEVEL OF 'T' STATISTIC (TWO-TAILED TEST)	NUMBER OF VALID CASES
51. Management team contains individuals with production backgrounds (+)									
No	37	51.4	67	43.8	0.356				225
Yes	35	48.6	86	56.2					
52. Management team contains individuals with finance backgrounds (+)									
No	34	47.2	66	43.1	0.666				225
Yes	38	52.8	87	56.9					
53. Management team contains individuals with marketing backgrounds (+)									
No	24	33.3	46	30.1	0.734				225
Yes	48	66.7	107	69.9					
54. Management team contains individuals with personnel backgrounds (+)									
No	57	79.2	100	65.4	0.051				225
Yes	15	20.8	53	34.6					
55. Management team contains individuals with R & D backgrounds (+)									
No	18	25.0	24	15.7					225
Yes	54	75.0	129	84.3	0.136				
56. Management team contains individuals with general management experience (+)									
No	28	38.9	51	33.3	0.506				225
Yes	44	61.1	102	66.7					
57. Management team contains individuals with experience of establishing a small company (+)									
No	43	59.7	82	53.6	0.472				225
Yes	29	40.3	71	46.4					
(k) Start-up Problems									
58. Shortage of supplies – problems during first year of operation (+/–)									
No	58	92.1	116	83.5	0.155				202
Yes	5	7.9	23	16.5					
59. Shortage of skilled labour – problem during first year of operation (+/–)									
No	52	80.0	105	76.1	0.686				203
Yes	13	20.0	33	23.9					
60. High labour turnover – problem during first year of operation (+/–)									
No	60	95.2	124	91.2	n.a.				199
Yes	3	4.8	12	8.8					
61. Wage costs – problem during first year of operation (+/–)									
No	59	92.2	121	88.3	0.557				201
Yes	5	7.8	16	11.7					
62. Government bureaucracy and red tape – problem during first year of operations (+/–)									
No	43	68.3	99	76.7	0.279				192
Yes	20	31.7	30	23.3					

SELECTED INDEPENDENT VARIABLES AND THEIR HYPOTHESISED DIRECTION OF ASSOCIATION WITH BUSINESS SURVIVAL	CLOSURES NO.	%	SURVIVORS NO.	%	SIGNIFICANCE LEVEL OF THE CHI-SQUARE STATISTIC	CLOSURES MEAN	SURVIVORS MEAN	SIGNIFICANCE LEVEL OF 'T' STATISTIC (TWO-TAILED TEST)	NUMBER OF VALID CASES
63. Obtaining payment from large debtors – problem during first year of operations (+/–)									
No	38	58.5	89	68.5	0.222				195
Yes	27	41.5	41	31.5					
64. Shortage of demand or markets – problem during first year of operation (+/–)									
No	49	73.1	102	75.0	0.908				203
Yes	18	26.9	34	25.0					
65. Shortage of key management skills – problem during first year of operation (+/–)									
No	47	74.6	95	68.8	0.506				201
Yes	16	25.4	43	31.2					
66. VAT registration – problem during first year of operation (+/–)									
No	59	95.2	118	95.9	n.a.				185
Yes	3	4.8	5	4.1					
67. Obtaining finance – problem during first year of operation (+/–)									
No	40	59.7	100	71.9	0.109				206
Yes	27	40.3	39	28.1					
68. Time constraints on management team – problem during first year of operation (+/–)									
No	31	49.2	61	46.6	0.848				194
Yes	32	50.8	70	53.4					
69. Any other problems during first year of operation (+/–)									
No	49	79.0	105	82.0	0.766				190
Yes	13	21.0	23	18.0					

Note: Due to the assumptions of the chi-square test it was not possible to calculate a coefficient.

ASSUMPTIONS/LIMITATIONS OF THE STRATEGY ADOPTED

In studies such as this there is a need to place some limits on the generalisations that can be made (Baum and Mezias, 1992, p.599; Aldrich, 1992, p.206). Therefore, to fully understand the conclusions of this paper it is important to be aware of the following key assumptions/limitations:

a) To assess the benefits of a Science Park location random samples of Park firms (in 1986) were matched with a similar sample of off park firms on the basis of four criteria (ownership, age, sector and geography). It must be emphasised here that the sample (in 1986) of off park firms were not identified and then matched with comparable Science Park firms on the basis of four criteria. The results from the latter matching procedure could have produced results different from those already presented in 1986 (Monck et al., 1988). As a result the random sample in 1986 of Science Park organisations

may include markedly more young firms and organisations located in the government designated 'assisted' areas.
b) The 'matching' methodology employed (also see Peck, 1985; Storey et al., 1987b) originally used by Monck et al., (1988) has been criticised by some commentators (Gibb, 1992, p.133 and p.140; Turok, 1991, pp.1547–1548). For example, it has been argued by Gibb (1992, p.133) that matching firms in policy-orientated research projects is nothing more than 'pseudo-scientific sampling'. We reject this view. The reason for matching firms was to make a genuine comparison between on and off park firms. The choice of matching criteria was influenced by previous empirical work which has indicated that organisation survival and growth is particularly associated with ownership, age, sector and geography factors (Storey, 1994).
c) The combined on and off park sample is not intended to be a representative random sample of high-technology firms in Great Britain in 1986.
d) Turok (1991, p.1547) has argued that direct interview surveys suffer from a range of problems. Most notable, responses from firms who have received assistance (such as firms located on Science Parks) are 'invariably threatened by respondent bias and post hoc rationalization'. We accept this criticism but find there to be no clearly superior method of eliciting responses.
e) It has also been asserted by Turok (1991, p.1546) that, 'Decisions about cut-off dates are inevitably arbitrary and the resulting snapshot comparisons do not capture processes of change effectively'. We believe this criticism is overcome by the use of 'follow-on' samples.
f) We only chart the survival of Science Park firms at three points in time whilst for the off park group we only record their survival at two points in time. It was not possible to ascertain the precise date of closure for surveyed firms nor was it possible to gather in-depth evidence on the exact reasons for closure. These remain areas for further research.
g) Science Park organisations are easier to track over a six year period. This could lead to bias since Science Park firms which changed their names would be known about by, for example, the Park personnel, whereas this was less likely to be the case for off park firms. Deriving a definition of 'closure' which both validly compared and measured Science Park with the off park firms is difficult. Nevertheless, we are confident that the wide definition of 'closure' defined above ensured that both groups of firms were treated comparably.
h) Only one narrow performance measure (Turok 1991 p.1545) was used in this paper – whether an independent firm interviewed in 1986 survived up to the 31st December 1992. For example, it has been argued by Cooper and Gimeno Gascon (1992, p.303) that, 'Survival versus discontinuance...[is a performance measure but it]...does not consider whether some 'survive' with higher performance than others'. Consequently, it is appreciated that the 'quality of the surviving firms may be variable in relation to their ability to generate new jobs, create wealth, export goods and services abroad and develop commercially viable new technological processes and products'.
i) Further, we only track the survival of the business interviewed in 1986 and we do not know whether some 'multiple business' starters (Birley and Westhead, 1993) who have closed down the surveyed firm are still in business elsewhere in another form.
j) It is acknowledged that cross-sectional analysis may not give a totally reliable picture of the dynamics of change (Mountfield, 1985, p.778). The 1986

interview survey was not specifically designed to identify all factors which may have a subsequent influence on new business survival. Nor was it originally designed to test the applicability of the resource exchange and population ecology theories. Further, like numerous earlier studies, 'the analysis is restricted to the survival or closure of the stock of plants which existed at time t0 and cannot incorporate new plants which entered between t0 and t1' (O'Farrell and Crouchley, 1987, p.313). Detailed accounting data on surveyed firms in 1986 was not collected and consequently the wide practice of predicting company failure based on financial ratios cannot be undertaken here (Altman, 1968; Taffler, 1982; Storey et al., 1987a; Shailer, 1992). We agree with Argenti (1976) who argued that business 'failure' is a dynamic event where financial ratios can only be seen as merely symptoms of business failure (also see Keasey and Watson, 1987). Unfortunately no time-varying explanatory variables were collected covering issues related to employment size, technological sophistication, management structures, competitive strategy, environmental characteristics, changes in demand growth, etc. It has also been warned by Cooper (1993, p.249 and p.250) that, 'Research to date has tended to focus upon variables that are relatively easy to gather information about or measure. This may not be the same as focusing upon the variables that most bear upon performance....(and)...we are dealing with variables that lend themselves to surveys, rather than examining the underlying factors that may be driving performance'. Nevertheless, some useful surrogate variables were collected during the original study in 1986 and they in part can be used to test the theories discussed above, particularly the resource exchange perspective. These variables have been found in earlier studies to be statistically associated with business survival. Also, collected variables were amenable to measurement but we appreciate that they will not isolate all proximate causes of business survival (Keasey and Watson, 1991, p.14).

k) To satisfy the assumptions of the Student's 't' test technique and logit analysis some explanatory variables with curvilinear distributions were transformed by natural log transformation.

l) O'Farrell and Crouchley (1987, p.313) in a review of their own logit analysis study of manufacturing firm closures in Ireland (O'Farrell and Crouchley, 1983, p.421) expressed serious reservations surrounding the multivariate technique. They warned 'the logit model is cross-sectional, which means that the independent variables for each plant and for each external factor are observed at time t0 values and no allowance can be made for changes after that date. This is a major flaw in any attempt to build an explanatory model of closure, since two of the most important factors which have been shown to relate to closure probability are dynamic, namely the size of the plant and the effect of the business cycle. More generally, there are problems in attempting to determine causality from cross-sectional data where several alternative models may describe the same cross-sectional pattern. Despite such equifinality, the temptation to interpret the parameter estimates as measuring the impact of 'explanatory' variables has frequently proved irresistible (Davies and Pickles, 1985). Some doubts as to the validity of this widespread practice are of concern where the process under study is suspected of being dynamic.

m) Logit models presented in Table 3 are based on data for less than 227 independent firms because a number of respondents in 1986 refused to answer all presented questions (valid cases for each independent variable are presented in Table 1). Further, it must be appreciated that the stochastic logit models deal with the probability of survival as opposed to success.

TABLE 3
Logit Models of Variables Associated with Business Survival

INDEPENDENT VARIABLES	MODEL 1	MODEL 2
CONSTANT	−1.9729	−2.3488
	(4.7786)	(3.6720)
BANK	−	−1.0796
		(7.4169)
ASSIST	−	0.7232
		(3.7076)
AGEBUS	0.1747	0.1150
	(5.4851)	(6.6900)
LOGSIZEU	−	0.7756
		(3.9693)
SHARE	1.8733	−
	(6.1140)	
COMP	−1.0240	−
	(4.0374)	
DEGREE	0.9579	−
	(3.4905)	
n=	97	157
Overall Predictive Accuracy	78.35%	71.34%
Survivors Predicted Correctly	92.31%	85.29%
Closures Predicted Correctly	50.00%	45.45%
−2LL	100.19	174.92
Model chi-square	22.8	28.4
d.f.	4	4
Goodness of fit significance	0.4398	0.3029

'Individual ventures may succeed against the odds or fail despite a favourable resource profile' (Cooper et al., 1991, p.72).

Chapter 5

RESULTS

Number of Independent High-Technology Firm Survivors

The basic data on changes in independent firms in the total sample over the six year period between the ends of 1986 and 1992 are detailed in Table 2 (2). Row 1 in Table 2 indicates that 154 independent firms have survived (68%). A further 50 firms (22%) have been confirmed as business closures (row 2), whilst 23 firms (10%) cannot be traced and do not appear to be trading in any identifiable form (even after field surveys, extensive telephone directory and local trade directory searches as well as searches through Companies House register) (row 3). The latter group of firms are also regarded as business closures for the remainder of this paper. Hence 154 independent firms have survived (68%) compared to only 73 independent organisation closures (32%).

TABLE 2
Surveyed Independent Organisations in 1986: Where Are They Now? (a)

ORGANISATION STATUS	TOTAL SAMPLE NO.	%
1. Survived at either original or new address	154	68
2. Confirmed organisation closure	50	22
3. No telephone listing/not recorded in telephone book or local trade directory	23	10
TOTAL	227	100
Total independent organisation closure rate (including no telephone listings)	73	32
Total independent organisation closure rate (excluding no telephone listings)	50	22

Note: (a) The 'tracking' of Science Park organisations was more successfully achieved because information was more extensive from Science Park managers surrounding organisation name changes and/or business relocations.

The above results are in line with those presented in a longitudinal panel study of independent small firms in eight manufacturing sectors in London over the 1979–89 period. North et al., (1992, p.14) found that 42% of the firms in the 1979 panel were no longer in existence by the end of 1989. Moreover, Garnsey and Cannon-Brookes (1992, p.26) in their longitudinal study of high-technology companies associated with the Cambridge Phenomenon concluded, 'Data available for the period since 1990 suggest a 10% fall in the number of active high technology companies in Cambridgeshire...The average annual failure rate increased from 1.5% per year in the early 1980s to 3.7% in the latter half of the decade. Since 1990, the available figures suggest that closures and moves have outnumbered start-ups by 3 to 1'.

It is very difficult to compare these findings with any official statistics on the survival of United Kingdom businesses in general, since the basis of the comparison is imperfect. Perhaps the nearest comparison is with businesses deregistered for VAT which generally show between 1980 and 1990 about 11% of the stock of firms de-registering each year (Daly, 1991, p.580). Based on an annual 11% deregistration rate over this six year period we would 'expect', if their age distribution was identical to that of Value Added Tax (VAT) registered firms, that 115 total sample firms would have closed. The 'observed' number of businesses closing in the total sample is 42 firms fewer than that 'expected' (73 'observed' closures compared with 115 'expected' closures). This suggests that, subject to the important provisos (3), the closure rate of independent essentially high-technology based firms is lower than that recorded by United Kingdom businesses in general. This latter result confirms the earlier findings presented by Storey and Strange (1992, p.18).

Univariate Analysis Results

FACTOR 1: PERSONAL BACKGROUND OF KEY FOUNDER No statistically significant differences were recorded between firms that closed and survived with regard to the personal background of the key founder (Table 1). Over 97% of founders in both groups were male and overall founders were on average 37 years of age when the business first started to trade. Contrary to expectation, founders of closing firms were equally likely to have a bachelor's degree or more and/or paper qualifications. Similarly, it can also be inferred from Table 1 that founders 'pushed' into entrepreneurship were not significantly more likely to have established a firm that was likely to close.

FACTOR 2: WORK EXPERIENCE OF KEY FOUNDER Three out of the seven variables measuring the work experience of the key founder were statistically significant at the 0.1 level of significance. In the opposite direction to that hypothesised, founders with management experience in their last organisation prior to start-up were more likely to have a business that closed. We infer from this that the 'type' and 'quality' of management experience may be the factor of considerable importance leading to subsequent new business survival. Moreover, founders who had gained their work experience and contacts in a non-manufacturing industry were significantly more likely to be still in business. There was no difference in the propensity for a business to survive with regard to whether a founder was last employed in a Higher Education Institute (HEI) and/or a public sector organisation. We infer here that individuals from non-profit making organisations have obtained skills necessary to manage the survival of an independent business. With regard to the employment size of the incubator worked in prior to start-up, as hypothesised, founders employed in large employment sized organisations had a significantly greater propensity to run surviving businesses. Supporting the evidence from previous studies, although not in a statistically significant direction, it can be inferred from Table 1 that business survivors were more likely to be headed by individuals who were not directors or owners of any other businesses and had not started the surveyed venture on a part time basis.

FACTOR 3: CHARACTERISTICS OF THE BUSINESS Fourteen characteristics of the surveyed businesses were explored and only five were found to be statistically associated with venture survival. As hypothesised, older firms and those with large employment sizes were significantly more likely to survive. This empirical evidence supports the view from the population ecology model that increased legitimacy leads to greater stability and business survival. Also, as posited, firms mainly engaged in manufacturing activities had a greater propensity to survive, although not in a statistically significant direction.

Contrary to expectation, firms located in government designated 'assisted' areas had a significantly greater propensity to survive. We infer here that government support services and grants may in part be responsible for the survival of high profile firms in these relatively depressed localities. Also, a 'northern' location was not found to be an impediment to business survival. On a note of caution, with regard to the location variables we believe that a recession lag effect may be influencing these results. Basically, the full force of the recession up to the end of 1992 had particularly been felt by firms located in 'non-assisted' and 'southern' locations. Moreover, no significant difference was recorded between the proportion of closures on and off Science Parks. In the short term Flynn's (1993) reservations surrounding sponsored environments have not been supported. It, however, must be appreciated that a number of off park firms were also located in sponsored 'assisted' area locations.

No statistically significant differences were recorded between surviving and closing firms with regard to the legal form of businesses. Also, firms with large absolute levels of sales and sales turnover as a proportion of the total employment size of the business were not significantly more likely to survive. In relation to the type of premises occupied by firms in 1986 no statistically significant difference was recorded between the two groups of firms. Contrary to expectation, firms located in leased premises were not significantly more likely to close. However, as posited, firms located in large sized units (with legitimacy and room for diversification into manufacturing activities) had a significantly greater propensity to survive. Finally, as hypothesised, businesses with more than one shareholder when it was set up were significantly more likely to survive. We infer here that firms with greater financial resources and depth of management expertise are more likely to overcome the survival hurdles.

FACTOR 4: CUSTOMER BASE In relation to the customer bases of closing and surviving firms no statistically significant differences were recorded. However, in the opposite direction to that hypothesised firms with larger numbers of customers sold to in the last twelve months were more likely to close. But as posited firms that had a greater dependency to sell their output (by value) to their three largest customers had a greater tendency to close. As hypothesised those firms that indicated that they had a stable (or captive) market where their customers depended entirely, or almost entirely, on their business for their supply of a particular product or service were more likely to survive. Moreover, as posited, firms that exhibited a greater tendency to rely upon the fortunes of local markets (in relation to the percentage of products/services (by value) sold to customers up to 10 miles away) had a greater propensity to close. Table 1 also shows that firms recording high proportions of output (by value) subcontracted to external manufacturers/assemblers were more likely to close, although not in a statistically significant direction.

FACTOR 5: COMPETITIVE STRUCTURE Contrary to expectation, firms that directly compete with a large number of organisations on a regular basis were significantly more likely to survive. However, as hypothesised, it can be inferred from Table 1 that firms regularly competing with small firms in potentially saturated (and price competitive) market niches were more likely to close.

FACTOR 6: NETWORKING Two variables exploring the development of networks by surveyed firms were collected. The vast majority of surveyed businesses had not established links with locally based government research institutions or large corporations in the area but those that had were more likely to survive, although not in a statistically significant direction. Further, as posited, a significantly larger proportion of businesses that had gained access to resources and skills from local HEI's recorded a significantly greater propensity to survive.

FACTOR 7: FINANCIAL BASE Only one out of the seven financial base variables was significantly associated with business survival. As suggested firms with diverse financial bases during the start-up period as well as during the last financial year were more likely to survive, although not in a statistically significant direction. Contrary to expectation, firms that indicated that personal savings were the main source of finance used during the start-up of the business were not significantly less likely to survive. A similar pattern was recorded in relation to this source of finance during the last financial year. However, as hypothesised those firms that had obtained a loan/overdraft from a clearing bank during the last financial year were significantly more likely to close. We infer here that high interest repayments may have pushed a number of firms out of business. Also, in the opposite direction to that hypothesised, firms that were making a profit during the last financial year were not more likely to survive up to the end of 1992. Finally, as posited, firms that had gained a grant from a local, national or European government during the last financial year (on potentially favourable terms) were more likely to survive, although not in a statistically significant direction.

FACTOR 8: TECHNOLOGY – SOPHISTICATION AND INPUTS No statistically significant differences between the two groups of firms were recorded with regard to technology sophistication and inputs. Over 63% of surviving as well as closing firms suggested that the technical novelty of their main product/service (as perceived by respondents) was at least advanced technology for manufactured products and/or at least a service based on knowledge new to the

United Kingdom. Moreover, it can be inferred that the profiles of firms in the two groups in relation to a commitment to research and development, levels of R & D expenditure as a percentage of turnover and number of qualified scientists and engineers engaged in R & D as a percentage of total employees are remarkably similar. It can be inferred from Table 1 that these variables cannot differentiate between surviving and closing ventures.

FACTOR 9: TECHNOLOGY DIFFUSION – R & D OUTPUTS Similarly, in relation to measures of technology diffusion very similar profiles were recorded by surviving and closing firms. However, as hypothesised surviving firms were more likely to have more new products/services launched in the last two years to existing customers and new markets and they had taken out in the last twelve months more patents or applications, although not in a statistically significant direction.

FACTOR 10: MANAGEMENT FUNCTIONS As hypothesised, those firms that had a diverse range of management skills and competencies – as reflected by a large number of management functions covered by individuals in the management team – had a significantly greater propensity to survive. However, in relation to only one management function (out of seven) was a statistically significant difference recorded between the two groups of firms. As hypothesised, those firms with a management team that contains individuals with personnel backgrounds were significantly more likely to survive.

FACTOR 11: START-UP PROBLEMS Previous research has inconclusively suggested that start-up problems may develop over time into life threatening problems. With reference to twelve cited start-up problems no statistically significant differences were recorded between surviving and closing firms. A similar conclusion was reached by Reynolds and Miller (1989) in their study. Nevertheless, it is interesting to note that larger proportions of closing firms suggested that they had experienced the following start-up problems: government bureaucracy and red tape, obtaining payment from large debtors, shortage of demand or markets, VAT registration, obtaining finance and other problems.

A Multivariate Logit Analysis of the Factors Associated with Business Survival

Many of the factors found to be associated with business closure are correlated with one another. Consequently, it is not surprising to note that relatively few studies of business closures have explored the factors associated with venture demise within a multivariate framework thereby enabling the effect of one factor, such as employment size to be identified while controlling for the effects of other influences such as age and location of the business. To achieve this objective two logit analysis models are detailed below.

Logit analysis has a number of advantages over dummy variable regression analysis or discriminant analysis. The technique is used to explain variations in a dependent variable with a binary form (for example, business survival or closure over two points in time t1 and t2). 'The models fitted analyse closure at the level of the individual plant and they are stochastic in that they predict the probability that a plant will close. The fundamental assumption of logit analysis is that the relationship between the probability of a plant closing and a (linear or non-linear) combination of the explanatory variables is logistic sigmoid' (O'Farrell and Crouchley, 1983, p.420).

The parameters of the multivariate linear logistic regression models for binary response data have been estimated by a maximum likelihood method using the SPSS/PC+ V4.0 programme (Norusis, 1990). Logit analysis is used to investigate the relationships between the response probability and selected independent (or explanatory) variables (Table 2). The status of a surveyed firm (Y) can take two values: here we have denoted '1' for survival and '0' for closure. If we denote X as a vector of explanatory variables then $P = Pr(Y=1/x)$ is the response probability modelled. This linear logit model has the form:

logit $(P) = \log (p/1-p) = a+b'X$

where a is the intercept and b the vector of slope parameters.

All independent variables discussed in stage 2 could potentially be placed in a multivariate logit model to predict business survival and closure. The final models presented in Table 3 are not the full saturated models involving a large number of parameters (or explanatory independent variables). On the grounds of parsimony it was decided to present models with fewer parameters, but which fit (and explain) the data to a relatively high level. Inevitably, in any model building process there is a trade-off between increasing goodness-of-fit and greater complexity and this research was guided by both theory and empirical evidence. Consequently, both the final 'good fit' models presented in Table 3 are theoretically as well as substantively meaningful and include parsimonious groups of parameters which are statistically significant. The criteria for model selection was −2 Log Likelihood statistic, lower values indicating a more desirable model. As noted earlier, there is a trade-off among the presented logit models because of the missing data problem for certain cases (or surveyed businesses). The more variables included in a logit model will result in a smaller number of cases that can be included in the model (a similar limitation was also recorded by Reynolds and Miller (1989, p.168) in their longitudinal study).

Table 3 shows the parameter estimates for the response probability and explanatory variables for two separate models. We have chosen to present the data in this way since incomplete information exists for certain variables. Model 1 is therefore calibrated on only 97 cases whilst Model 2 is based on 157 cases. The results in both models show a strong positive effect upon survival as age of business increases (AGEBUS – see Table 2 for variable definition). It is a consistent finding in empirical studies of small business survival/non-survival (Daly, 1987; Evans, 1987).

In Model 2 there is a strong negative effect upon business survival for those firms that had bank loans outstanding in 1986 (BANK). This can be interpreted as a proxy for size and profitability. A growing, successful business will generate profits to reinvest in the business. At the same time this profit stream will enable the firm to raise external finance from a variety of sources, including venture capitalists. The small firm literature consistently points to the high incidence of bank lending amongst the smallest businesses, who tend to have restricted access to other sources of finance. Thus any sample of businesses using only bank finance will be biased toward the smallest and youngest of firms. However, the government's recent policy of high real interest rates has certainly played its part in reducing the likelihood of survival for small businesses in general. There is a dual effect here; firstly borrowers faced higher borrowing costs, and secondly the rise in interest rates over the period exerted a strong downward effect on demand.

Model 1 reports more than one shareholder (SHARE) had a positive effect on survival probability. This can be interpreted as a 'two-heads are better than one' effect in terms of the skills and diversity of knowledge that each shareholder brings to the business. On the capital side there is the potential for firms with larger numbers of shareholders to raise more capital, either internally or externally. It can also be inferred from Model 1 that a positive correlation is apparent between a founder having a bachelor's or higher degree (DEGREE) and subsequent business survival. Supporting earlier evidence that a founder with a diverse skill and experience base is more likely to operate a business that surmounts survival obstacles.

Also, Model 1 shows that surveyed businesses competing with fellow small employment sized firms (COMP) are less likely to survive. This already reflects the conditions of perfect competition where there is free entry and exit into the market. That is to say individual firms without market power are price takers with prices driven below those in mature oligopolistic markets.

Model 2 found a positive relationship between business survival and location (in 1986) in a government designated 'assisted' area (ASSIST). We infer here that government assistance (directly or indirectly) has created a 'munificent' environment for new ventures. Government support measures and particularly financial assistance may have supported high-technology firms over some of the initial surival hurdles. Moreover, the employment size (log) (LOGSIZEU) of the business exerted a significant and positive influence on survival. The larger the business the greater its survival chances. Explanations for this are fundamentally the same as explanations discussed regarding age of firm. Again, we infer supporting the population ecology model, businesses with increased legitimacy are more likely to survive.

Many of the variables discussed can derive support from a vast literature of theoretical and empirical work. However, variables such as age of business, size and level of competition to some degree affect all businesses. Government policy can have only a very modest impact in the short term on these variables in order to encourage high-technology business survival. With this in mind, there are two variables which are potentially amenable to policy intervention – high educational level of the key founder and more than one shareholder in the business. It is these factors that can be determined within the firm in ways that can affect the probability of business survival. Government can directly influence the science research budget. By increasing the budget more individuals with degrees can potentially found their own technology-based ventures. Additionally, government can continue to support management training programmes that espouse the virtues of establishing new ventures with balanced management teams containing individuals with a variety of competencies.

Finally, Table 3 shows the predictive accuracy of the logit models, with about 75% of firms correctly specified as either survivors or closures. However, the closures are only predicted with an accuracy level of 50% or less, even when conducting a reclassification rather than a formal 'hold out' test. This suggests that the forecasting power of the models, as they stand currently, are not suitable for operational use.

CONCLUSIONS

This paper addresses the question: what factors influence the survival, over time, of a group of high-technology small firms. It uses data on independently owned high-technology firms in Great Britain in 1986 and reviews the factors which influence their survival or non-survival in 1992. The first part of the paper presents hypotheses of the factors which might be expected to influence survival/non-survival and the second part of the paper presents the empirical results.

The key findings are as follows: the first is that the high-technology sample overall had a lower closure rate than would be expected from comparing those firms with VAT registered businesses which cover (virtually) all sectors of the economy in the United Kingdom.

The second finding is that despite 69 variables being included in the univariate analysis, all of which are derived directly from a literature search, only 13 are shown to be statistically significantly associated with survival/non-survival. Perhaps, most interestingly, none of the technology-related variables were significant, suggesting that the factors influencing survival/non-survival of independent technology-based firms are no different to the factors influencing similar firms operating outside high-technology.

The third finding from the use of logit regression models is that, irrespective of other included variables, the key influence on survival is firm age, with young firms being least likely to survive. This serves to re-emphasise the point that the high-technology firms in this analysis are no different to smaller firms generally, since firm maturity is consistently shown to be associated with survival.

Finally, we conclude that, whilst other factors such as mode of financing and number of shareholders do help to explain survival/non-survival the overall explanatory power of Model 1 is not sufficient for them to be used as a forecasting tool. Given that the models are constructed using existing theoretical and empirical studies, it suggests more work needs to be conducted before a satisfactory forecasting model of survival/non-survival is available for use.

NOTES

1. In our definition we specifically include, as closures, businesses moving off the Science Park to an alternative location at which they ceased to trade. UKSPA, in principle, include these firms but its tracking procedures have less precision once the firm has left the Park. Such firms would not then, normally, be included in the UKSPA list of closures.
2. Several criticisms may be made surrounding the adopted definition of business closure. The central criticism, however, is that the definition we have employed of closure fails to recognise in full the contribution which a Science Park makes to technical and economic development. For example, where a business ceased to trade, even in the form of liquidation, the technology may still be developed by another business and the Science Park may claim some 'credit' for enabling that technology to become commercially tested. The implied assumption of our closure measure is that all is lost in these cases.

    We have some sympathy with this point of view since, in some instances, it is clearly valid. However, it can be argued that this issue is equally likely to arise in the case of the off park firms. To resolve this matter a much more intensive verification of the implications of closures would have to be conducted than is possible here.

3. There are a number of problems in making this comparison. The most important of these concerns ownership change. Where, for example, firm X is acquired by firm Y, the latter may or may not choose to include firm X under its VAT registration number. If it chooses to, then firm X is de-registered. This means that some firms which are located on Science Parks, but which have changed ownership, would be regarded as de-registrations for the VAT data, but not for the Science Park data. Conversely, some firms which have moved off the park, but which continue to trade under their VAT number would be regarded as losses to the Park, but would not be so identified in the official data. We have no way of definitively resolving these conflicting influences.

REFERENCES

ALDRICH HE (1992) Methods in Our Madness? Trends in Entrepreneurship Research, in Sexton DL and Kasarda ID (eds) The State of the Art of Entrepreneurship, Boston, Massachusetts: PWS-Kent Publishing, pp.191–213.

ALDRICH HE AND AUSTER E (1986) Even Dwarfs Started Small: Liabilities of Age and Size and their Strategic Implications, in Staw B and Cummings LL (eds) Research in Organizational Behavior, Greenwich, CT: JAI Press, pp.165–198.

ALDRICH HE, MCKELVEY B AND ULRICH D (1984) Design Strategy from the Population Perspective, Journal of Management, 10, pp.67–86.

ALTMAN EI (1968) Financial Ratios, Discriminant Analysis and the Prediction of Corporate Bankruptcy, Journal of Finance, 23, pp.589–609.

ARGENTI J (1976) Corporate Collapse – the Causes and Symptoms, Maidenhead: McGraw-Hill.

AUDRETSCH DB (1991) New-Firm Survival and the Technological Regime, Review of Economics and Statistics, 60, pp.441–450.

AUDRETSCH DB AND FRITSCH M (1992) Market Dynamics and Regional Development in the Federal Republic of Germany, Berlin, Germany: Wissenschaftszentrum Berlin fur Sozialforschung, Discussion Paper FS IV, 92–6.

AYDALOT P AND KEEBLE D (eds) (1988) High Technology Industry and Innovative Environments: The European Experience, London: Routledge.

BADEN-FULLER CWF (1989) Exit from Declining Industries in the Case of Steel Castings, Economic Journal, 99, pp.949–961.

BATES T (1990) Entrepreneur Human Capital Inputs and Small Business Longevity, Review of Economics and Statistics, 72, pp.551–559.

BATES T AND NUCCI A (1989) An Analysis of Small Business Size and Rate of Discontinuance. Journal of Small Business Management, 27, pp.1–7.

BAUM IAC AND MEZIAS SI (1992) Localized Competition and Organizational Failure in the Manhattan Hotel Industry 1898–1990, Administrative Science Quarterly, 37, pp.580–604.

BEESLEY ME AND HAMILTON RT (1984) Births and Deaths of Manufacturing Firms in the Scottish Regions, Regional Studies, 20, pp.281–288.

BIRLEY S (1986) The Role of New Firms: Births, Deaths and Job Generation, Strategic Management Journal, 7, pp.361–376.

BIRLEY S AND WESTHEAD P (1990) North-South Contrasts in the Characteristics and Performance of Small Firms, Entrepreneurship and Regional Development, 2, pp.27–48.

BIRLEY S AND WESTHEAD P (1993) A Comparison of New Businesses Established by 'Novice' and 'Habitual' Founders in Great Britain, International Small Business Journal, 12, pp.38–60.

BREHENY M AND MCQUAID W (1987) High Technology UK: The Development of High Technology Industry, in Breheny M and McQuaid W (eds) The Development of High Technology Industry, London: Croom Helm, pp.297–354.

BRUNO AV, MCQUARRIE EF AND TORGRIMSON CG (1992) The Evolution of New Technology Ventures Over 20 Years: Patterns of Failure, Merger, and Survival, Journal of Business Venturing, 7, pp.291–302.

BULLOCK M (1983) Academic Enterprise, Industrial Innovation, and the Development of High Technology Financing in the United States, London: Brand Bros and Co.

CARROLL GR (1983) A Stochastic Model of Organizational Mortality: Review and Reanalysis, Social Science Research, 12, pp.303–329.

CHILD J (1974) Management and Organisation, New York, Halstead Press.

CHURCHILL NC (1992) Research Issues in Entrepreneurship, in Sexton DL and Kasarda ID (eds) The State of the Art of Entrepreneurship, Boston, Massachusetts: PWS-Kent Publishing, pp.579–596.

COOPER AC (1981) Strategic Management, New Ventures and Small Business, Long Range Planning, 14, pp.39–45.

COOPER AC (1993) Challenges in Predicting New Firm Performance, Journal of Business Venturing, 8, pp.241–253.

COOPER AC AND BRUNO A (1977) Success Among High Technology Firms, Business Horizons, 20, pp.16–22.

COOPER AC, DUNKELBERG WC AND WOO CV (1988) Survival and Failure: A Longitudinal Study, in Kirchhoff BA, Long WA, McMullen WE, Vesper KH and Wetzel WE, (eds) Frontiers of Entrepreneurship Research 1988, Wellesley, Massachusetts: Babson College, pp.225–237.

COOPER AC, GIMENO GASCON FI AND WOO CV (1991) A Resource-Based Prediction of New Venture Survival and Growth, in Wall JL, Jauch LR, Roberts D, Ross R and Kelly C, Proceedings of the Annual Meeting of the Academy of Management, Madison, Wisconsin: Omnipress, pp.68–72.

COOPER AC AND GIMENO GASCON FI (1992) Entrepreneurs, Processes of Founding, and New Firm Performance, in Sexton DL and Kasarda ID (eds) The State of the Art of Entrepreneurship, Boston, Massachusetts: PWS-Kent Publishing, pp.301–340.

CRESSY RC (1992) U.K. Small Firm Bankruptcy Prediction: A Logit Analysis of Financial Trend-Industry, and Macro-Effects, The Journal of Small Business Finance, 1, pp.233–253.

DALY M (1987) Lifespan of Businesses Registered for VAT, British Business, 3 April, pp.28–29.

DALY M (1991) VAT Registrations and Deregistrations in 1990, Employment Gazette, 99, pp.579–588. Revised in Bannock G and Daly M (1994) (eds) Small Business Statistics, Paul Chapman, London.

DAMESICK P (1987) The Evolution of Spatial Economic Policy, in Damesick PI and Wood PA (eds.) Regional Problems, Problem Regions and Public Policy, in the United Kingdom, Oxford: Clarendon Press, pp.42–63.

DAVIES RB AND PICKLES AR (1985) Longitudinal Versus Cross-Sectional Methods for Behavioural Research: A First-Round Knockout, Environment and Planning A, 17, pp.1315–1329.

DE MEZA D AND WEBB DC (1988) Credit Market Efficiency and Tax Policy in the Presence of Screening Costs, Journal of Public Economy, 36, pp. 1–22.

DONCKELS R AND SEGERS JP (1990) New Technology Based Firms and the Creation of Regional Growth Potential, Small Business Economics, 2, pp.33–44.

EVANS DS (1987) The Relationship Between Firm Growth, Size, and Age: Estimates for 100 Manufacturing Industries, Journal of Industrial Economics, 35, pp.567–581.

FLYNN DM (1993) A Critical Exploration of Sponsorship, Infrastructure, and New Organizations, Small Business Economics, 5, pp.129–156.

FLYNN JE (1991) The Determinants of Exit in an Open Economy, Small Business Economics, 3, pp.225–232.

FOTHERGILL G AND GUDGIN G (1982) Unequal Growth: Urban and Regional Employment Change in the UK, London: Heinemann.

FREEMAN L, CARROLL GR AND HANNAN MT (1983) The Liability of Newness: Age Dependence in Organizational Death Rates, American Sociological Review, 48, pp.692–710.

GARNSEY E AND CANNON-BROOKES A (1992) The 'Cambridge Phenomenon' Revisited: Aggregate Change Among Cambridge High Technology Companies Since 1985, Cambridge: Judge Institute of Management Studies, Working Paper (New Series) No.3.

GARNSEY E AND CANNON-BROOKES A (1993) The 'Cambridge Phenomenon' Revisited: Aggregate Change Among Cambridge High-Technology Companies Since 1985, Entrepreneurship & Regional Development, 5, pp.179–207.

GIBB A (1992) Can Academe Achieve Quality in Small Firms Policy Research? Entrepreneurship & Regional Development, 4, pp.127–144.

GORT M AND KLEPPER S (1982) Time Paths in the Diffusion of Product Innovations, Economic Journal, 92, pp.630–653.

GOUDIE AW AND MEEKS G (1991) The Exchange Rate and Company Failure in a Macro-Micro Model of the UK Company Sector, Economic Journal, 101, pp.444–457.

GRAYSON L (1993) Science Parks: An Experiment in High Technology Transfer, London: The British Library.

GUDGIN G (1978) Industrial Location Processes and Regional Employment Growth, Farnborough: Saxon House.

HANNAN MT AND CARROLL GR (1992) Dynamics of Organizational Populations: Density, Legitimation and Competition, New York: Oxford University Press.

HANNAN MT AND FREEMAN IH (1977) The Population Ecology of Organisations, American Journal of Sociology, 82, pp.929–964.

HANNAN MT AND FREEMAN IH (1988) Density Dependence in the Growth of Organisational Populations, in Carroll GR (ed) Ecological Models of Organizations, Cambridge, Massachusetts: Ballinger, pp.1–32.

HAWLEY AH (1950) Human Ecology: A Theory of Community Structure, New York: Ronald Press.

HENDERSON RA (1980) An Analysis of Closures Amongst Scottish Manufacturing Plants Between 1966 and 1975, Scottish Journal of Political Economy, 27, pp. 152–174.

HOAD WM AND ROSCO P (1964) Management Factors Contributing to the Success or Failure of New Small Manufacturers, University of Michigan: Ann Arbor.

JENSSEN S AND KOLVEREID L (1992) The Entrepreneurs' Reasons Leading to Start-Up as Determinants of Survival and Failure Among Norwegian New Ventures, in Birley S and MacMillan IC (eds) International Perspectives on Entrepreneurship Research, Amsterdam: North-Holland, pp.120–133.

KALLEBERG AL AND LEICHT KT (1991) Gender and Organizational Performance: Determinants of Small Business Survival and Success, Academy of Management Journal, 34, pp.136–161.

KEASEY K AND WATSON R (1987) Non-Financial Symptoms and the Prediction of Small Company Failure: A Test of Argenti's Hypothesis, Journal of Business Finance & Accounting, 14, pp.335–354.

KEASEY K AND WATSON R (1991) The State of the Art of Small Firm Prediction: Achievements and Prognosis, International Small Business Journal, 9, pp.11–29.

KEEBLE D, WALKER S AND ROBSON M (1993) Spatial and Temporal Variations in New Firm Formation, Small Business Growth and Firm Dissolution in the United Kingdom, 1980–90, Cambridge, UK: University of Cambridge, Department of Geography and Small Business Research Centre, Working Draft.

LOW MB AND MACMILLAN LC (1988) Entrepreneurship: Past Research and Future Challenges, Journal of Management, 14, pp.139–161.

MAHMOOD T (1992) Does the Hazard Rate for New Plants Vary Between Low- and High-Tech Industries? Small Business Economics, 4, pp.201–209.

MANSFIELD E (1962) Entry, Innovation and the Growth of Firms, American Economic Review, 52, pp.1002–1051.

MARTIN R (1985) Monetarism – Masquerading as Regional Policy? The Government's New System of Regional Aid, Regional Studies, 19, pp.379–388.
MASSEY D, QUINTAS P AND WIELD D (1992) High Tech Fantasies: Science Parks in Society, Science and Space. London: Routledge.
MINER IB, SMITH NR AND BRACKER IS (1992) Predicting Firm Survival from a Knowledge of Entrepreneur Task Motivation, Entrepreneurship & Regional Development, 4, pp.145–153.
MONCK CSP, PORTER RB, QUINTAS P, STOREY DJ AND WYNARCYK P (1988) Science Parks and The Growth of High Technology Firms, London: Croom Helm.
MOUNTFIELD PR, UNWIN DI AND GUY K (1985) The Influence of Size, Siting, Age, and Physical Characteristics of Factory Premises on the Survival and Death of Footwear Manufacturing Establishments in the East Midlands, UK, Environment and Planning A, 17, pp.777–794.
NORTH D, LEIGH R AND SMALLBONE D (1992) A Comparison of Surviving and Non-Surviving Small and Medium-Sized Manufacturing Firms in London During the 1980s, in Caley K, Chell E, Chittenden F and Mason C (eds) Small Enterprise Development: Policy and Practice in Action, London: Paul Chapman, pp.12–27.
NORUSIS MJ (1990) SPSS/PC+ Advanced Statistics 4.0, Chicago: SPSS INC.
OAKEY R (1984) High Technology Small Firms, London: Pinter.
OAKEY R (1985) British University Science Parks and High Technology Small Firms: A Comment on the Potential for Sustained Industrial Growth, International Small Business Journal, 4, pp.58–67.
O'FARRELL PN (1976) An Analysis of Industrial Closures: Irish Experience 1960–1973, Regional Studies, 10, pp.433–448.
O'FARRELL PN AND CROUCHLEY R (1983) Industrial Closures in Ireland 1973–1991: Analysis and Implications, Regional Studies, 17, pp.411–427.
O'FARRELL PN AND CROUCHLEY R (1987) Manufacturing-Plant Closures: A Dynamic Survival Model, Environment and Planning A, 19, pp.313–329.
PECK FW (1985) The Use of Matched-Pairs Research Design in Industrial Surveys, Environment and Planning A, 17, pp.981–989.
PENNINGS JM (1982) Elaboration on the Entrepreneur and his Environment, in Kent CA, Sexton DL and Vesper KH (eds) Encyclopedia of Entrepreneurship, Englewood Cliffs, New Jersey: Prentice Hall, pp.307–315.
PFEFFER J AND SALANCIK GR (1978) The External Control of Organizations: A Resource Dependence Perspective, New York: Harper & Row.
PHILLIPS BD AND KIRCHHOFF BA (1989) Formation, Growth and Survival: Small Firm Dynamics in the U.S. Economy, Small Business Economics, 1, pp.65–74.
REID GC (1991) Staying in Business, International Journal of Industrial Organization, 9, pp.545–556.
REYNOLDS PD, AND MILLER B (1989) New Firm Survival: Analysis of a Panel's Fourth Year, in Brockhaus RH, Churchill NC, Katz IA, Kirchhoff BA, Vesper KH and Wetzel WE (eds) Frontiers of Entrepreneurship Research, Wellesley, Massachusetts: Babson College, pp.159–172.
REYNOLDS PD STOREY DJ AND WESTHEAD P (1993a) Cross-National Comparisons of the Variation in New Firm Formation Rates, Coventry: SME Centre, University of Warwick.
REYNOLDS PD, MILLER B AND MAKI WR (1993b) Regional Characteristics Affecting Business Volatility in the United States, 1980–4, in Karlsson C, Johannisson B and Storey D (eds) Small Business Dynamics: International, National and Regional Perspectives, London: Routledge, pp.78–116.
ROBERTS EB (1991) Entrepreneurs in High Technology: Lessons from MIT and Beyond, New York: Oxford University Press.
ROMANELLI E (1989) Environments and Strategies of Organization Start-Up: Effects on Early Survival, Administrative Science Quarterly, 34, pp.369–387.
SCHARY MA (1991) The Probability of Exit, Rand Journal of Economics, 22, pp.339–353.

SCOTT MG AND LEWIS J (1984) Re-Thinking Entrepreneurial Failure, in Lewis J, Stanworth J and Gibb A (eds) Success and Failure in Small Business, Aldershot: Gower, pp.29-56.

SHAILER GEP (1992) Composite Accounting Variables in Failure Prediction Models for Small Privately Held Companies, Piccola Impresa, 4, pp.55-80.

SMILOR RW AND FEESER HR (1991) Chaos and the Entrepreneurial Process: Patterns and Policy Implications in Technology Research, Journal of Business Venturing, 6, pp.165-172.

SPECHT PM (1993) Munificence and Carrying Capacity of the Environment and Organization Formation, Entrepreneurship Theory and Practice, 18, pp.77-86.

STINCHCOMBE AL (1965) Social Structure and Organizations, in March IG (ed) Handbook of Organizations, Chicago: Rand McNally, pp.153-193.

STOREY DJ (1994) The Role of Legal Status in Influencing Bank Financing and New Firm Growth, Applied Economics, 26, pp.129-136.

STOREY DJ AND STRANGE A (1992). Where Are They Now? Some Changes in Firms Located on UK Science Parks in 1986, New Technology, Work and Employment, 7, pp.15-28.

STOREY DJ, KEASEY K, WATSON R AND WYNARCYK P (1987a) The Performance of Small Firms: Profits, Jobs and Growth, London: Croom Helm.

STOREY DJ, WATSON R AND WYNARCYK P (1987b) Fast Growth Small Businesses: Case Studies of 40 Small Firms in North East England, London: Department of Employment Research Paper No. 67.

TAFFLER RJ (1982) Forecasting Company Failure in the UK Using Discriminant Analysis and Financial Ratio Data, Journal of the Royal Statistical Society, Series A, 143, pp.342-358.

TUROK I (1991) Policy Evaluation as Science: A Critical Assessment, Applied Economics, 23, pp.1543-1550.

VAN DE VEN AH (1992) Longitudinal Methods for Studying the Process of Entrepreneurship, in Sexton DL and Kasarda ID (eds) The State of the Art of Entrepreneurship, Boston, Massachusetts: PWS-Kent Publishing, pp.214-242.

VESPER K (1980) New Venture Strategies, Englewood Cliffs, New Jersey: Prentice Hall.

WATSON J AND EVERETT J (1993) Defining Small Business Failure, International Small Business Journal, 11, pp.35-48.

WEDERVANG F (1965) Development of a Population of Industrial Firms: The Structure of Manufacturing Industries in Norway, 1938-1948, Oslo: Scandinavian University Books.

WESTHEAD P (1988) Manufacturing Closures in Wales, 1980-1984, Cambria, 15, pp.11-36.

WESTHEAD P AND BIRLEY S (1994) Environments for Business Deregistrations in the United Kingdom, 1987-1990, Entrepreneurship & Regional Development (forthcoming).

WESTHEAD P AND MOYES A (1992) Reflections on Thatcher's Britain: Evidence from New Production Firm Registrations 1980-88, Entrepreneurship & Regional Development, 4, pp.21-56.

WILKENS J (1987) Her Own Business: Success Secrets of Entrepreneurial Women, New York: McGraw-Hill.

WINTER SG (1984) Schumpeterian Competition in Alternative Technological Regimes, Journal of Economic Behavior and Organisation, 5, pp.287-320.

CHAPTER 6

Employment Generation and Small Business Growth in Different Geographical Environments

DAVID NORTH AND DAVID SMALLBONE

AIMS OF THE PAPER

This paper explores the relationship between the growth of SMEs and their ability to generate employment over a ten-year period using data from a detailed empirical study of the development of established manufacturing SMEs during the 1980s. The first part of the paper considers the employment generation potential of mature SMEs focusing on the extent to which job creation is concentrated in the most successful, growth orientated firms. A key question will be the degree to which the relationship between growth and employment creation in SMEs varies between different types of geographical environment by comparing the experiences of SMEs in urban, outer metropolitan, and remote rural locations. In the final section of the paper we examine some of the reasons for these differences by comparing SMEs in inner city and remote rural locations in terms of the factors which have influenced employment change over the decade.

THE DATA BASE

The empirical evidence is drawn from a project entitled 'A Longitudinal Study of Adjustment Processes in Mature SMEs during the 1980s' which was part of the Economic and Social Research Council's (ESRC's) Small Business Research Initiative (1). The firms were drawn from 8 manufacturing sectors and their mature nature is reflected in the fact that to be included, a firm had to be in existence in 1979 and therefore at least 10 years old when the interviews were carried out in 1990/91. The other definitional criteria were that a firm had to be independently owned and employing less than 100 employees in the base year i.e. 1979.

The main panel on which the study is based consists of SMEs which were located in London in 1979 and were originally surveyed in 1979 and again in 1981 as part of a previous research project (Leigh et al 1983). Out of the 293 firms from our original panel which satisfied the above criteria and formed the basis of the present study, 169 (or 58%) of the firms were still in existence in 1989 and of these, 126 were included in the present study (North et al 1992).

In order to compare the experiences of SMEs in London with those in other types of location, 2 other sample panels of SMEs which met the same criteria as those in London were selected for the purpose of the project. The second panel comprises 100 SMEs in Hertfordshire and Essex, these being chosen to represent outer metropolitan locations in the London region (this will be termed the OMA panel). The third panel comprises 80 SMEs drawn from a rural area, these being settlements with a population of less than 10,000 in northern rural counties and which may be considered to be 'remote rural' firms rather than 'accessible rural' firms (Keeble et al 1992).

Table 1 shows the sectoral breakdown of the 3 different panels, the main difference between them being the weighting of the rural panel towards the

TABLE 1
Sectoral Distribution of the London, OMA, and Rural Panels

SECTOR	LONDON PANEL	IL STAYERS	OMA PANEL	RURAL PANEL	COMBINED PANEL
Clothing	12	(7)	9	10	31
Electronics	22	(6)	15	7	44
Furniture	26	(17)	19	19	64
Ind. Plant	20	(10)	16	15	51
Instruments	10	(3)	14	4	28
Pharm'cals	6	(5)	4	n.a.	10
Printing	26	(16)	14	23	63
Toys & Games	4	(1)	9	2	15
Total	126	(65)	100	80	306

craft-based sectors compared with the London and OMA panels. However, given the steps taken to find rural firms in the electronics, instruments, and pharmaceutical sectors, we can say that one of the characteristics of established SMEs in these northern rural areas is a higher proportion of craft-based firms and a lower proportion of firms in the science and technology-based sectors than is the case in both London and the OMA (Smallbone et al 1994).

In this paper we have subdivided the London panel into inner and outer London firms in order to focus particularly on the performance of those firms which stayed in inner city locations during the 1980s. Sixty five of the London panel were inner London firms (we will refer to these as the 'inner London stayers') and 48 were outer London firms. A further 13 firms moved out of inner London during the decade.

EMPLOYMENT CHANGE AND THE GROWTH PERFORMANCE OF FIRMS

Before comparing the employment performance of the SMEs in different geographical environments, we start by making some observations about the changes in employment within the panel as a whole over the decade.

(i) Our evidence provides clear support for the view that if they can manage to survive the critical early years after formation, SMEs are capable of generating additional jobs over an extended period of time.

In aggregate the 306 surviving SMEs provided more jobs in 1990 than in 1979, there being a net increase of 18%. This represents a mean increase of 3.8 jobs per firm, but a median increase of only 1 job; the discrepancy is an indication of the disproportionate effect of a minority of firms which increased their employment substantially. Just over half of the surviving firms (52%) increased their employment over the period compared with just over a third (36%) which decreased it. As expected, there were some marked sectoral differences in the employment generation potential of the SMEs, although it is perhaps surprising that a favourable employment performance by the surviving SMEs is found in all sectors apart from clothing where there was a net employment decrease of 18%. The SMEs in the instruments sector showed the best employment performance, with a net increase in employment of 51% and a mean increase of 13 additional jobs (and a median of 5 jobs) being generated per firm.

We now turn to consider the relationship between employment change and the overall growth performance of the firms over the 1979–90 period. Others have argued that employment generation is closely associated with the growth of firms and that a substantial proportion of new job creation is concentrated in just a few firms. For example, Storey argues that 'analysis of employment trends in several European countries suggests that significant employment creation takes place in relatively few but fast growing firms' (Storey 1988). We are interested to see to what extent employment generation in the firms in our panel is dependent on their growth in output over the decade and whether the success of the firms in these terms guarantees job creation. Alternatively, is there evidence of jobless growth in the SME sector, with some firms achieving substantial growth on the basis of a stable or even declining workforce as for example where the increased output results from capital substitution for labour?

(ii) Our evidence shows unequivocally that job creation was closely tied to the growth of the firms in output terms (measured in terms of deflated sales turnover 1979–90) and that nearly all the new jobs were created by firms which at least doubled their output over the decade.

As Table 2 shows, relative changes in employment were closely associated with relative changes in real turnover in all 8 sectors. However, because of increases in productivity, firms needed to at least double their output in real terms in order to make much employment impact. For the panel as a whole, a firm had to typically increase its real sales turnover by two and half times in order to double its employment, and in the printing and electronics sectors it was necessary to more than treble sales turnover. Job generation will only occur on any significant scale in mature manufacturing SMEs if major increases in output are achieved and this is demonstrated clearly when we look more closely at the performance of the firms to see where the additional jobs were created.

When the surviving firms were assigned to five groups(2) on the basis of their growth performance over the decade, we find that 83% of the additional jobs which were created were in those firms which had at least doubled their sales turnover in real terms (i.e. the 'high growth' and 'strong growth' groups in Table 3). Nearly three quarters (71%) of all new jobs were created by the 70 firms

Chapter 6

TABLE 2
The Results of Regressing Relative Changes in Employment Against Relative Changes in Real Turnover for the Period 1979–90

SECTOR	NO. OF FIRMS	R VALUE	INTERCEPT 'A' COEFF. VALUE	SLOPE 'B' COEFF. VALUE	STANDARD ERROR	INCR. IN T'OVER FOR 100% INCR IN EMPT.
Clothing	29	0.938**	−0.198	0.462	0.727	259%
Elect'nics	44	0.926**	−0.261	0.362	1.190	348%
Furniture	63	0.732**	0.129	0.457	1.204	190%
Ind. Plant	47	0.844**	0.415	0.201	1.112	291%
Instruments	28	0.474*	0.425	0.236	1.324	244%
Pharm'cals	10	0.957**	−0.607	1.147	1.688	140%
Printing	61	0.670**	0.557	0.143	1.797	309%
Toys & Games	14	0.989**	−0.219	0.959	0.656	127%
Total Panel	296	0.747**	0.335	0.259	1.835	257%

* significant at the .01 level
** significant at the .001 level
NB There was insufficient data to include 10 cases

TABLE 3
Employment Change 1979–90 by Growth Performance Groups for the Combined Panel

	79 EMPLOY.	90 EMPLOY.	NET CHANGE	% CHANGE	MEAN CHANGE PER FIRM
High Growth (70 firms)	1864	3573	+1709	91.7%	+24.6
Strong Growth (42 firms)	213	513	+300	140.8%	+7.2
Moderate Growth (52 firms)	935	1133	+198	21.2%	+3.8
Stable (65 firms)	1521	1351	−170	−11.2%	−2.6
Declining (73 firms)	1779	901	−878	−49.3%	−2.6
Total Panel (302 firms)	6312	7471	1159	18.4%	+3.8

NB There was insufficient data to include 4 firms

which achieved high growth status over the period, creating on average 25 additional jobs each and, in aggregate, nearly doubling their employment over the decade. The most impressive performance was achieved by the high growth firms in the instruments, pharmaceuticals, and electronics sectors, creating on average 38, 35, and 30 jobs respectively. There were some examples of jobless growth amongst those firms achieving high growth, but they were few in number; just 5 high growth firms reduced their employment over the decade and 7 increased their employment by less than 25%.

THE EMPLOYMENT GENERATION POTENTIAL OF SMES IN DIFFERENT GEOGRAPHICAL ENVIRONMENTS

There is now an increasing amount of evidence to show that the employment performance of small businesses varies geographically. In particular, the employment creation potential of small firms in urban areas appears to be less than that of comparable firms in non-urban areas. For example, it has been shown that the employment performance of small, independent firms located in the conurbations is inferior to that in smaller urban areas (e.g. Coombes et al 1991) and two other recent studies have shown that rural SMEs outperform their urban counterparts in terms of employment growth (Keeble et al 1992; University of Cambridge 1992). Our own findings are broadly consistent with these other studies.

(i) In aggregate the surviving SMEs located in urban areas generated fewer jobs than those based in outer metropolitan and rural areas, the SMEs in rural areas showing the highest rate of employment growth.

Whilst in aggregate the surviving SMEs in all 3 panels increased their employment over the decade, there are clear differences in the magnitude of the increases. As Table 4 shows it is the SMEs in the northern rural areas which achieved the best employment performance and the inner London firms the worst. It might be thought that the better employment performance of the rural firms is the result of them tending to be younger and smaller than their urban counterparts although our evidence shows that it was the more established rural firms (and particularly those in the 20–49 size band in 1979) which had the greatest capacity to expand their employment. The younger and smaller rural firms did in fact generate fewer jobs on average than comparable firms in the London and OMA panels (Smallbone et al forthcoming).

(ii) The propensity of an SME to grow appeared not to vary with location, there being a similar proportion of growing firms in all 3 panels.

It might be expected that the different rates of employment change in the surviving SMEs in the 3 panels are the result of differences in their growth performance over the decade, with the rural panel being weighted towards fast growing firms and the London panel towards stable and declining firms. However, our evidence shows that this is not the case.

When we compare the distribution of the surviving SMEs in each panel between the five performance groups (Table 5), we find that the pattern is remarkably similar in each panel. There is certainly no indication that the firms which stayed in the inner city during the 1980s were unable to achieve the growth rates experienced by their counterparts in other types of location.

TABLE 4
Employment Change 1979–90 by SMEs in Different Locations

	LONDON PANEL (126 FIRMS)	IL STAYERS (65 FIRMS)	OMA PANEL (100 FIRMS)	RURAL PANEL (80 FIRMS)	TOTAL PANEL (306 FIRMS)
1979 Employ't	3611	(1682)	1634	1067	6312
1990 Employ't	3852	(1729)	2013	1606	7471
Net Absolute Change	241	(47)	379	539	1159
% Change	7%	(3%)	23%	51%	18%
Change per firm					
Mean	1.9	(0.7)	3.8	7.0	3.8
Median	0	(0)	2	2	1

TABLE 5
The Distribution of SMEs by Performance Group in Different Locations

PERFORMANCE GROUP	LONDON PANEL NO.	%	IL STAYERS NO.	%	OMA PANEL NO.	%	RURAL PANEL NO.	%	TOTAL PANEL NO.	%
High Growth	31	25%	16	25%	24	24%	15	19%	70	23%
Strong Growth	12	10%	5	8%	15	15%	16	20%	43	14%
Moderate Growth	25	20%	14	22%	13	13%	15	19%	53	17%
Stable	25	20%	13	20%	23	23%	18	23%	66	22%
Declining	33	26%	17	26%	25	25%	16	20%	74	24%
Total	126	100%	65	100%	100	100%	80	100%	306	100%

(iii) For a given increase in output, the number of jobs created directly in urban firms, and especially those in inner city locations, was substantially less than that generated by similar firms in other locations. The growth of the firm was most likely to be translated into direct job creation in rural areas.

It follows from the above findings on the employment and growth performances of the SMEs in the 3 panels that whilst the location of the firm appears to make little difference to its growth chances, it does affect its employment generating potential. This is clearly demonstrated when we consider the average employment changes for firms in each of the performance groups in the different panels (Table 6). The sharpest difference is between the rural firms and those in inner London. Despite their favourable sales growth performance, inner London SMEs appear to have generated significantly fewer jobs than the growth of firms in other locations. The rate at which growth in output leads to job creation is greatest amongst SMEs based in rural areas.

TABLE 6
Mean (and Median) Employment Change per Firm by Growth Performance Group for the Inner London and Rural Firms

PERFORMANCE GROUP	INNER LONDON STAYERS	RURAL PANEL	TOTAL PANEL
High Growth	18.9 (5)	34.8 (22)	24.6 (16.5)
Strong Growth	6.8 (5)	5.9 (5.5)	7.2 (6)
Moderate Growth	−0.3 (0)	8.4 (3.5)	3.8 (2.5)
Stable	−2.9 (0)	0.7 (0)	−2.6 (0)
Declining	−11.1 (−2)	−13.8 (−4)	−12.0 (−4)
All Firms	1.6 (0)	7.0 (2)	3.8 (1)

Although there were relatively few examples in the panel as a whole of firms achieving rapid growth without significant employment creation (i.e. jobless growth), most of them were firms which managed to attain high growth whilst remaining in inner London. This applies to 4 of the 5 high growth firms which reduced their employment over the decade and to 4 of the 7 which increased their employment by less than 25% (the other 3 being outer London firms). Thus whilst growth strategies which avoid or minimise employing additional labour tend to be the exception, it is interesting that those cases which did occur were all urban firms, and especially inner city firms.

It is also interesting to look briefly at the 13 firms which moved away from inner London over the decade. Although our evidence indicates that there was not a general tendency for growth to require SMEs to move away from inner city locations, the growth performance of the 13 firms which did leave suggests that the inner city economy is losing some of the best performing firms which do have considerable job generation potential. In fact, the best employment performance of the London SMEs was achieved by these 13 firms; in aggregate, their employment increased by a third over the decade, with a median increase of 5 jobs. Although admittedly modest in number, these examples provide some support for the argument that inner city locations are most likely to lose those firms which have embarked on strategies which involve investing in production directly and expanding their direct workforce.

The marked disparities between the employment generation potential of growing SMEs in different geographical environments is made clear when we consider the results of regressing employment change against changes in real turnover for the firms which grew over the decade (i.e. groups 1–3). Employment creation was dependent upon a much larger increase in output being achieved in urban SMEs than their rural counterparts. Using the regression coefficients to predict changes in the average SME in each type of location, the addition of 10 more employees typically required an increase in sales turnover of £1,284m (at 1990 prices) in inner London firms compared with an increase of £0.336m in rural firms and £0.677m in OMA firms. Put differently, a 200% increase in sales turnover would result in an average 66% increase in employment in an inner London firm compared to a 175% increase in a rural firm. SMEs may have similar opportunities to grow in different locations, but their means of achieving it would seem to have very different employment consequences.

FACTORS INFLUENCING EMPLOYMENT CHANGE IN INNER LONDON AND RURAL FIRMS

Having established that a given increase in real turnover typically produced a lower increase in employment in inner London during the 1980s compared with firms in rural areas, we now consider some of the factors which may help to explain this phenomenon focusing on the inner London firms at one extreme and the rural firms on the other. A comparison is made between them in terms of labour constraints (as perceived by managers), labour productivity and their flexibility in the use of labour.

LABOUR CONSTRAINTS

If firms based in inner London have found it more difficult to recruit labour or if they have been more likely to have experienced 'labour problems' than similar firms based in rural areas, this may have encouraged managers to find ways of minimising the impact of labour on the development of the firm e.g. by substituting capital for labour. Our evidence is that:

(i) Inner London firms showed a higher propensity to report labour constraints as an influence on the development of the firm during the 1980s than firms located in rural areas.

In each interview, managers were asked to identify the main constraints which had influenced the development of the firm during the period 1979–90. Although inner London firms showed a higher propensity to report all types of constraints (except for space/site constraints) than rural firms, the difference is greatest in the case of labour. The proportion of firms located in inner London reporting labour constraints (such as difficulties in obtaining labour, labour attitudes and poor quality labour), was three times that of rural firms (38% in inner London compared with 16% in the rural areas). If we focus just on those firms which had been aiming to grow over the study period, 44% of those located in inner London reported labour-related constraints as an influence on the development of the firm compared with just 8% in the rural areas.

(ii) 'Skill shortages' and 'recruitment problems' were by far the most frequently reported labour problems by firms in both the inner city and the rural areas.

In an attempt to examine the nature of the labour constraint in more detail, we also asked managers about any specific labour problems which the firm had faced during the 3 years prior to the interview (i.e. 1987–90) and their responses are summarised in Table 7.

TABLE 7
Labour Problems Facing Firms in the Late 1980s

TYPE OF PROBLEM	INNER LONDON FIRMS %	RURAL FRIMS %
Skill shortages	65%	59%
Recruitment problems	52%	46%
Labour turnover	12%	6%
Motivation to work	22%	11%
Absenteeism	8%	6%
Ageing workforce	23%	8%
Other labour problems	14%	–
At least 1 problem	82%	69%
No. of firms	100% (65)	100% (80)

The problem of skilled labour shortages is a national one and a major national investigation of the constraints on the growth of small firms concluded that the shortage of skilled labour was much more of a constraint on growth than finance, for example (DTI 1991). However, in this study skills shortages were most acute in the craft-based sectors. In clothing and industrial plant the majority of firms had experienced skills shortages in both locations, whereas in printing and furniture inner London firms showed a higher propensity to face skills shortages than rural firms: 69% of printing and 82% of furniture firms in inner London compared with 35% and 53% respectively of rural SMEs. On the other hand, in the more technologically based electronics and instruments sectors skilled labour seemed more difficult to find in the rural areas (64% rural, 33% inner London).

(iii) SMEs in Inner London were more likely to have experienced other types of 'labour problem' than their rural counterparts.

When 'labour problems' other than skills shortages and recruitment problems are considered, a more marked difference is apparent between firms in inner London and those in rural areas. Managers of inner London SMEs were more likely to report problems associated with an ageing workforce, labour turnover and with (what they judged to be) poor worker motivation. When all types of labour problem are combined, there is a tendency for labour problems to be more commonly reported by the managers of inner city firms than for rural firms. Although the difference is a matter of degree rather than a major contrast, there is some support for the hypothesis that the managers of SMEs in inner London have more incentive to seek ways to achieve growth which avoid the constraining effects of labour than their rural counterparts.

(iv) There is evidence that wage costs in inner London are significantly higher than those in rural areas.

Although the cost of labour was not identified by inner London managers as a major constraint on the development of their firms during the 1980s, it was undoubtedly one factor encouraging them to seek ways of using labour more efficiently. Whilst it is notoriously difficult to make accurate comparisons of wage levels between SMEs because of differences in factors such as job specification and the terms of employment, some comparison is possible from our data. In each case we asked managers for the maximum and minimum wage for a basic week for a particular grade of worker. For example, in printing the median maximum and minimum wage in inner London for a machine-minder was £300 per week in 1990 whilst in the rural firm the median minimum wage was £169 and the median maximum £195. In the case of furniture, the median minimum and maximum wages for a skilled machinist in inner London firms were £197.50 and £200 respectively compared with £154 and £177 in rural firms. From this evidence, it would seem that the incentive to maximise the return from each worker employed is likely to be considerably greater in inner London.

LABOUR PRODUCTIVITY

(i) Labour productivity in the rural SMEs was generally lower than that of firms in inner London in 1979 and by 1990 the gap had widened in all 3 sector groups.

With the exception of the printing sector, average productivity levels actually declined over the 1979–90 period in the rural SMEs (see Table 8). By contrast, in inner London productivity increased in all three sector groups over the decade; in the case of printing the increase was an impressive 85%.

Of course, the contrast in the trend of the sales/employment ratio between inner London and rural firms is really just another way of describing the difference in the relationship between a change in real turnover and employment change in the two types of location. We therefore need to consider the extent to which it reflects a real difference in the priority given to productivity increases by managers in the two types of location and in the means by which they have achieved it.

(ii) There is evidence to suggest that productivity increases based on intensifying the use of labour were more common in inner London SMEs than in the rural firms.

The interviewed managers were asked to identify up to 3 reasons for any increases in productivity during the 1980s and the results are shown in Table 9. Although investment in new machinery is the most common reason given for

TABLE 8
Productivity Levels and Change 1979–90 by Sector for Firms in the Different Locations (productivity is measured by real sales turnover £'000 per employee in 1979 and 1990)

SECTOR	1979 MEDIAN	1990 MEDIAN	CHANGE (%)
CRAFT SECTORS			
Inner London	11.0	14.6	33%
Rural	11.0	10.5	–5%
MEDIUM/HIGH TECH SECTORS			
Inner London	16.3	18.7	15%
Rural	15.6	12.6	–19%
PRINTING			
Inner London	14.7	27.2	85%
Rural	11.5	12.6	10%

NB In order to ensure sufficient numbers of firms in each category, the sectors have been combined in the following ways:

craft-based sectors = clothing, furniture, industrial plant & toys
medium-high technology sectors = electronics, instruments & pharmaceuticals

productivity improvements by firms in both types of location, it was more frequently seen as the basis of productivity increases in the rural firms. This is supported by a higher propensity to achieve increased productivity through workforce training among rural firms. On the other hand, SMEs located in inner London more frequently attributed their productivity increases to steps designed to make more intensive use of labour such as a greater flexibility in working practices, a closer supervision of labour and offering greater incentives to the workforce. SMEs in inner London were therefore more likely to look to make adjustments to their labour processes as a way of achieving improvements in productivity, and less likely to simply rely on investment in new machinery. If the increased output was more likely to be achieved by the existing workforce working more intensively, this is an additional factor which helps to explain the poorer employment performance of London firms over the decade compared with those in the remote rural areas.

(iii) The annual rate of capital investment per employee varied considerably between sectors as well as between locations.

Since new machinery was the most common reason given for increased productivity in both inner London and rural firms, we have also compared their rates of investment per employee (see Table 10). However, given the difficulties of collecting accurate investment data from firms for a ten-year period, we asked firms for their capital investment in plant and machinery for the 3 years prior to the interview.

The sectoral variations shown in Table 10 reflect variations in technological conditions in the different sectors. For example, in the printing sector, the impact of technological change on capital requirements is demonstrated by the

TABLE 9
The Basis of Productivity Improvements for Inner London and Rural SMEs

REASON	INNER LONDON	RURAL
New Machinery	45%	68%
Greater Flexibility in Work Practices	43%	16%
Closer Supervision of Labour	31%	11%
Incentives to Workforce	21%	8%
Training of Workforce	14%	29%
More Careful Recruitment	5%	5%
Redesign of Products	24%	13%
Wihdrawal from Low Productivity Areas	12%	8%
Management Training	5%	5%

fact that in both types of location, the median investment levels were more than three times those of the other types of sector. Although there is evidence that many rural printing firms had been significantly upgrading their production base over the decade (Smallbone et al, forthcoming), their median rate of capital investment was still below that of printing firms in inner London. London is a very competitive market for printing firms and firms needed to invest to survive in this sector.

TABLE 10
Average Annual Capital Investment per Employee in the Late 1980s for Inner London and Rural SMEs

(using median £ per employee)

SECTOR	INNER LONDON FIRMS	RURAL FIRMS
Craft-based	£147	£333
Med-high tech	£410	£360
Printing	£1970	£1667
All firms	£380	£500

NB In order to ensure sufficient numbers of firms in each category, the sectors have been combined as follows:

craft-based sectors = clothing, furniture, industrial plant & toys
medium-high technology sectors = electronics, instruments & pharmaceuticals

On the other hand, in the other craft-based sectors (i.e. clothing, furniture, toys) the median investment level of inner city firms was less than half that of their rural counterparts. The latter typically had a higher commitment to in-house manufacturing than their inner London counterparts, a typically lower level of externalisation of production and a lower degree of diversification into non-manufacturing activity. A combination of these characteristics resulted in the rural firms being more substantial investors in capital equipment than similar firms in London. It is in these sectors where we find some of the best examples of inner London firms growing over the decade using strategies which have not involved increasing employment.

LABOUR FLEXIBILITY

If it can be demonstrated that inner London firms have been highly active in their management of labour to increase labour flexibility, this would help to explain why their rate of employment growth has typically been below that of sales turnover. Our definition of labour flexibility includes both numerical and functional flexibility (Atkinson 1985). Numerical flexibility describes the ease with which a firm can acquire and dispose of labour and usually implies a change in the balance between the employment of full-time 'core' labour and the employment of 'peripheral' labour (i.e. part-time workers, homeworkers, self-employed). Functional flexibility refers to job content and in our case focuses specifically on the reduction of demarcation and the movement of workers between different tasks. The externalisation of production is also considered since it provides a means of achieving both numerical and functional flexibility.

(i) Although an active strategy to manage labour to increase labour flexibility over the decade is only apparent in a minority of firms, it is more common in inner London than in the rural SMEs.

In order to summarise the overall changes in labour flexibility, we will focus on those firms which made significant increases in numerical or functional flexibility during the 1980s (for a full discussion of labour flexibility in the 3 panels see North et al forthcoming). Firms were judged to have significantly increased their numerical flexibility if by the end of the decade they were making much greater use of one or more of the various peripheral sources of labour. In addition we have also included those firms which sought cost reductions and increased flexibility by means of subcontracting out a greater share of their production. Defined in this way just 15% of inner London firms and 6% of rural firms had significantly increased their numerical flexibility over the decade and it is striking that more than half of these firms were in either clothing or electronics. In terms of functional flexibility, firms were judged to have significantly increased flexibility if there had been a significant reduction in the level of job demarcation over the period; just 11% of inner London firms and 5% of rural SMEs met this criterion. If we combine firms which have increased either (or both) numerical or functional flexibility then 23% of inner London firms and 11% of rural firms can be said to have significantly increased labour flexibility over the decade. On this basis we can suggest that as a result of a combination of factors a minority of inner London firms may have reduced their demand for additional labour as a result of increasing their flexibility in the use of labour. The difference between inner London and rural firms in this respect would seem to result from more labour constraints, more competitive market pressure in some sectors, greater opportunities for externalisation and less underlying flexibility at the start of the decade than their rural counterparts.

(ii) Inner London firms have typically been more active in subcontracting out production than their rural counterparts thus reducing their demand for labour within the firm.

Whilst externalisation may be a strategy more usually associated with large firms, there is a growing recognition that small firms themselves often contract work out to other firms (Blackburn 1992). Indeed in this particular study, a majority of SMEs in all types of location subcontracted out production at some time during the study period. However, when the frequency and the extent of the use of subcontractors are taken into account, differences between inner London and rural firms are clearly apparent. Whereas 54% of Inner London SMEs used subcontractors on a regular basis only 30% of rural firms did so. Similarly whilst only 1 rural firm subcontracted out more than a quarter of the value of its turnover in 1990, 12% of inner London firms did so. The difference probably reflects the fewer opportunities that exist for subcontracting out to other local firms in rural areas which means that rural SMEs have to be more self sufficient in terms of the functions which they provide. Thus another reason why employment growth in the inner London firms was less than expected on the basis of sales growth was that some of the jobs were being created in other supplying companies. Unfortunately our data does not enable us to assess the scale of this indirect job creation nor where such jobs are located.

CONCLUSIONS

It is now generally accepted that there has been an urban-rural shift in manufacturing employment within the UK over the last 3 decades and that this is largely the result of the differential expansion and contraction of firms rather than the movement of firms from urban to rural areas (for example, see Fothergill & Gudgin 1982; Fothergill et al 1985). More recent work has focused on comparing the employment performance of small firms in urban and rural areas and shown that the employment performance of urban firms is inferior to that of rural firms (Keeble 1992). This paper provides further evidence in support of this urban–rural contrast, but goes beyond previous work in showing that the weaker employment performance of urban SMEs (particularly those in inner city locations) appears not to result from their growth in output terms being any worse than that of similar SMEs in other types of location. Whilst SMEs in urban areas would appear to have a similar ability to achieve growth as firms elsewhere, they are more likely to achieve it in ways that minimise the number of additional workers employed directly by the firm. Thus the number of jobs generated by a given increase in turnover tends to be significantly lower in urban areas, and especially in inner city locations, than in outer metropolitan and rural locations.

There is clearly no single explanation for these spatial differences in the relationship between the growth of the small firm and employment creation and the relative importance of different factors varies from one sector to another.

For example, we have shown that labour constraints have had a particular impact upon firms in the craft sectors in inner city locations and that this has been a factor in encouraging inner city firms to try to reduce their dependence on their own core workforce. Higher wage costs in inner city areas compared to rural areas have also led to inner city firms adopting approaches to growth which reduce their dependence upon labour, especially in the printing sector. It also appears that labour productivity improvements, often involving the more intensive use of labour as well as capital substitution, have been a greater priority for urban firms than rural firms. As well as experiencing different constraints and competitive conditions which lead to different approaches to the use of labour, it is also important to recognise that firms in different types of geographical environment face different possibilities for achieving growth. For example, because of the higher density of firms in urban areas and the interdependence that is often found between them, there are better opportunities for adopting growth strategies involving the externalisation of production than is the case in rural areas. The options facing rural firms are more likely to be limited to those that require the internal expansion of the firm's activities and therefore increasing the workforce directly.

From a policy point of view, our findings suggest that the best way of generating employment in the longer term is to focus policy on those firms with the greatest growth potential and particularly those with the characteristics of the high growth and strong growth firms in this study. Although this applies in both urban and rural locations, policy-makers clearly need to take account of the fact that the employment implications of growth vary between different geographical environments as a result of differences in the way growth is achieved.

NOTES

1 The ESRC's Small Business Research Initiative includes financial contributions from Barclays Bank, the Commission of the European Communities (DG YXIII), Department of Employment and the Rural Development Commission. This particular project also received some additional funding from the Department of Trade and Industry. The views expressed in this paper do not necessarily reflect those of the sponsoring organisations.

2 Definition of the 5 performance groups:

Group 1 'High Growth Firms' i.e. firms that more than doubled their turnover in real terms over the decade, that reached a size by 1990 likely to ensure continuing viability (£0.5m turnover), and that were consistently profitable in the late 1980s.

Group 2 'Strong Growth Firms' i.e. firms that at least doubled their turnover in real terms over the decade, but failed to reach a large enough size or to maintain the consistent profitability needed to be amongst the higher performing firms. Their success was arguably less secure than that of the high growth firms in that they remained small and lacked consistent profitability but on the criterion of sales growth they were clearly successful.

Group 3 'Moderate Growth Firms' i.e. firms which increased their turnover in real terms by a factor of between 1.5 and 2 over the decade.

Group 4 'Stable Firms' i.e. firms that stayed at about the same size in terms of the real value of their output, having increased their turnover by a factor of between 1.0 and 1.5. These are survivors rather than growers.

Group 5 'Declining Firms' i.e. firms which actually declined in terms of their real turnover 1979-90 and were therefore the weakest firms in the panel.

REFERENCES

ATKINSON J (1985) Flexibility, Uncertainty and Manpower Management, IMS Report No 89, Institute of Manpower Studies, Falmer, Sussex.

BLACKBURN R (1992) Small Firms and Subcontracting: What Is It and Where?, in Leighton P and Felstead A (eds) The New Entrepreneurs Self Employment and Small Businesses in Europe, Kogan Page, London.

COOMBES M, STOREY D, WATSON R AND WYNARCYK P (1991) The Influence of Location upon Profitability and Employment Change in Small Companies, Urban Studies, Vol 28 No 5.

DTI (DEPARTMENT OF TRADE AND INDUSTRY) (1991) Constraints on the Growth of Small Firms, HMSO, London.

FOTHERGILL S AND GUDGIN G (eds) (1982) Unequal Growth Urban and Regional Employment Change in the UK, Heinemann, London.

FOTHERGILL S, KITSON M AND MONK S (1985) Urban Industrial Change, HMSO, London.

KEEBLE D, TYLER P, BROOM G AND LEWIS J (1992) Business Success in the Countryside: the Performance of Rural Enterprise, PA Cambridge Economic Consultants for the Department of the Environment, HMSO, London.

LEIGH R, NORTH D, GOUGH J AND ESCOTT K (1983) Monitoring Manufacturing Employment Change in London 1976–81, Report for the Department of the Environment, Middlesex Polytechnic.

NORTH DJ, LEIGH R, AND SMALLBONE D J (1992) A Comparison of Surviving and Non-Surviving Small and Medium Sized Manufacturing Firms in London during the 1980s, in Caley K, Chell E, Chittenden F and Mason C (eds) Small Enterprise Development: Policy and Practice in Action, Paul Chapman, London.

NORTH DJ, SMALLBONE DJ, AND LEIGH R (1994) Employment and Labour Process Changes in Small & Medium Sized Manufacturing Enterprises during the 1980s, in Atkinson J and Storey D (eds) Employment, The Small Firm and the Labour Market, Routledge, London.

SMALLBONE DJ, NORTH DJ, AND LEIGH R (1994) The Growth and Survival of Mature Manufacturing SMEs in the 1980s, Urban-Rural Comparison, in Curran J and Storey D (eds) Small Firms in Urban and Rural Locations, Routledge, London.

STOREY D (1988) The Role of SMEs in European Job Creation: Key Issues for Policy and Research, in Giaoutzi M, Nijkamp P and Storey D (eds) Small and Medium Sized Enterprises and Regional Development, Routledge, London.

UNIVERSITY OF CAMBRIDGE (1992) The State of British Enterprise: Growth, Innovation and Competitive Advantage in Small and Medium Sized Firms, Small Business Research Centre, University of Cambridge.

CHAPTER 7

Longitudinal Study of Small Enterprises in the Service Sector

ADRIAN WOODS, ROBERT BLACKBURN
AND JAMES CURRAN

INTRODUCTION

The central role small businesses now play in the UK economy cannot be disputed. In 1991, for example, private sector businesses employing less than 20 people accounted for over one- third of those employed in the non-public sector or around seven million jobs (McCann, 1993: Table 3). Other data confirms this trend. During the last decade, for example, self-employment has risen from 2.7 million to 3.2 million (Labour Force Survey, 1993). This growth in small-scale enterprise is also shown in its superior employment and job generation performance compared with large firms (Daly et al., 1991).

The success of small firms has led to rising expectations about their contribution to the economy more generally in terms, for example, of exporting and innovation. These expectations were especially important in relation to their role in the recession of the early 1990s. Politicians, government and business groups stressed the importance of small firms in overcoming the recession and their ability to contribute substantially to the green shoots of recovery. The then Secretary of State for Employment, Michael Howard, epitomised this view:

'Small firms played a crucial role in leading the economy out of the recession in the mid-1980s. I am confident that they will play a similar role in the months ahead'. (Department of Employment, 1992:1).

The view has received further support from a recent CBI survey of small firms which claimed that 'small firms are leading the recovery, with the first increase in output for three years' (CBI, 1993:2).

However, as with most aggregate data, overall figures on the contribution of small firms to the economy and employment mask large inter-sector variations. The 1980s saw a continued shift towards the service sector so that by 1992 manufacturing industries (SIC categories 2–4) constituted 10 per cent of businesses, and services (SIC categories 6–9) around 66 per cent (Business Monitor, 1992). Small firms, in the main, are in the service sector so the relatively superior performance of small firms is partly a reflection of this sector's performance.

Two much remarked upon main weaknesses of small business research to date have been its over-concentration on manufacturing firms and its reliance on comparing single 'snapshot' surveys unable to take into account variations between methods of data collection, sectors, or changes over time (Mason, 1989). This chapter discusses data from a longitudinal survey of small, service sector enterprises which started in 1990 and compares the results obtained from the surviving firms in 1993 with those in 1990 and 1992. It analyses in detail the experiences of the businesses over the last two years. In doing so, it helps provide an assessment of the contribution small, service sector enterprises can make to the economy and highlights their potential to meet the expectations of policy makers and other interested parties.

METHODOLOGICAL BACKGROUND

The data in this chapter is drawn from three surveys of a sample of small, service sector enterprises. Originally, 350 business owners were interviewed face-to-face in 1990. This first interview comprised a detailed in-depth study of a wide range of aspects of the owner-managers, the businesses and their employees.[1] The businesses were drawn from five different localities to represent spatial variations in socio-economic conditions throughout the economy. They included a prosperous local economy in the South East (Guildford), a relatively depressed locality in the North East (Doncaster), a Midlands economy (Nottingham), an inner city area in London (Islington) and a rural area (North East Suffolk).[2] The businesses were randomly drawn from seven carefully selected areas of services to represent consumer, producer and mixed types of service activities, as well as old and new types of business (Curran et al., 1991)

A follow-up telephone survey was conducted in February 1992 to investigate how the businesses were performing (Curran and Blackburn, 1992). This chapter reports the next stage of this tracking exercise and analyses results from a telephone survey undertaken in March 1993. Overall, the sample had declined from the original 350 in 1990 to 204 in 1993 (Table 1). This is a result of business closures,[3] difficulty in tracing some firms and variations in response rates. Overall, between the first interviews in 1990 and the telephone survey in 1993, 122 businesses (34.9 per cent) had ceased to trade or were not traceable. Most are likely to have ceased trading since interviewers using directory enquiries were able to confirm the non-existence of these businesses in most instances.[4]

Thus, of the original 350 businesses interviewed in 1990, 65 per cent were known to be still trading in 1993 (respondents plus those who were in existence but were unable or unwilling to participate in the 1993 survey). This survival rate is similar to that of the analyses of Value Added Tax registrations and deregistrations reported in the 1980s (see, e.g., Department of Employment, 1992:Table 5). This is somewhat surprising given the depth of the recession of the early 1990s. The biggest fall-out was in the Video Hire, Health, Beauty and Leisure[5] sector which declined from 49 firms in 1990 to 24 in 1993 (a 49 per cent survival rate) and among the Employment Training and Secretarial Agencies which declined from 52 to 24 (a 46 per cent survival rate). In contrast, the Garages and Vehicle Repairers and Plant and Equipment Hire businesses showed the highest survival rates at 84 per cent and 79.6 per cent respectively.

The decline in the numbers of businesses in the Video and other leisure activities sectors might have been expected for a number of reasons. For example, video hire has been declining as satellite viewing increases and as more videos are purchased outright through high street chains such as W H Smith. Concentration of ownership has also increased among the remaining video hire outlets producing fewer, larger outlets. In a severe recession, expenditure on leisure activities more generally will also decline as consumers reduce less essential expenditure. Employment Agencies might also be expected to have suffered as activity in the labour market declined further in 1992 as a result of the recession.

TABLE 1
Sample Size and Response Rates 1990–1993

	1990	1992	1993
Number Interviewed	350	274	204
Too Busy/Declined Interview*	–	9	24
Changed Hands/Not Traceable/No Longer In Business	–	67	55
Response Rate	56.1	96.8	89.5

Note: * Counted as non-response although some owner-managers were prepared to undertake interviews at a later date. Two firms were interviewed in 1993 which were not interviewed in 1992. Therefore, 202 of the firms interviewed in 1992 were interviewed in 1993.

The buoyancy in the Garage and Vehicle Repairs sector, also recorded in the 1992 survey, probably reflects the fact that people have been keeping their vehicles longer and buying new cars less frequently.[6] The data on the Plant and Equipment Hire sector is the most unexpected given its close links with the very depressed construction sector. However, other research conducted on these firms (Dickson et al., 1993) suggests that these businesses are highly flexible in their responses to the market and show considerable ingenuity in seeking customers, often accepting very low profit margins to continue in business.

BUSINESS CONDITIONS 1992–1993

In general, the surviving firms experienced a rather better year than in 1991–1992. The percentage of firms reporting 'a good year' rose from 29.2 to 34.5 per cent. Similarly those reporting a 'bad year' fell from 46.4 to 35 per cent (Table 2). Together, almost two-thirds of the sample reported that 1992–1993 had been about the same or better than 1991–1992 compared with only just over half in the 1992 survey. Broadly, therefore, the findings provide limited support for government's view that recession flattened out in 1992–1993. They are also broadly in line with other surveys of small businesses such as those of the Small Business Research Trust (1993).

TABLE 2
Respondents' Views on How 1992–1993 Compared with the Previous Year

	PER CENT	
PROPORTIONS REPORTING 1992–1993 WAS...	1992	1993
'A bad year'	46.4	35.0
'A good year'	29.2	34.5
'About the same'	22.6	29.6
Other	1.8	1.0
	N = 274 100.0	N = 203 100.0

However, as already noted, there were large sectoral differences in the economic experiences among the firms over 1992–1993. One way of analysing the changes in business conditions experienced by businesses over time is to use a 'balance approach' calculated by subtracting the percentage of firms that report a 'bad' year from those who report a 'good' year in both the 1992 and 1993 surveys (Table 3).

TABLE 3
A Balance Assessment of How Business in the Seven Sectors Experienced 1992–1993 Compared with 1991–1992

TYPE OF BUSINESS	BALANCE 1992	BALANCE 1993
Advertising, Marketing and Design	–30.0	7.1
Computer Services	–2.4	27.2
Employment Training and Secretarial Services	–24.2	0
Free Houses, Wine Bars and Restaurants	–5.3	9.1
Garage and Vehicle Repairs	–2.2	–7.7
Plant and Equipment Hire	–34.0	–23.5
Video and Leisure	–23.6	–9.1
All	–17.2	–0.5
N=	274	203

Note: Where respondent replied that the year had been the 'Same' it is considered neutral for this calculation.

Overall, the trend was still downwards but much less steeply than in 1991–1992 and there have been some striking changes in business conditions in some of the sectors (Table 3). Plant and Equipment Hire firms, for instance, continued to report poor market conditions even if not quite so poor as for 1992–1991. In contrast, Advertising, Marketing and Design went from a negative balance of –30 per cent to a positive one of 7.1 per cent. Computer Services went from –2.4 per cent to 27.2 per cent. All told, whereas in 1992 every sector reported a negative balance, in 1993 three of the sectors reported a positive balance and one a neutral balance overall. These results must be put in context. They are from surviving businesses, that is, they exclude those firms who experienced such poor trading conditions that they were unable to continue in business and did not take part in the surveys.

Table 4 analyses the data in the same way in relation to the five localities in which the businesses were operating. The table needs careful interpretation since, obviously, all the localities did not start from the same level of prosperity. Businesses in Guildford, for example, show high negative balances in both surveys but started from a high level of prosperity. Guildford, however, demonstrates how the experiences of the sample of small firms bear out the severity of the recession in the South East. Businesses in Doncaster, one of the two poorest localities in the study, showed a modest upturn in the 1993 survey though it should be kept in mind that they started from a relatively low level of prosperity, measured for example by size. Nottingham also showed a marked recovery compared with the experiences of firms in 1991–1992. North East Suffolk, the rural locality, also continued to decline on balance. Islington showed the distinctive character of an inner city economy in not reflecting the wider pattern found in the South East region exemplified by Guildford.

TABLE 4
A Balance Assessment of How Businesses in the Five Localities Experienced 1992–1993 as Compared With 1992–1991 and the Previous 12 Months

LOCALITY	BALANCE 1992	BALANCE 1993
Nottingham	−31.3	5.1
Guildford	−27.9	−18.2
North East Suffolk	−5.6	−5.1
Doncaster	−7.2	7.3
Islignton	−12.9	13.6
N=	274	203

Note: Percentages expressed as a balance over the previous year.

TURNOVER CHANGES

Another way of assessing how trading in 1992–1993 was for the businesses is to look at changes in turnover (Table 5). The results show again that for the surviving firms who responded in 1993, business conditions had improved. Just over 40 per cent reported turnover up on 1991–1992 (allowing for inflation) compared with 33 per cent in 1992. As for the 1992 results, this data shows that, even in recession, a substantial proportion of small businesses are able to go against the trend and achieve real growth. Breaking down the results by sector using a balance approach again shows large differences (see Table 6). As in the 1992 survey, Computer Services showed an ability to achieve growth even in very adverse trading conditions generally. Garage and Vehicle Repairers also did well although less well than Computer Services firms. The catering sector which was doing unexpectedly well in the 1992 survey, appeared to have been hit much harder by the recession in 1992–1993.

The fact that in some sectors a substantial proportion of firms were continuing to suffer from a depressed turnover but were continuing to trade shows the resilience of small firms. This is particularly marked in Advertising, Marketing and Design and Plant and Equipment Hire. In sectors where there has been a substantial decline in the number of firms remaining in the sample such as among Employment, Training and Secretarial Agencies and, to a lesser extent, Video Hire and Leisure, the surviving firms managed a better overall performance than firms in their sectors in 1991–1992. There are always small firms whose owner-managers run their businesses more effectively than other managers or whose market conditions are more favourable than other businesses in the same sector and hence enjoy higher levels of prosperity.

TABLE 5
Changes in Business Turnover 1992 and 1993

	1992 %	1993%
Lower	44.3	38.1
Higher	33.0	41.6
About the same	21.2	20.3
N=	272	203

Note: Based on a question which asked how business turnover had changed during the last year *allowing* for inflation.

TABLE 6
Allowing for Inflation was Business Turnover for 1992 Higher, Lower or About the Same in Relation to 1991?

TYPE OF BUSINESS	% BALANCE 1992	% BALANCE 1993
Advertising, Marketing and Design	−30.0	−11.1
Computer Services	12.2	27.2
Employment Training and Secretarial Services	−3.1	9.1
Free Houses, Wine Bars and Restuarants	3.3	−9.1
Garage and Vehicle Repairs	4.5	10.8
Plant and Equipment Hire	−27.5	−5.9
Video and Leisure	−41.2	−4.5
All	−11.3	3.5
N=	272	203

A locality analysis confirms the finding earlier that trading conditions were worst in Guildford (Table 7). It also shows how the firms in the poorer localities, Doncaster and North East Suffolk, were able to weather the recession overall showing, on balance, an increase in turnover in both the 1992 and 1993 surveys. Both Nottingham and, to a lesser extent, Islington, showed marked improvements in 1992–1993 compared with 1991–1992.

Again, however, it should be kept in mind that the localities started from different levels of prosperity. For example, in 1990, the year all the firms were first interviewed, almost half of the firms in Guildford had turnovers of £250,000 or more while in North East Suffolk less than 30 per cent of firms had turnovers of over £250,000.

TABLE 7
Allowing for Inflation was Business Turnover for 1992 Higher, Lower or About the Same in Relation to 1991?

AREA	% BALANCE 1992	% BALANCE 1993
Nottingham	−9.8	7.7
Guildford	−24.6	−16.2
North East Suffolk	5.8	2.7
Doncaster	3.6	24.4
Islington	−29.6	0
N=	273	203

COPING WITH THE RECESSION

The respondents were asked in 1993, as in 1992, what strategies they had used to cope with the recession (Table 8). The results highlight the continuing cautious approach of owners and a reluctance to switch, overall, to more positive strategies. No method increased its use by any significant percentage in 1993 compared with 1992. However, several methods declined in their use including cutting fixed costs/overheads, cutting labour costs, delaying payments to creditors, introducing new working methods and reducing borrowing. Apart from new working methods, these are defensive strategies and clearly, there is a limit to how long these strategies can be used or will continue to produce real benefits. After having used them extensively in the first years of the recession, their use was bound to decline as the recession wore on. In the 1993 survey, two new items were introduced into the interviews schedule[7] – reducing prices or special price promotions – and both were used by a substantial minority of owner-managers. There is, however, only a marginal increase in the use of more proactive strategies. For instance, expanding into new markets rises from 35.8 to 37.4 per cent and increased expenditure on marketing/advertising goes from 17.9 to 18.7 per cent.

What these results show is that as the recession ends defensive strategies are being less used, perhaps because their effectiveness has declined and owner-managers have become slightly more proactive. However, it is difficult to interpret their behaviour as showing small firms leading the economy out of the recession. Instead it shows a very cautious attitude to expansion and a 'wait and see' attitude to signs of recovery in the economy. This is very much what might be expected among a sample of small business owners facing continuing uncertainties and having experienced the several proclaimed but false economic dawns of the 12 months to March 1993.

Obviously, different sectors face different economic conditions as well as different technological and labour constraints. As a result, the scope for using any of the above strategies differs across the sectors. The survey revealed strong differences in the relative importance of each method in each sector.

TABLE 8
Percentage Who Have One or More of the Following 1991–1992 and 1992–1993

STRATEGY	1992 SURVEY %	1993 SURVEY %
Cut fixed costs/overheads	75.5	55.6
Cut labour costs	56.2	33.9
Delayed payments to creditors	50.0	38.9
Pressured debtors to pay more quickly	69.7	66.0
Introduced new services or products	48.5	51.7
Expanded into new markets	35.8	37.4
Introduced new equipment	36.1	39.9
Introduced new working methods	47.4	36.5
Reduced marketing/advertising expenditure	45.6	47.8
Increased marketing and advertising expenditure	17.9	18.7
Reduced borrowing	48.2	36.5
Increased borrowing	15.7	11.8
Reduced prices	not asked*	39.9
Special price promotions	not asked*	27.6

Note: See Note 7.

Advertising, Marketing and Design firms were the most likely to use the most favoured overall strategies reported in the 1992 survey, cutting fixed and labour costs as ways of coping with the recession (Table 9). In contrast, in Plant and Equipment Hire pressuring debtors to pay more quickly was a favoured strategy. The most proactive sectors, that is, those most likely to use positive strategies to counter the effects of recession, were Employment, Training and Secretarial Agencies, Free House, Wine Bars and Restaurants and Video and Leisure businesses. In all these, half the firms claimed to be trying to expand into new markets. It has to be remembered, however, that the choices open to businesses in particular sectors may be limited by market, labour, product and technological factors. For instance, Garage and Vehicle Repairers would have difficulties expanding into new markets but may be constrained to purchase new equipment to stay abreast of technological change in their sector. Similarly, the low use of a particular strategy such as cutting labour costs may reflect a lower need for this in a sector. For instance, as noted earlier, Garage and Vehicle Repairers were continuing to experience a fairly strong market for their services.

EMPLOYMENT CHANGES

The emphasis on the ability of small firms to generate jobs has received support from several studies (see e.g. Daly et al., 1991; Storey, 1994). The 1993 survey results show the employment trends in the surviving businesses (Table 10). The total number of jobs created by the firms in 1990 was almost 2,500 but by 1993 this had fallen to just under 2,000. However, as noted earlier, the total number of businesses about which full data on employment is known had fallen in this period from 349 to 203. (Data was not available for one firm in the 1990 survey.)

TABLE 9
Highest and Lowest Percentage Use of Particular Strategies By Sector 1993

STRATEGY	HIGHEST USE	LOWEST USE
Cutting fixed costs/overheads	Advertising, Design and Marketing (89%)	Garages and Vehicle Repair (62%)
Cutting labour costs	Advertising, Design and Marketing (70%)	Garages and Vehicle Repair (27%)
Delaying payments to creditors	Advertising, Design and Marketing (52%)	Plant and Equipment Hire (32%)
Pressuring debtors to pay more quickly	Plant and Equipment Hire (85%)	Video and Leisure Services (23%)
Introducing new services or products	Video and Leisure Services (82%)	Garages and Vehicle Repair (24%)
Expanding into new markets	Employment, Training and Secretarial Agencies (50%) Free House, Wine Bars and Restaurants (50%) Video and Leisure Services (50%)	Garages and Vehicle Repairs (19%)
Introduced new equipment	Garages and Vehicle Repairs (57%)	Employment, Training and Secretarial Agencies (18%)
Introduced new working methods	Computer Services (52%)	Free House, Wine Bars and Restaurants (27%)
Reduced marketing/advertising expenditure	Free House, Wine Bars and Restaurants (64%)	Advertising, Design and Marketing (19%)
Increased marketing and advertising expenditure	Employment, Training and Secretarial Agencies (32%)	Garages and Vehicle Repairs (11%)
Reduced borrowing	Garages and Vehicle Repairs (45%)	Advertising, Design and Marketing (30%)
Increased borrowing	Free House, Wine Bars and Restaurants (18%)	Employment, Training and Secretarial Agencies (0%)
Reduced prices	Plant and Equipment Hire (53%)	Video and Leisure Services (18%)
Special price promotions	Video and Leisure Services (59%)	Advertising, Design and Marketing (0%)

What is noticeable, however, is the rise in the average size of the businesses between 1990 and 1993. Even though the number of firms for which data is available declined by well over one-third to 204 in 1993, total employment compared with 1990 declined by less than one-quarter.[8] Again, the surviving firms in the sample show considerable overall strength in swimming against the tide of poor economic conditions generally.

TABLE 10
Employment 1990–1993

SURVEY	TOTAL FIRMS	TOTAL EMPLOYMENT	MEAN	MEDIAN	MAXIMUM
1990	349	2465	7.1	5.0	54
1992	272	2389	8.7	5.0	152
1993	204	1887	9.3	6.0	124

Notes: Figures exclude owner-managers or directors.
Two firms interviewed in 1993 were not interviewed in 1992.

An alternative analysis of the data reveals the growth rates of the surviving businesses based on their employment in 1990 (Table 11). The surviving firms increased employment between 1990 and 1993 by over 250 jobs and their average size increased to just over nine (median 6). This supports other research which has found small firms' contribution to employment to be continuing despite the recession. The data also reveals that, among the surviving 203 firms, 31.5 per cent reduced employment, 48.3 per cent maintained the same level and only 20.2 per cent expanded. In other words, the growth in total employment was confined to one-fifth of the surviving firms. Within this expanding cohort one firm expanded to 124 people. These findings add substantial weight to the view that out of any group of firms, only a few are likely to grow to any significant size and job creation tends to come from a few small firms rather than small firms generally (Storey and Johnson, 1987; Storey, 1994).

TABLE 11
Employment Change in Surviving Firms 1990–1993

	TOTAL EMPLOYMENT	MEAN	MEDIAN	MAXIMUM
1990	1606	7.9	5.0	54
1993	1872	9.2	6.0	124
Change 1990–1993	+266	+1.3	+1.0	+99

Notes: 203 firms in analysis. Figures exclude owner-managers or directors. One firm employing 15 people in 1993 was unable to provide accurate employment data in 1990.

One aspect of the discussion of job generation has been an emphasis on the contribution of new sectors in the economy. The survey results displayed a variation in employment trends by sector, although these did not necessarily support conventional wisdom (Table 12). Higher than average growth was seen in Computer Services and Free Houses, Wine Bars and Restaurants. Conversely, Advertising, Marketing and Design and Plant and Equipment Hire showed minor declines in their employment levels. Computer Services, one of the sectors which showed clear growth over the 1990–1993 period, showed only moderate employment expansion over the most recent period.

Caution must be exercised in this analysis. For example in Computer Services a single firm had a very large impact on the growth figure for that sector increasing from 25 in 1990 to 152 in 1992 and declining to 124 in 1993.

However, what the data does reveal is the relative stability in employment in sectors such as Garages, Plant and Equipment Hire and Video Shops, albeit it must be remembered, among surviving businesses only.[9]

TABLE 12
Employment Change by Sector 1990–1993

	AVERAGE SIZE 1993	TOTAL CHANGE	AVERAGE CHANGE	N=
Advertising, Marketing and Design	8.8	−3	−0.1	29
Computer Services	13.8	+203	+5.9	34
Employment Agencies	7.5	+15	+3.7	23
Free Houses, Wine Bars and Restaurants	11.8	+33	+1.5	22
Garage and Vehicle Repairers	5.6	+28	+0.7	40
Plant and Equipment Hire	11.1	−18	−0.5	34
Video and Leisure	5.4*	+8	+0.4	21
All	9.3	+266	+1.3	203

Note: * Includes 22 firms.

RELATIONS WITH BANKS

In the first interviews in the research programme carried out in 1990, just over 75 per cent of the owner-managers felt that their relations with their bank were 'good' or 'satisfactory' and only 10 per cent described them as 'poor'. In the 1992 telephone survey just over 70 per cent felt that their relations with their bank had stayed the same or improved. But nearly a quarter reported relations had worsened. This pattern was repeated in the 1993 survey with three-quarters of owner-managers reporting relations had improved or remained the same and just under a quarter (23.4 per cent) believing that relations had worsened.

Overall, therefore, although some business owners were complaining of poor relations with banks, these findings continue to show a more satisfactory position than other surveys (Binks, 1991:155–156) or the characterisation of these relations generally in the media in the recent past (see e.g. The Mail on Sunday, 20.01.91 and The Sunday Times, 26.05.91).

What is the influence of the business conditions a business faces on its view of its bank? As business conditions worsen for a firm it is more likely to need the understanding and help of its bank. Popular views often suggest that banks are unhelpful when this happens and, hence, we might expect that owner-managers would report a worsening of relations. Table 13 gives an indication of how well such a supposition is supported.

TABLE 13
Relations with Bank and Business Conditions

	BUSINESS CONDITIONS			
RELATIONS WITH BANK	'BAD' YEAR	'GOOD' YEAR	'SAME'	ALL
'Improved'	9 (13%)	14 (20%)	2 (4%)	13.0
'Stayed the same'	41 (58%)	37 (53%)	42 (75%)	62.5
'Worsened'	19 (27%)	16 (23%)	12 (21%)	23.4
N=	69	67	56	192

Note: 192 firms in analysis.

Of those reporting a 'bad' year, 13 per cent said that relations with their bank had improved. This compares with 20 per cent for those reporting a 'good' year. Among those reporting a 'bad' year 27 per cent said relations had worsened. This compares to 23 per cent among those who reported a 'good' year. There is very little evidence from this that the conditions experienced by a business overly influence relations with banks or alternatively that the businesses found their banks unsympathetic when they faced poor trading conditions.

TRAINING AND ENTERPRISE COUNCILS

One of the key new bodies established to support small businesses in the 1990s are the Training and Enterprise Councils (TECs). When the 1992 survey was carried out the TECs were only two years old. Results from the 1992 survey revealed that although most business owners were aware of TECs, few had approached them for advice or believed they would use them in the future. Now, a year later, most TECs have had a chance to establish themselves and to start to offer more help to local firms.

The results from the 1993 survey show only a marginal increase from 1992 in the use of TECs by the business owners (Table 14). In all, 24 firms (11.8 per cent) had approached their TEC for advice or help. (The corresponding proportion in the 1992 survey was 11 per cent but because the total number of firms in 1993 was lower, the actual number of firms contacting their TECs fell from 29 to 24). Of these, 11 were satisfied and 10 dissatisfied with the service they received. What was noticeable were the considerable sector variations in the percentage that had approached their local TEC (Table 15).

There appear to be three groups. Advertising, Marketing and Design and Computer Services have a relatively high percentage (around a quarter) of business owners using their local TEC for help or advice. A second group consisting of Free Houses, Wine Bars and Restaurants, Plant and Equipment Hire, and Video and Leisure has about average percentage use (around 10 per cent). Finally, Garages and Vehicle Repairers and Employment Training and Secretarial Agencies made no use at all of their local TECs.

One possible explanation for this uneven use by sector is that business owners vary their external links according to their different business needs. For example, some local Advertising, Marketing and Design firms may be approached by TECs to help them meet their marketing requirements. Another possibility is that these firms are approaching their TECs as a source of business for their services.

TABLE 14
Have you Approached your Local TEC for Help or Advice?

	PER CENT
Have approached	11.8
Have not approached	88.2
N=203	100.0

TABLE 15
Have you Approached your Local TEC for Help or Advice, by Business Type?

TYPE OF BUSINESS	PER CENT
Advertising, Marketing and Design	25.0
Computer Services	24.2
Employment Training and Secretarial Agencies	0.0
Free Houses, Wine Bars and Restuarants	13.6
Garages and Vehicle Repairers	0.0
Plant and Equipment Hire	8.8
Video and Leisure	9.1
N=203	11.8

The low level of use by Garages and Employment, Training and Secretarial Services may result from different reasons. Garage owners have been shown to have a restricted level of networking in the research conducted earlier in the research programme (Curran et al., 1991). This may be related to the nature of their business, a quick turnaround of customers, mainly private customers, means there is little time or need to make formal connections with local business institutions. The Employment, Training and Secretarial sector's low use may be a result of these firms requiring other services than those offered by the TECs. Their low use of TECs in 1992–1993 is set against a relatively high use reported in the 1992 survey. Alternatively, this fall in use may be unrelated to what TECs provide. This sector appeared one of the most depressed in the 1993 survey and this may have affected the type of support received or sought.

Of those business owners who had not approached their local TEC so far, only seven (4 per cent) said they intend to in the future. It appears that the TECs have already reached their market level with their present products and marketing strategies. There are new local initiatives taking place aimed at increasing the use of the TECs and there is a major national initiative, the One-Stop-Shop (Business Link), which could lead to an increase in use and it will be interesting to see whether these help TECs achieve greater contact with the small business sector.

While there appear to be some marked differences in the use of TECs between type of business and year of survey, differences between the localities are much less marked. However, in general the TECs have clearly not made a substantial impact on this sample of businesses (see also Curran, 1993). At best, a quarter of the businesses in any sector have approached their TEC for help or advice and the overall level seems stuck at the 1992 level of around a little over 10 per cent. Moreover, the proportion who think they might approach their TEC in the future was lower in 1993 than 1992.

THE OUTLOOK FOR 1993

When asked about future business conditions owner-managers are usually optimistic. One advantage of a longitudinal study is the ability to compare how business owners expected their firm to perform and compare it with their actual performance later. If we look at the percentage balances from the 1992 survey and compare them to the actual results from this survey, this commonly recorded optimism is clearly shown in every sector (Table 16).

TABLE 16
Future Business Conditions Predicted in 1992 Compared With Actual Conditions

TYPE OF BUSINESS	BALANCE PREDICTED 1992	BALANCE REPORTED 1992
All	28.1	−0.5
Advertising, Marketing and Design	45.0	7.1
Computer Services	39.0	27.2
Employment Training and Secretarial Agencies	24.2	0
Free Houses, Wine Bars and Restuarants	42.1	9.1
Garages and Vehicle Repairers	34.1	−7.7
Plant and Equipment Hire	−2.3	−23.5
Video and Leisure	14.7	−9.1
All	28.1	−0.5

Note: These calculations are made by deducting those owners who stated that they expected 1992 to be a worse year from those who stated that it would be better.

What the above table also shows is the difficulty firms have in accurately predicting their future business conditions especially in a period of economic uncertainty. However, in any assessment of the future a degree of optimism is almost certainly required by business owners in order to sustain their efforts and especially through a recession.

When asked about their expectations for the next 12 months, this high level of optimism was again expressed (Table 17).

Overall business owners were more optimistic about the forthcoming trading period than in the 1992 survey, with almost two-thirds expecting a better year.

There were some minor sector differences but what is more significant is the finding that even those sectors that had experienced recession in the last three years, such as Video Hire and Leisure, were more optimistic about the future than a year ago. Alternatively, Garage and Vehicle Repairers were the least optimistic, although they experienced relatively buoyant trading conditions in the last three years.

TABLE 17
Will 1993 Be A Better Year For Business Than 1992?

	WORSE	BETTER	SAME	OTHER/ DON'T KNOW
Advertising, Marketing and Design	10.3	72.4	17.2	0.0
Computer Services	9.1	63.6	27.2	0.0
Employment Training and Secretarial Agencies	4.3	60.9	30.4	4.3
Free Houses, Wine Bars and Restuarants	4.5	68.2	22.7	4.5
Garages and Vehicle Repairers	12.5	57.5	25.0	5.0
Plant and Equipment Hire	5.9	67.6	23.5	2.9
Video and Leisure	9.2	63.6	22.7	4.5
All	8.4	64.5	24.1	1.0

Note: 203 firms in analysis. Percentages may not add to 100 due to rounding.

SUMMARY AND CONCLUSIONS

The contribution of small businesses to the UK economy is widely recognised as important. Small firms are very strongly represented in services, now the most important sector of the UK economy in terms of jobs and its contribution to national output. While there has been a lot of research on the small business in the UK, much of it has been of the 'snapshot' kind with much less devoted to seeing how particular small businesses survive or prosper over time.

This chapter presents findings from a survey in 1993 of small service sector firms, originally interviewed in 1990. The firms were also interviewed in 1992 and over the period 1990–1993, a substantial proportion have participated in other projects in a large-scale research programme. In the 1993 survey, the aim was to collect information on how the businesses had fared over the period February 1992 to March 1993, a period in which the UK economy continued to suffer severe recession despite official claims of indications of recovery.

Of the 350 firms interviewed in 1990, 65 per cent were still known to be trading in March 1993. The biggest reductions were in the Video Hire, Beauty and Leisure sector which had lost 40 per cent of the firms interviewed in 1990. In contrast, the Garage and Vehicle Repairers showed the highest survival rate with 84 per cent of the original sample still trading. Leisure sector businesses are likely to suffer in a recession as consumers cut back on non-essential expenditure. People have been keeping their vehicles longer and increasingly see a car as an essential means of transport and this probably helps explain the garage sector's survival.

As the 1992 survey showed, even in recession, a substantial proportion of small businesses will continue to do well and even grow. In the 1993 survey, almost two out of three of the surviving firms reported that compared with 1991–1992, business had been the same or better in 1992–1993. Just over 40 per cent reported a real growth in turnover (allowing for inflation) over the previous 12 months compared with a third in the 1992 survey.

Again, the sectors showed marked differences. Computer Services firms, for example, did relatively much better than other sectors in 1992–1993 while sectors such as Plant and Equipment hire, as expected, did much less well. The data from the five contrasting localities in which the firms operated, showed that the recession in the South East continued to hit businesses hard. Firms in less prosperous areas such as Doncaster and Nottingham had done better overall though, of course, they started from a lower overall level of prosperity.

The 1993 survey asked owner-managers what strategies they were using to cope with recession. As in the 1992 survey, the results showed an emphasis on defensive strategies – cutting costs, pressuring debtors to pay more quickly etc – and rather less on proactive strategies such as seeking new markets and customers. But the use of defensive strategies had declined in 1992–1993, compared with 1991–1992, perhaps because the potential of such strategies to help the business had declined: there is a limit to how far costs can be cut and the business remain viable. Yet, there had been no dramatic increase in positive strategies. There had been only a small increase in their use, indicating a cautious, wait-and-see attitude to hopes that the recession was coming to an end. Certainly, there were few indications that these small firms were spearheading any expansion out of recession as some observers have claimed.

Between them, the 204 surviving firms were responsible for creating almost 2,000 jobs. This total had declined since 1990 but since there were fewer firms, the average number of jobs in each firm had increased. In short, the surviving firms showed their overall strength by adding to employment. However, most new jobs were created by a few firms with one firm in particular showing substantial growth. This is exactly the pattern reported by other research on small firm job creation.

The 1990 and 1992 surveys showed that relations between the small businesses in this sample and the banks were generally good. The 1993 survey confirmed these previous findings. The proportions reporting that their relations with their banks had become 'poor' remained low and there were few differences between the firms reporting a 'bad year' in terms of trading and a 'good year' in 1992–1993. In other words, there were few indications that firms experiencing poor trading felt that their banks were treating them badly compared with other firms in the survey.

In 1992, the survey showed that the TECs had not made much of an impact on the small firms. Only a little over 10 per cent had used their TEC for help or advice in 1991–1992. The 1993 survey shows the situation has not improved much. In fact, only just under 12 per cent of firms had used their TEC in 1992–1993. The results appear to show that the TECs' difficulties in reaching small businesses remain.

The owner-manager respondents are, overall, optimistic about the coming year. But as the 1992 survey showed, small business owners are usually optimists. They have to be, given all the risks and uncertainties of running a small business. The results of the 1993 survey confirm the resilience of the surviving small businesses with over 40 per cent achieving higher turnover in 1992–1993 than in 1991–1992. But taking the findings for the 1993 survey overall, the picture offered is one of optimism tempered with a wait-and-see attitude. Recovery in the economy may be coming but these owner-managers are reluctant to abandon the careful, cautious strategies which have kept them going since 1990.

ACKNOWLEDGEMENTS

We wish to acknowledge the financial contributions from the Economic and Social Research Council, Barclays Bank, Commission of the European Communities (DGXXIII), Department of Employment and the Rural Development Commission for the original survey in 1990 and the survey carried out in February 1992. The survey carried out in March 1993 was funded internally by Brunel University and Kingston University. Any views expressed do not necessarily reflect those of the sponsoring organisations.

NOTES

1. For further details and a full report, see Curran et al., 1991. Other reports examining a wide variety of aspects of the operations of the businesses, owner-managers' strategies and employee experiences have also been produced. A list of the reports, papers, articles and books in which results from the various projects in the research programme are reported is obtainable from the Small Business Research Centre, Kingston University.
2. For example on an index of local prosperity of 280 local labour markets, Doncaster ranked 274 while Guildford ranked 15 (Champion and Green, 1988).
3. The phrase 'business closure' is used here rather than phrases such as 'business deaths'. Some of the businesses undoubtedly failed but others may well have been taken over or closed by the owners in order to open up elsewhere. The data does not allow the various causes of closure to be separated out.
4. This exercise in 1992 did, however, identify that 10 businesses had changed ownership and had therefore fallen out of the scope of the study.
5. These figures cover firms that are known to be in business in 1993 although some were too busy or unwilling to be interviewed.
6. None of the garage businesses were franchised dealers selling new cars. The exclusion of the latter kind of business was deliberate (see Curran et al., 1991).
7. The main reason for adding these two items to the 1993 interview schedule was that they were mentioned unprompted by a proportion of respondents in the 1992 survey. The 1993 results suggest that had these items been among the prompted list offered in the 1992 interviews, a substantial proportion of owner-managers would have reported their use.
8. To some extent this gives a misleading picture for the base year includes 349 firms and in 1993 this is 204. It must be noted that new firms will have been started in the sectors covered which would counterbalance the absolute decline in businesses and the people they employ. To generate a full assessment would entail a full components of employment change analysis (see Storey, 1994).
9. Detailed data on the employment practices, employment relations and training strategies of a sub-sample of 81 firms in the research programme is given in Curran (1993).

REFERENCES

ABBOTT B (1993) Small Firms and Trade Unions in the 1990s, Industrial Relations Journal, 24, 4.

BINKS M (1991) Small Businesses and Their Banks in the Year 2,000, in Curran, J and Blackburn, R A (Eds) Paths of Enterprise, The Future of the Small Business, Routledge, London.

BUSINESS MONITOR (1992) Size Analysis of United Kingdom Businesses 1992, PA 1003, Central Statistical Office, HMSO, London.

CBI (1993) News Release. Speech by Howard Davies to the British Venture Capital Association, Manchester, 5 May.

CHAMPION T AND GREEN A (1988) Local Prosperity and the North South Divide: Winners and Losers in 1980s Britain, Department of Town Planning, University College Cardiff, Wales.

CURRAN J (1993) TECs and Small Firms: Can TECs Reach The Small Firms Other Strategies Have Failed To Reach?, Paper presented to the All Party Social Science and Policy Group, House of Commons, April.

CURRAN J AND BLACKBURN RA (1992) Small Business Survey, February, ESRC Centre for Research on Small Service Sector Enterprises, Kingston University.

CURRAN J, BLACKBURN RA AND WOODS A (1991) Profiles of the Small Enterprise in the Service Sector, ESRC Centre for Research on Small Service Sector Enterprises, Kingston University.

CURRAN J, KITCHING J, ABBOTT B AND MILLS V (1993) Employment and Employment Relations in the Small Service Sector Enterprise – A Report, ESRC Centre for Research on Small Service Sector Enterprises, Kingston University.

DALY M, CAMPBELL M, ROBSON G AND GALLAGHER C (1991) Job Creation in 1987–89: The Contributions of Small and Large Firms, Employment Gazette, November, 589–596, reprinted in Bannock G and Daly M (1994) (eds) Small Business Statistics, Paul Chapman, London.

DEPARTMENT OF EMPLOYMENT (1992) Small Firms in Britain 1992, HMSO, London.

DICKSON K, SMITH S AND WOODS A (1993) Technological Innovation and Cooperation In Selected Service Sectors, ESRC Centre for Research on Small Service Sector Enterprises, Kingston University.

LABOUR FORCE SURVEY (1993) Historical Supplement – April 1993, Spring 1979 to Autumn 1992, Department of Employment, London.

MASON CM (1989) Explaining Trends in New Firm Formation in the UK, Regional Studies, 23, 331–346.

McCANN A (1993) The UK Enterprise Population 1979-1991, The NatWest Review of Small Business Trends, 3, 1, 4–13, reprinted in Bannock G and Daly M (1994) (eds) Small Business Statistics, Paul Chapman, London.

SMALL BUSINESS RESEARCH TRUST (1993) NatWest SBRT Quarterly Survey of Small Business in Britain, August, 9, 3.

STOREY D (1994) Understanding the Small Business Sector, Routledge, London.

STOREY DJ AND JOHNSON S (1987) Job Generation and Labour Market Change, Macmillan, London.

THE SUNDAY TIMES (1991) Banks Hammer Customers With Penal Rates as Bankruptcies Soar by David Smith and Mark Skipworth, 26 May.

THE MAIL ON SUNDAY (1991) How Banks' Help Has Been Hit For Six, by Timon Day, 20 January.

CHAPTER 8

Quality Assurance and Business Support Organisations:Chaos or Coherence?

HELEN WINNIFRITH

The recent publication from GFA Consulting, Quality in Enterprise Development – A Guide to Models and Approaches (GFA Consulting, 1993) takes 67 fact-filled pages to describe some of the range of quality assurance methods currently used to measure quality in business support organisations. This paper does not seek to duplicate or precis that valuable guide. It rather seeks to examine the principles and assumptions underlying these quality assurance methods, and to consider whether the range of methods constitutes chaos or coherence.

Any sample of literature from business support organisations, whether leaflets or annual reports, will contain statements of objective such as 'To provide a high quality free counselling service to people'; 'Our aim is to encourage the growth of small businesses in the area with helpful, friendly guidance'; 'You'll find friendly experts ready to listen and advise'. We may accept that the writers of all these statements, many of which were written five or more years ago, were and are genuinely committed to giving their clients a high quality service. Five years ago, an organisation stating that it provided a high quality service might not have offered any definition or proof that it succeeded in this aim. However we should not go on to assume that this absence of definition or proof means that it did not succeed in providing a high quality service, whatever it meant by that. I have found no evidence to prove that the recent attention to 'quality' with all the range of models, yardsticks, badges and defined standards has in fact added one iota to the effectiveness of business support organisations or to the satisfaction of their clients. This may sound like heresy, so I shall go on to explain in more detail why for me all our attempts to codify, measure and control may be worthy steps in the right direction, but cannot ensure what they go to such pains to achieve.

Firstly we need to examine the concept of quality in business support organisations. Each approach – BS 5750, Investors in People, occupational standards – comes at the concept of quality in a slightly different way. Pragmatically we shall concentrate now on the approach of the Employment Department (ED), as they hold strings to a large purse and they require all Training and Enterprise Councils (TECs) to have 'robust quality assurance systems' in place for all their functions, including business support, by April 1994. Their approach puts supplier capability central to the quality of TEC service provision, and makes the department responsible for ensuring that TECs have the capability to deliver services or products to specified standards (Employment Department 1992). The ED's Quality Assurance Division now requires TECs to ensure (Employment Department 1993):

1. Clear and measurable outputs and standards are specified for each service/product.
2. TECs and their suppliers have the resources and skills required to meet their obligations before contracting.
3. A documented delivery process on the part of the supplier, with:
   - identification of individuals responsible for the delivery of each service or product
   - identification by suppliers of the competences needed by their staff, and staff development to ensure staff possess these competences
   - identification of the physical resources and training methods needed.
4. Agreed and documented arrangements for review of progress, covering service or product and also the delivery process where appropriate:
   - documented system for monitoring the business process and identifying outputs.
5. Systematic evaluation and development of delivery of products and services:
   - Customer feedback leading to appropriate action.
6. Continuous improvements by suppliers.

I shall focus on three of these requirements:
- clear and measurable outputs and standards
- identification of required competences and staff development
- customer feedback leading to appropriate action.

My observations are based on three years of working alongside TECs and business support organisations in connection with my work with Business in the Community as its Training Manager, responsible for a nationwide training programme for business counsellors and others working in business support; also particularly on information and knowledge obtained this summer from telephone conversations and interviews with 32 TECs, when I contacted them to discuss how close they were to achieving the ED requirements. This was in the course of consultancy work I was undertaking for GFA Consulting.

The first evidence for the very different approaches TECs take to this question of quality in business support organisations came from the differing titles of the people in each TEC whom I eventually found to be responsible for that work. These titles included Head of Personnel and Corporate Planning, Quality Manager, Development Manager, Head of Business and Enterprise. In some TECs I could not identify anyone with knowledge of the Employment Department's requirements for supplier management. Clearly different TECs have different structures, and some have no quality team. However there was also a difference of functional responsibility, as some TECs with a quality team assigned this work to the quality team, some to the enterprise team. It was apparent that in some cases there was friction over whether the Enterprise section (with understanding of business support, but perhaps not of quality issues) or the Quality section (with knowledge of quality issues, but probably not of business support) should take overall responsibility for the ED's requirements. This decision may have clear implications for the way the work is undertaken.

The first of my three focal points concerns 'clear and measurable outputs and standards'. 'Outputs' are easier to measure than 'standards' as they tend to be quantitative: examples of outputs are the number of business plans produced, the number of businesses started. When we look at 'standards' we have more difficulty with measurements. We are dealing primarily with service standards, but even these cover a huge area. If we look at the service of business counselling and advice, the Enterprise Support Services Quality Standards used in Wales (Enterprise Support Services 1992) take the following as their 'specific standards':

'Business Counselling should be delivered by individuals with key competencies of:
- good interpersonal and communications skills to create a relationship of trust and openness with the client
- a good contact network and knowledge of the small business environment, so that clients can be advised on specific follow-up actions and/or referred to other sources of help
- sound analytical and problem solving skills to gain an understanding of the client's project, pin-point areas of weakness or concern, and develop strategies for dealing with these
- a depth of business knowledge and experience sufficient to portray a credible image with the client and to deal with a wide range of business situations.'

Indicators of these 'standards' are 'possession of qualifications/memberships, adoption of external accreditation, use of BS 5750, monitoring of counsellors' competences, having a register of approved business counsellors, ensuring confidentiality'. Monitoring measures include 'inspecting records, reading development plans for counsellors, analysing customer response, observing counsellors' performance and inspection of premises.'

We may query where in this are the 'clear and measurable standards'. There is no yardstick against which to measure the statements. There is no definition of what is acceptable and what is not.

A TEC which tries to grapple with this vexed question and seems to emerge triumphant with the Holy Grail of 'clear measurable outputs and standards' is Hereford and Worcester (Hereford and Worcester TEC 1992). Its counselling quality manual incorporates indicators to measure such specific outputs as the percentage of actions agreed between counsellor and client which the client has implemented. For example, an agreed action plan could perhaps list specific outputs such as – 'complete an analysis of prices charged by ten competitors in this town', or 'send press releases to five local papers this month'. Client and counsellor can then at a later meeting (the number of repeat sessions is another output indicator to be measured) identify what percentage of the agreed actions has been achieved, and we have the clear measurable output we are seeking. Or do we? What if the client has found that the first three competitors' prices he analyses are so low that he sets about reformulating his entire business plan? What if the client's press releases are delayed because an unexpected large order suddenly overwhelms her, and press coverage becomes inappropriate? Is the counsellor's service any less good because of the external factors? Are we not hunting for clear and measurable outputs and standards in an area of human and commercial activity where life cannot be so simple and so clear cut? We find echoes here of the difficulties faced by a business working towards Investors in People which has to 'evaluate the investment in training and development' to 'assess achievement and improve future effectiveness', 'evaluating how its development of people is contributing to business goals and targets'. This indicator can be a stumbling block for some organisations who are faced with the difficulty of linking, for instance, customer care training for support staff to increased profits, when again there are so many variables and no possibility of control experiments.

Moving on to our second ED requirement, we must ensure 'identification of required competences and relevant staff development'. Here do we not have the cavalry galloping to the rescue in the form of the Small Firms Lead Body (SFLB) with their draft standards for business counselling and the provision of business information and advice? In the Lead Body documents (Small Firms Lead Body 1993) we find performance criteria, evidence requirements and range statements which have been developed from earlier competence work and have been widely circulated around the sector. We see the combination of National Vocational Qualification (NVQ) experience merging with specialised knowledge of the sector, with the Royal Society of Arts (RSA) and the Institute of Business Counsellors (IBC) becoming the Joint Awarding Body. In the level 4 NVQ (business counsellors) we find a national, externally assessed competence based award which will certify that those business counsellors achieving it are competent to do their work. Business counsellors will be assessed on their observed behaviour with clients, where previously many have counselled exclusively behind closed doors.

But can we let the matter rest there? Will TECs rush to make the possession of the NVQ their only criterion by which individuals are acceptable to them as business counsellors? The IBC has been concerned that people could achieve the NVQ without having the in depth business experience required to be a member of the IBC; what of this discrepancy? What of the Catch 22 classically faced by actors, that you can't get a job if you haven't got an Equity card and you can't get an Equity card if you haven't got a job? That is, how do you build up the portfolio necessary to gain an NVQ if you can't do the work till you've got an NVQ? We have heard very little about any requirement within the NVQ framework for people to be assessed after acquiring their NVQ, to see if they are still competent 3 or 5 years later – what of counsellors who acquire the NVQ and then rest on their laurels, getting out of date, complacent and rusty? What of the problem of the Advice Counselling and Guidance Lead Body, which has yet to define its competency standards for the Business Enterprise Sector? What about other relevant occupational standards and competencies, outside the SFLB's remit, which are important in business support organisations, such as management of the business support organisation, sales and marketing? All these unanswered questions show that it is over simplistic to seize on the very welcome arrival on the scene of the NVQ for business counsellors as the answer to all our problems in the area of identifying competences and relevant staff development.

The third and last ED standard on which I wish to focus is 'customer feedback leading to appropriate action'. The concept of 'satisfying customer needs' is of prime importance in quality management thinking, and this requires feedback from customers. However we must remember that the needs of a client in a business support organisation presumably relate to some aspect of business development: thus it is not enough to concentrate on whether they are 'satisfied' with the service they have received at the point of contact.

It has been common, though not universal, practice in enterprise agencies to follow up clients a month or two after a counselling session. This usually has two functions: to find out whether the client is making progress and/or needs more help, and to find out whether the client is satisfied with the service. The Business in the Community accreditation scheme showed many methods of follow up:

- Some agencies followed up all clients by post with a questionnaire and reply paid envelope
- Some followed up a percentage of clients by post
- Some followed up all or a percentage of clients by telephone
- Some used another organisation to follow up by telephone in an attempt to gain a degree of objectivity.

All these methods have obvious flaws – postal follow up has a low response rate: telephone follow up is time consuming: clients may be inhibited if the original counsellor carries out the feedback, etc. A grave problem with using follow-up results concerns interpreting clients' replies. Deborah Knox's (Knox 1992) recent research project on the effectiveness of local enterprise agencies, working on 20 client questionnaires, showed 100% satisfied response to the question 'Were your needs highlighted, discussed and analysed, and a satisfactory conclusion reached?'. The question 'Were you satisfied with the outcome of the meeting, ie were your expectations satisfied?' showed 55% were satisfied, 45% somewhat satisfied, with no client recording any dissatisfaction. When we ask clients if they were 'satisfied with the service', we do not know what their measures of satisfaction are – do they answer yes because they are comparing the service with the long queues, uncomfortable waiting rooms and lack of privacy they may have found in the benefit office? Do they answer 'Yes' because the counsellor was friendly and interested, but they do not realise he or she has given them out of date or inaccurate information about a specific question they asked? Do they answer 'No' because they wanted a start-up grant for which they were correctly told they were ineligible and they are not satisfied with this rejection?

In customer feedback we receive subjective impressions from people with different expectations and different experiences. These impressions are themselves difficult to measure objectively and clearly. To bring more clarity into our measurements, we may try to obtain client feedback on two separate areas, both important: process and outcome. Thus we might ask questions about the client's views on the friendliness of the reception staff, the rapport established by the counsellor, the length of time spent waiting; all these deal with process. We would then ask questions about whether the client's behaviour or understanding changed as a result of the counselling, in terms of acting on agreed decisions; that is, outcomes. Claude Lambshead (1991) argues persuasively that in the case of owner-managed businesses, any impact by a business support organisation on the business can come about only through a change in the behaviour of the owner-manager. If we accept the truth of this statement, should we not attach less significance to customer satisfaction with service at the point of contact (process), important though that is, than to information on the main outcome: change in the behaviour of the owner-manager?

If this change in behaviour is what we are seeking to achieve, should we not concentrate on measuring that change rather than isolating factors in the process and measuring those? If a client is empowered by the process of counselling to achieve his business start-up, is it very significant whether he says he is 'satisfied' by the process itself, given the difficulties described earlier in measuring satisfaction? If the outcome of counselling or training is that the client knows how to keep the books, where before she did not, does it matter whether the counsellor concerned has an NVQ or belongs to the IBC, or whether the organisation has got BS 5750? We may agree that desirable outcomes are more likely if the processes are properly ordered and monitored, but we must not lose sight of why we are putting so much time and effort into ordering and monitoring these processes. Neither must we be trapped into thinking that because the processes are ordered and monitored, it will necessarily follow that we achieve positive impact on businesses.

An analogy: let us consider a sixteen year old who wants to grow taller and to prove that she has done so. She knows that good diet and exercise affect health and that health influences growth. She eats good food and records what she eats. Noncompliance is rigorously investigated. She takes plenty of exercise and is never ill. Unfortunately she has no accurate tape-measure. So she asks people who know her, 'Have I grown?' but they give vague or contradictory replies. She is convinced that she has grown and shows them that her skirt is too short, her shirts don't cover her elbows. Sceptics say 'That is no proper measure – how do you know they haven't shrunk?' However, is not the proof of growth less important than the existence of health which has promoted growth?

On this analogy, we may take it that the action TECs are taking to meet the ED requirements is designed to promote health or measure growth, or both. If we study the variety of models and approaches they are adopting, using for instance the GFA guide, we do seem to come closer to chaos than to coherence. We find accreditation processes, self-scoring quality manuals, external assessment of counsellors, external assessment of a TEC's own quality standards. We also find TECs acting unilaterally on quality: this may lead to clashes where one business support organisation has several funders, each making their own quality requirements, or where one business support organisation contracts with two or more TECs.

Greater coherence could come about if we concentrated all our powers of thought, measurement and analysis on the client. Clients can, if we ask the right questions, help us to understand how we can improve our service for the future 'process'. Clients can also, again if we ask them the right questions, help us learn whether their behaviour and understanding have been changed through the intervention of the business support organisation – 'outcome'.

The questions we need to ask are detailed and necessarily have to be asked over a period of time. We can obtain much useful feedback immediately from an exit questionnaire, when the experience of having been counselled is still uppermost in the client's mind. We can obtain further useful information about how the client has digested information or ideas, perhaps by asking questions a month later. We may then need to ask further questions six or twelve months after that to understand whether there are changes in performance such as increased profit, increased sales, new markets, savings in costs, improved productivity, better morale. If we are interested in attesting the quality of the business support organisation, then once we have ascertained that such changes have taken place, we must identify whether these changes can be attributed to the intervention of the business support organisation or to external factors. In such complicated questions, with no possibility of control experiments or isolating any one factor, we cannot hope for 'clear and measurable outputs and standards'. However, if we were to concentrate our time and money into constructing intensive studies of a sample of clients over a long period of time, we would at least be trying to answer the vitally important question – has positive change taken place as a result of the business support organisation's intervention?

Should we not accept that 'clear and measurable outputs and standards' will necessarily elude us in this area of life, and put our limited resources less into measuring for the sake of measuring but rather into improving? Better training for counsellors may result in measurable NVQs; but it is not to measure NVQs that we should train, rather to improve the likelihood of the counsellor having a positive impact on the behaviour and understanding of the client. Similarly the motivation of an organisation in working towards BS 5750 should not be to achieve a badge of quality, rather to streamline and clarify the internal processes of that organisation in the knowledge that this should facilitate purposeful dialogue between counsellor and client which can alter the client's behaviour and understanding.

Only by making this simple client-centred approach central to all our thinking and actions can we hope to achieve postive change – measuring it may continue to elude us.

REFERENCES

EMPLOYMENT DEPARTMENT (1992) TEC Quality Assurance:Supplier Management, Consultative Report, October.

EMPLOYMENT DEPARTMENT (1993) Quality Assurance Division, TEC Quality Assurance; Supplier Management.

ENTERPRISE SUPPORT SERVICES (1992) Quality Standards for Wales Handbook, December.

GFA CONSULTING (1993) Quality in Enterprise Development: A Guide to Models and Approaches, GFA Consulting/Employment Department/South Thames TEC.

HEREFORD AND WORCESTER TEC (1992) Counselling Quality Manual.

KNOX D (1992) The Effectiveness of Local Enterprise Agencies, MBA research project, University of Warwick.

LAMBSHEAD C (1991) paper delivered to 21st European Small Businesses Seminar, Barcelona, September.

SMALL FIRMS LEAD BODY (1993) consultation document, NVQ/SVQ in Business Counselling and NVQ/SVQ in Business Information and Guidance, March.

CHAPTER 9

Small Firms and BS 5750: A Preliminary Investigation

JULIAN NORTH, JAMES CURRAN
AND ROBERT BLACKBURN

INTRODUCTION

In recent years there has been an increasing emphasis on 'quality' and 'quality management', in attempts by governments, advisers and other interested parties to improve the performance and efficiency of British industry (see, for example, Department of Trade and Industry, 1992; Yates, 1992).[1] One result has been the promotion of formal quality standard, BS 5750. The standard was originally published in 1979, and was based on existing standards for the management of product quality in the electronics and defence industries (Sherwood, 1986). It is not surprising, therefore, that of the estimated 20,000 BS 5750 registrations, a large majority are medium and large manufacturing businesses (BSI, 1992). However, it is apparent that small firms are beginning to be affected by the standard. For example, research by Curran and Blackburn (1992a) and the Small Business Research Trust (1992) indicates that over 40 per cent of small firms sampled, were affected by BS 5750.

However, more specific information about how small firms are being affected is lacking. For example, it is unclear why small firms are initially motivated to implement BS 5750, especially in the light of claims that the standard is irrelevant to their needs, and also costly and time consuming to implement (Bannock, 1991). So far discussion of the issue has largely taken place through media coverage, consultancy and management literatures. However, such sources have drawn criticism for their methodological weakness and, as such, are unsuitable materials to use as a basis for academic discussion (Hill, 1991; North et al., 1993).

This chapter has two main aims. The first is to provide a general overview of the issues concerning quality and quality standards in small firms. This will involve developing an alternative definition of quality, demonstrating how individuals and owner-managers formulate ideas and expectations about 'standards' of quality and how these 'standards' are interpreted in terms of BS 5750. This will give us a conceptual framework from which the cited advantages and disadvantages of the standard can be discussed. The chapter will then provide the preliminary results of research investigating small business owners' opinions on quality and BS 5750.[2]

QUALITY AND BS 5750

Although a majority of the quality management literature talks openly about the notion of 'quality', it fails to provide an explicit definition, opting instead for banal or meaningless phrases such as 'fitness for purpose'. An alternative approach might argue that the notion of 'quality' in any context (economic or otherwise) is relative and socially constructed or negotiated. That is, the definition of 'quality' in relation to the production of a good or service will be a joint construction of the producer (the owner-managers and others who constitute the small firm, for example) and others external to the enterprise. The most obvious external others are customers. The latter have expectations and desires concerning the performance and appearance of a product or the content of a service activity, which they believe they should, or could, obtain under given circumstances. Probably the most important of these circumstances is price, though time (for instance, length of waiting for delivery) are other aspects likely to be relevant. It is also likely that producers and customers may have differing or poorly formulated expectations or desires about product performance or service content in relation to other exigencies such as price. When transactions occur those involved may well become clearer in their ideas and even be able to generate written precise 'quality standards'[3] as part of a purchasing contract or as a result of negotiation.

However, 'quality standards', even those which are very precisely formulated, are never fixed. For instance, the expectations and desires of customers, as well as the producers' production strategies, are subject to changing awareness of how others in the market are behaving. The equation between the product or the content of a service and its price is unstable where, for instance, competition occurs or in a recession. New technology also emerges, new firms enter the market and knowledge of how other producers and customers are behaving changes. Influences of these kinds may therefore lead to new notions of 'quality' and 'quality standards'. The above offers a way to generate a much more specific conceptualisation of 'quality' than attempts to talk in terms of some mystical notion of 'quality' which firms, their customers and employees should be seeking.

Furthermore, it fits neatly into our understanding of BS 5750. The standard specifies the organisational framework for a quality assurance management system (Fox, 1991). Quality assurance contains all those planned and systematic actions required to provide adequate confidence that a product or service will satisfy a given requirement for 'quality' (BS 4778 – BSI, 1987a). In other words, BS 5750 provides a managerial framework that, in theory, will consistently deliver a final product or service to the agreed 'quality standard'.

BS 5750 AND SMALL FIRMS

When embarking on a new project, small firm owner-managers will consciously or subconsciously employ some form of cost/benefit evaluation. The decision to implement BS 5750 is, however, complicated by understanding that not all the motivations for implementing the standard are positive, and that the implications of introducing the standard are not always easy to predict. Small firms may be motivated to implement BS 5750 for one or a combination of the following reasons.

The first relates to the realisation of 'procedural benefits'. Fox (1991) suggests that implementing the standards procedures may improve the firms 'shipped quality level' through the 'quality improvement of all functions ..[such as].. education, training and communications' (Fox, 1991). However, recent studies have questioned this belief (Small Business Research Trust, 1992; Holliday, 1993). It is argued that if the design or manufacturing process results in the production of low quality goods, the standard will ensure that all subsequent goods are of equally low quality (Woodcock, 1992a). It is unclear whether this is simply a result of the poor application and maintenance of the standard or a shortcoming of the standard itself.

However, this function is seen as of secondary importance to other disciplinary advantages it can give the firm. Fox (1991) suggests implementing the standard as a means of ensuring 'cost-effective quality management ... is the only valid objective ...[for]... seeking BS 5750 approval' (Fox, 1991). Indeed, there is anecdotal evidence that BS 5750 may reduce operating costs as a result of increased managerial control (Woodcock, 1992b). However, research by Blackham (1992) provides conflicting evidence. In a sample of 100 UK firms, 31 per cent experienced an increase in costs after introducing BS 5750 compared with 6.1 per cent who experienced a cost reduction.

Alternatively, small firms may decide to implement BS 5750 as a general strategy of moving upmarket. In other words, small firms may implement BS 5750 to distinguish themselves from their domestic and international competition or as a means of occupying a protected niche and/or higher added value market position. This may create a situation where other small firms in the market are then forced to implement BS 5750 to remain competitive. Of course this will depend upon how competitive the industry is and how much importance customers within the industry attribute to BS 5750. Indeed, it is claimed that some small firms are being forced to implement the standard by large customers (Tisdall, 1990; Bannock, 1991; Batchelor, 1992). If so, it is likely that such pressures will vary according to economic sector and market position (Curran and Blackburn, 1992b; North et al, 1993).

Small firms are confronted with a number of potential problems associated with implementing and maintaining the standard which may make registering impractical. The first concerns the relevance of BS 5750 to small firms. It is a system designed primarily for managing product quality in large manufacturing firms. Indeed, the relevance of the standard to very small firms (ie less than 20 employees) is highly questionable, since the system of management it advocates is more compatible with businesses structured like large firms (North et al, 1993).[4] Moreover, it is argued that complying with BS 5750 will erode the often cited main economic advantage of the small firm, namely, its flexibility (Bannock, 1991).

Further questions about the standard's relevance to small firms concern its applicability to the service sector, especially since approximately 90 per cent of small firms are in services and construction (Curran and Burrows, 1988). Despite attempts to modify the standard for services, it has yet to shake much of its product orientated wording (North et al., 1993).[5] Furthermore, it is argued that there is a problem finding a suitable definition of quality in the absence of a tangible final product in service businesses (Fennel, 1991).

Furthermore, it is argued that many small firms will find implementing and registering for BS 5750 over complex, time consuming and costly (Bannock,

1991; Pengelly in Rock, 1992). For some, these problems may prove to be prohibitive. For others, the chosen method of implementation and registration are likely to be determined by available resources. For example, many owner-managers complain that they do not have the time to interpret and implement BS 5750 (Jay Communications, 1991). In this situation they may be forced to employ a consultant. However, this method is costly and does not guarantee benefits from registration (Bannock, 1991; Blackham, 1992). It is likely that larger small firms will find implementation and registration less of burden since they have a greater capacity to spread financial costs and may also have the in house resources to afford a member of staff with specific responsibility for implementing the standard.

In summary, small firms may be motivated to implement BS 5750 for a number of reasons. However, many will consider the standard irrelevant to their needs as a result of size, sector or a combination of the two. Others may consider that the problems associated with implementation and registration are prohibitive. Of those firms implementing BS 5750, the extent of the anticipated problems are likely to be inversely related to firm size.

A NEW STUDY ON BS 5750 AND SMALL FIRMS

The above represents an attempt to identify and conceptualise the possible motivations for, and implications of, implementing (or not implementing) BS 5750. However, it draws on a literature which has been criticised for its theoretical, conceptual and methodological weaknesses. For example, Hill (1991) suggests that much of the quality management literature ignores systematic analysis and data collection in favour of prescription and argument by anecdote. North et al. (1993) illustrate how previous research into BS 5750 has tended to concentrate on medium and large firms. These sources are inadequate in absolute terms for assessing the impact on small firms but provide a number of possible areas to explore in relation to small firms and BS 5750.

This chapter presents some new evidence on BS 5750 and small firms. The results were gathered through 150 telephone interviews with small business owner-managers and form part of a larger project investigating quality, quality standards and small firms. Each firm was selected to ensure a balance between services and manufacturing in general accordance with the small firms sector overall.

Accordingly, there was an 80/20 split between services and manufacturing, comprising of 120 service firms and 30 manufacturing firms in the sample. Consideration was also given to ensure a wide representation of economic activities (electronics, printing, advertising, computers, employment services, garages and plant hire). The survey produced a 90.4 per cent response rate.[6]

THE RESULTS

It is clear that small business owners' awareness of BS 5750 is increasing. The study indicated that 94.7 per cent of the sample were aware of BS 5750. This demonstrates a significant increase on previous recorded levels of awareness (eg 63 per cent – Curran and Blackburn, 1992a) and indicates that BS 5750 is becoming more of an issue for small firms. The government has taken an active interest in the promotion of BS 5750, especially through Department of Trade and Industry (DTI) advice and financial support. However, awareness of the DTI scheme (48.7 per cent of sample) was not as high as expected in relation to the general awareness of BS 5750. This poses questions about how effective the DTI scheme has been in promoting the standard, especially in the light of criticism relating to its exploitation by consultants (Rock, 1992). However, other organisations are taking an active interest in the promotion of BS 5750. For example, 62.7 per cent of respondents had their awareness raised partly through the media; 45.0 per cent through their customers; and 38.7 per cent through trade associations.[7] The source and flow of information tended to vary with economic sector. For example, garage and plant hire firms were more likely to have received information about BS 5750 from their trade associations than from other sources.

Despite the high level of awareness of BS 5750 it is clear that a majority of small firms remain unaffected by the standard. About two-thirds of the sample were either unaware of, or had no intention of implementing BS 5750 (Table 1). Just under a quarter of the sample were either still thinking about or intending to register but had taken no significant steps towards implementation (ie they had not begun to develop a quality manual), and 8.0 per cent were operating in accordance with BS 5750 procedures and 2.7 per cent were actually registered. As expected, there was a clear inverse relationship between implementation rates and firm size (Table 2). Over a quarter of small firms with over 20 employees were implementing or registered BS 5750, but only 2.2 per cent of small firms with between one and four employees had considered the same option (Table 2).

TABLE 1
Small Firms' Intentions Towards Implementing and Registering for BS 5750

	PER CENT
No Intention/Unaware	66.0
Thinking About It	10.7
Intending to Register	12.7
Currently Implementing	8.0
Registered BS 5750	2.7
N=	150

TABLE 2
Small Firms' Intentions Towards Implementing and Registering for BS 5750 by Firm Size Per cent

	1-4	5-9	10-19	20+
No Intention/Unaware	84.8	67.9	41.9	55.0
Thinking/Intending	13.0	30.2	32.3	15.0
Implementing/Registered	2.2	1.9	25.8	30.0
N=	46	53	31	20

Indeed, a large proportion of the latter category (84.8 per cent) were unaware of, or had no intention of implementing the standard. It is obvious from the above figures that size has a definite influence on owner-managers' attitudes towards registration. Though systematic analysis of this relationship is beyond the scope of this chapter, it is clear that many smaller firms consider the standard irrelevant to their needs. For example, a number of owner-managers suggested that because they had survived a recession in a highly competitive environment, they were confident of their management approach. In other words, if a firm has a management approach able to survive extreme market conditions, what is the point of risking a totally new system through the implementation of BS 5750?

Implementation rates vary according to economic sector, for example, from 22.2 per cent of electronics firms to no garages (Table 3). The relatively high rates of implementation in the electronics sector are probably a result of the existing use of formal written procedures, for example, through Ministry of Defence and large firm specifications. As a result, a large majority of firms in the electronics sector had a good working knowledge of BS 5750 and its implications. However, half of the electronics firms had still decided not to implement it. Many were satisfied to select what they saw as the best aspects of the standard and adjust them to their own requirements ie owner-managers would develop those procedures considered most relevant or beneficial to the firm. It also appears that the 'paper value' of registration has reduced in the electronics sector and is no longer significant enough to encourage many firms to register. This may be a result of two developments. The first relates to the novelty value of BS 5750. Originally, electronics firms may have used registration to distinguish themselves from each other. Now that a significant proportion of firms in the sector have BS 5750, it can not be used for that purpose. Second, large customers are themselves beginning to question the value of registration. For example, there is anecdotal evidence of at least one large electronics business changing its purchasing policy from insisting on BS 5750 to its old criteria, when it could not find the quality it required from BS 5750 registered suppliers.[8] This presents us with a situation where many electronics firms are keen to use written procedures but no longer see the value of registration.

TABLE 3
Small Firms' Intentions Towards Implementing and Registering for BS 5750 by Firm Size Per cent

	ELECTRONICS	PRINTING	ADVERTISING MARKETING & DESIGN	COMPUTER SERVICES	EMPLOYMENT AGENCIES	GARAGES	PLANT & EQUIPMENT HIRE
No Intention/Unaware	50.0	81.3	76.5	57.7	33.3	79.4	70.8
Thinking/Intending	27.8	6.3	17.6	23.1	53.3	20.6	20.8
Implementing/Registered	22.2	12.5	5.9	19.2	13.3	–	8.3
N=	18	16	17	26	15	34	24

On the other hand, according to the data collected professional service activities such as employment agencies are becoming increasingly interested in BS 5750. Preliminary results indicate that as the industry has become more competitive, firms are using BS 5750 as a competitive weapon.[9] For example, 80 per cent of firms who are interested in or have implemented BS 5750 consider this to be a significant motivation. This may explain why 53.3 per cent of employment agencies are either thinking about, or intend to implement, BS 5750, and why there are fewer firms in this sector rejecting the standard than in even the electronics sector. It could be that in time employment agency owner-managers may experience similar doubts about the standard to those appearing to have occurred in the electronics sector when a significant proportion of firms have become registered.

The conditions which stimulated an interest in BS 5750 in the above sectors may not occur, for the short term at least, in other sectors. For example, the study indicated that garage and vehicle repairers have yet to be significantly affected. A majority of the garages interviewed dealt with individual private customers who are less likely to be impressed by registration, and the use of BS 5750 as a marketing tool may not be relevant in this context. Many garages are also very small and may consider the standard irrelevant. Therefore, the implementation of BS 5750 by a majority of small garages may be very slow or not occur at all.

A range of problems associated with BS 5750 implementation and registration were expressed in the survey (Table 4). Of the firms not intending to implement BS 5750, 54.1 per cent considered the standard irrelevant to their needs. This included 34.7 per cent of firms who were either unaware of the standard or believed it inappropriate as a result of the firms' size and/or economic sector, and 19.4 per cent who believe it is 'over-bureaucratic'. The latter suggest that BS 5750 is incompatible with their flexible and informal styles of management. A further 39.8 per cent of firms believed the standard was too costly and time consuming to implement. In other words, firms in this category might possibly want to implement the standard but find the potential demands on financial and time resources prohibitive. Firms thinking about or intending to implement BS 5750 appear more concerned with the problems of implementation than the standard's relevance to their business. Indeed, 76.3 per cent believed that implementing the standard will be costly and time consuming. If it were implemented, 13.2 per cent believed BS 5750 would be over-bureaucratic to maintain and may affect the flexibility of the firm.

TABLE 4
Main Problems with BS 5750 by Intention Towards Implementation and Registration Per cent

	NO INTENTION/ UNAWARE	THINKING/ INTENDING	IMPLEMENTING/ REGISTERED
Not Relevant	34.7	–	–
Too Costly	30.6	34.2	21.4
Over-bureaucratic	19.4	13.2	28.6
Time consuming	9.2	42.1	21.4
Other	–	5.3	–
Don't Know/No Answer	6.1	5.3	28.6
N=	98	38	14

The most interesting results relate to those firms who are implementing or registered BS 5750. As expected, a significant proportion (21.4 per cent) in this category considered the standard costly to implement. However, it may be too early to assess whether the disciplines introduced by BS 5750 will reduce operating costs. Just over a fifth believe the standard is time consuming to maintain despite all but one of the firms having a member of staff specifically responsible for operating the standard's procedures. Similarly, just over a quarter believe that the standard is over-bureaucratic. BSI contend that this problem may be countered by implementing the standard in a manner appropriate to the requirements of the firm (Harland in Rock, 1992; Woods in Woodcock, 1992b). However, it is so far unclear whether the above firms have considered this advice or could implement it, and, therefore the issue of bureaucracy and BS 5750 remains unresolved. A further 28.6 per cent of this category (represented by the 'Don't know/No Answer' response) believed that there were no problems with implementing BS 5750 and that the standard was clearly beneficial to their business. Table 5 illustrates what these benefits may be.

TABLE 5
Main Motivation For or Perceived Benefit From Implementing BS 5750 by Intention Towards Implementation and Registration Per cent

	THINKINK/INTENDING	IMPLEMENTING/REGISTERED
Procedural Benefits	23.7	57.1
Market Image	31.6	14.3
External Pressure	36.8	21.4
Other	5.3	7.1
Don't Know/No Answer	2.6	–
N=	33	22

As with Table 4, Table 5 has been separated into the respondent categories 'thinking/intending' or 'implementing/registered BS 5750'. This is to distinguish the main motivations for implementing BS 5750 from the main perceived benefits of registration according to category type.[10] A majority of firms thinking or intending to register BS 5750 (36.8 per cent) suggested that they were reacting to external market conditions. In other words, they were being forced (or expected to be forced in the future) to implement the standard as a result of customer pressure or because their competitors are already registered. This finding supports the view that many small firms are implementing BS 5750 not out of choice but out of necessity. If so, it will be interesting to see how this affects the long term success of the system. For example, North et al. (1993) argue that firms pressured to implement BS 5750 are likely to consider it an unwanted burden and may decide to cut corners in both implementing and maintaining the standard, thus affecting the success of the system.

Almost a third of firms thinking/intending to introduce BS 5750 consider that registering will improve their marketing image. This means that over two-thirds (73.7 per cent) of firms in this category would do so for reasons beyond the original purpose of the standard, namely to realise procedural benefits. In fact, only 23.7 per cent of firms thinking about or intending to implement BS 5750 consider the latter motivation the most important.

The figures on motivation differ slightly from those who are implementing or registered BS 5750. Respondents in this category stated that procedural benefits were the most important benefit from implementing BS 5750. This might reflect a change in attitude resulting from a greater understanding of what the standard is about. Moreover, it appears as if experienced firms are more convinced about the value of implementing written procedures than the marketing value of registration. Correspondingly, only 14.3 per cent of this category suggested they perceived the main benefit of registration to be improved marketing image. However, despite implementing BS 5750, just over a fifth still suggested that external pressure was the main reason for their action. This indicates the latter are not enjoying any benefits of registration other than retaining existing contracts.

CONCLUSIONS

It can be seen that though awareness of BS 5750 amongst small firms is very high, a majority consider the standard to be irrelevant to their requirements. For example, over two-thirds of respondents are unaware of or do not intend to register for the standard. Of these, 34.7 per cent consider the standard irrelevant by virtue of their size (only 2.2 per cent of firms with one to four employees are implementing or registered) or sector (no garages are implementing or registered). Almost a third of those unaware of or not implementing the standard said that it was too costly and a fifth that it is over-bureaucratic and incompatible with their style of management.

Those small firms who are thinking about or intending to implement BS 5750 are doing so for a number of reasons. The most significant reason appears to be as a reaction to external market conditions, that is pressure from larger customers. However, as firms gain more experience of the standard they appear to become more impressed by the procedural aspects. Moreover, some firms (in sectors that have experienced BS 5750 for a long time) are now realising that they can achieve greater benefits by choosing those procedures strictly relevant to their business. They may not then register for BS 5750 but it may be argued that the marketing value of registration is already declining in some sectors.

Though enthusiasm for the standard is growing in some sectors, it is likely that as more firms register its novelty will decrease, as will the value of registration. It may then be considered to be an expensive luxury, when firms can operate efficiently using only the procedures they require. In this sense it could be argued that BS 5750 is, as Bannock (1991) suggests, just another managerial fashion that will eventually pass, and that its effect has been to introduce small firms to methods of managerial control only previously accessible to large organisations.

NOTES

1. This is not merely a UK phenomena, BS 5750 has international and European equivalents ISO 9000 and EN 29000.
2. The data used in this paper has been updated after cleaning and, therefore, is slightly different to that presented in the original paper. However, this does not affect the arguments in any way.

3. The use of the term 'quality standard' in this sense should not be confused with BS 5750, which is often referred to as a 'quality standard'. The former refers to an agreement on product performance or service content between producer and customer through the transaction process. BS 5750, on the other hand, is not concerned with defining product 'quality' but rather the processes within which 'quality standards' are interpreted and attained.
4. A 'structured business' is one where there are a number of personnel performing differing and identifiable jobs (see North et al, 1993).
5. BSI has attempted to remedy the situation by re-writing BS 5750 parts 1–3 and introducing Part 8, a guide to quality management and quality system elements for services (BSI, 1987.).
6. The high response rate can be attributed to a sampling frame used on previous ESRC projects. Therefore, many of the respondents had already indicated their willingness to co-operate with research projects.
7. The above represents data gathered through a multiple response answer.
8. From case study evidence given to the Small Business Research Centre, Kingston University.
9. The Federation of Recruitment and Employment Services Limited (1989) notes a 23 per cent growth of the number of firms in the industry between 1988 and 1989, a growth that occurred as trade was slowing down as a result of recession, thus making the industry more competitive.
10. The above does not imply that respondents only have one motivation for, or perceived benefit from, implementing BS 5750. However, respondents tended to be very clear about what the main ones were. Therefore, this approach was seen as logical and consistent.

REFERENCES

BANNOCK G (1991) Opinion – BS 5750:No Rush To Register, Small Business Perspective, pp 15–16, Jan–Feb.
BATCHELOR C (1992) Badge Of Quality, Financial Times, 4 September.
BLACKHAM A (1992) The Value Of ISO 9000 Registration – Conclusions Of International Survey, Paper Presented at The UK Quality Management Exhibition, November.
BRITISH STANDARDS INSTITUTE (1987a) BS 4778 : Terms and Definitions, London.
BRITISH STANDARDS INSTITUTE (1987b) BS 5750 Part 8, Guide to Quality Management and Quality System Elements for Services, London.
BRITISH STANDARDS INSTITUTE (1992) Information provided to the Small Business Research Centre, Kingston University.
CURRAN J AND BURROWS R (1988) Enterprise in Britain: A National Profile of Small Business Owners and the Self Employed, London, Small Business Research Trust.
CURRAN J AND BLACKBURN RA (1992a) Small Business Survey, February 1992, Kingston upon Thames, Small Business Research Centre, Kingston University, March.
CURRAN J AND BLACKBURN RA (1992b) Small Firms and Local Economic Networks, Relations Between Small and Large Firms in Two Localities , Kingston Upon Thames, Small Business Research Centre, Kingston University, March.
DEPARTMENT OF TRADE AND INDUSTRY (1992) BS 5750/ISO 9000: 1987 A Positive Contribution To Better Business, London, Department of Trade and Industry, August.
FENNEL E (1991) 'Kite Marks Call for Legal Eagles', The Times, 23 April.
FOX MJ (1991) Ensuring Your Business Achieves and Profits from BS 5750 Registration, Hertfordshire, Technical Communications (Publishing) Ltd.
FEDERATION OF RECRUITMENT AND EMPLOYMENT SERVICES LIMITED (1989) Yearbook of Recruitment and Employment Services, Harlow, Essex, The Longman Group.
HILL S (1991) How Do You Manage a Flexible Firm? The Total Quality Model, Work, Employment and Society, Vol 5, No 3, pp 397–415.

HOLLIDAY R (1993) Small Firms and the Organisation of Production, Unpublished Phd thesis, Business School, Staffordshire University.
JAY COMMUNICATIONS (1991) Attitudes Within British Business To Quality Management Systems, Burnham, Buckinghamshire, The CMC Partnership Ltd.
NORTH J, CURRAN J AND BLACKBURN RA (1993) Quality Standards and Small Firms: A Position Paper, Kingston Upon Thames, Small Business Research Centre, Kingston University, September.
ROCK M (1992) Twist and Turns on Quality Street, Director, December.
SHERWOOD KF (1986) A Guide To Quality, Institution Of Production Engineers.
SMALL BUSINESS RESEARCH TRUST, (1992) Quality Procedures: BS 5750, Natwest Quarterly Survey of Small Business, Vol 8, No 3, pp 18–22, August.
TISDALL P (1990) National Council Gets Its Big Break, The Times, 25 October.
WOODCOCK C (1992a) The Cost of Keeping Up The Standard, The Guardian, 31 August.
WOODCOCK C (1992b) Computer Firm Gauges Success By Clients' Standard Response, The Guardian, 19 October.
YATES I (1992) Why Manufacturing Industry Must Come First, The Observer, 15 November.

CHAPTER 10

Multinational/Supplier Linkages in the Scottish Electronics Industry

IVAN TUROK

Linkages between foreign investment and the domestic economy are an important concern in economic development. Backward linkages to indigenous suppliers of materials, services and machinery have traditionally been considered one of the main ways in which benefits from inward investment filter through to the host region (e.g. Hirschman, 1958; Kennedy, 1991). A well-developed supplier base may also attract further investment.

Historically, emphasis has been placed on the scale and value of local linkage effects and the volume of jobs generated among suppliers, within a static framework. This is the chief concern of mainstream economic research, reflected in input–output and multiplier studies seeking to quantify the short-term impact on employment and income. It is also reflected in attempts by government bodies to impose fixed local content quotas on foreign investment.

The linkage issue has reappeared recently in a different guise, in the burgeoning literature on new forms of industrial organisation, termed 'flexible specialisation' or 'post-Fordism' (e.g. Harrison, 1992; Piore and Sabel, 1984; Storper and Walker, 1989). Greater emphasis is given to the 'quality' and dynamic nature of linkages, and the long-term implications for regional economic development. Two distinctive scenarios are emerging in the literature, which I shall term 'developmental' and 'dependent' (Table 1). This is a stark dichotomy, but it helps to distinguish key features of linkage development discussed in the subsequent empirical material.

Both scenarios recognise the imperative for major corporations to be more responsive to fluctuating global economic conditions and increasing market diversity. This is reflected in the need to accelerate product development and production cycles, and to improve product quality and price competitiveness. It is also associated with certain tendencies towards decentralisation and localisation.

In the developmental scenario, economic pressures are alleged to promote fragmented structures of production for greater flexibility. The processes of vertical disintegration of large corporations and decentralisation of decision-making demand closer, more collaborative relationships between individual plants, suppliers and distributors within the value chain. These encourage stronger geographical clustering to minimise transaction and transport costs, and to facilitate high level exchange of technical ideas, market awareness and corporate plans.

TABLE I
Alternative Linkage Scenarios: A Summary of the Main Tendencies

	DEVELOPMENTAL	DEPENDENT
Nature of local linkages:	Collaborative, mutual learning. Based on technology and trust. Emphasis on added value	Unequal trading relationships. Conventional sub-contracting. Emphasis on cost-saving.
Duration of linkages:	Long-term partnerships.	Short-term contracts.
Meaning of 'flexibility':	High-level interaction to accelerate product development and increase responsiveness to volatile markets.	Price-cutting and short-term convenience for multinationals.
Inward investors' ties to the locality:	Deeply embedded. High investment in decentralised, multi-functional operations.	Weakly embedded. Branch plants restricted to final assembly operations.
Benefits for local firms:	Markets for local firms to develop and produce their own products. Transfer of technology and expertise strengthens local firms.	Markets for local firms to make standard, low-tech components. Sub-contracting means restricted independent growth capacity.
Quality of jobs:	Diverse including high skilled, high income.	Many low skilled, low paid, temporary and casual.
Prospects for the local economy:	Self-sustaining growth through cumulative expansion of the industrial cluster.	Vulnerable to external forces and corporate decisions.

Such 'clusters' may become the cores of internally generated growth poles, since the desire of major corporations to increase local sourcing creates market opportunities for new business formation and development. In the process of interaction they transfer valuable technology and expertise to local firms, which become 'specialist suppliers'. They develop the products and know-how for cumulative growth and the wherewithal to tap new markets at home and abroad. The emphasis in this perspective is clearly on the potential of inward investment to induce all-round development. Corporations get deeply embedded in the local economy through the creation of a network of sophisticated, interdependent linkages, which support the expansion of local firms and generate self-sustaining growth of the cluster as a whole (see e.g. Best, 1990; Piore and Sabel, 1984).

In the dependent scenario flexibility has negative connotations. Local clusters are weak nodes within a wider network of powerful multinationals. The direct global connections expose local economies to volatile world markets and make them vulnerable to forces of international competition. Moreover, the motives for multinationals extending local linkages are driven more by cost-cutting than by a desire to add value through the exchange of technology and information. Linkages with suppliers are hierarchical and the relationships adversarial rather than co-operative. Considerations of price or short-term convenience are uppermost. Proximate suppliers save corporations labour costs, capital investment and overheads at times of increased competition and falling profits. Suppliers do not participate in the development and technical evolution of the product.

Examples might include the use of sub-contractors to make standard components previously produced in-house, or to absorb short-term or cyclical variations in demand – 'capacity sub-contractors'. Their gross margins are tightly controlled through competitive bidding for contracts. They may be labour intensive to manage large fluctuations in orders without bearing the costs of expensive plant and machinery used discontinuously. Their work processes are likely to be simple and unskilled staff recruited, often on a temporary, even casual basis. They add much less value to the overall production process than specialist suppliers. Some may be 'labour-only subcontractors', where the customer provides whatever components, equipment and expertise are needed on a 'free-issue' basis.

Such linkages could promote economic and technical dependence. They may undermine the capacity of suppliers to upgrade themselves, by pruning overheads to the bone and depriving them of the resources required to develop the functions of a rounded enterprise, including product development, marketing and strategic management. From this perspective more numerous linkages do not imply improved regional development prospects, stronger local industrial capability or evolution towards a higher skill, higher income economy. Links may prove short-lived or restricted in scope. Inward investments may remain weakly embedded (see e.g. Amin and Malmberg, 1992; Morris and Lowder, 1992; Perrons, 1992).

This paper contributes to the debate by assembling evidence about the scale and nature of linkages in the Scottish electronics industry (1). This is an interesting case given its sharp growth and the proposition that a 'critical mass' of electronics and supply companies has been established in what is often known as 'Silicon Glen'. Are the developmental and dependent scenarios relevant, and do the linkages conform more closely to one than the other? The paper begins by contrasting the spectacular growth in electronics sales and gross output during the last decade with the modest rise in actual production and employment. Consequently, input purchases have risen steeply and there have been great opportunities for local suppliers of electronic and related components. Section two examines how far this potential has been realised in aggregate terms. The third section looks at the detailed purchasing practices of a sample of major companies in computers and consumer electronics. Section four explores some of the reasons for the pattern of local sourcing, focusing on issues concerning technology, quality, responsiveness and price. The conclusion outlines some implications for policy.

ELECTRONICS GROWTH IN SCOTLAND: A POTENTIAL MARKET FOR SUPPLIERS

Electronics gross output in Scotland increased four-fold during the 1980s, a very substantial compound growth rate of 14% per annum, while the rest of manufacturing experienced stagnation (Scottish Office, 1992a). By 1990 electronics was a sizeable part of the Scottish economy in some respects, accounting for 20% of gross manufacturing output and 42% of manufactured exports (Turok, 1993a). Nearly half of all UK exports of computers and peripheral equipment originate in Scotland. However, the direct benefits for the local economy are far less than this suggests, apparent in the relatively slow rise in employment and value added (Figures 1 and 2). Gross output increased at a compound rate of 16% per annum between 1983 and 1989 (the latest date for consistent data available), compared with 7.1% for value added and only 1.8% for employment.

FIGURE 1
Index of Gross Output and Employment for Electronics.

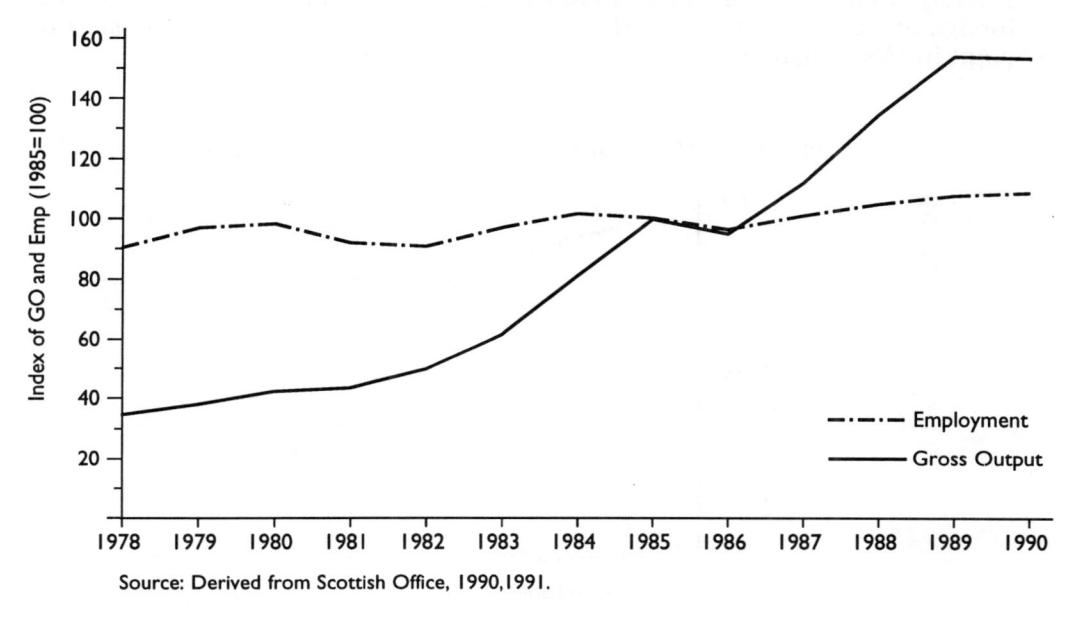

Source: Derived from Scottish Office, 1990, 1991.

FIGURE 2
Electronics' Gross Output and Value Added.

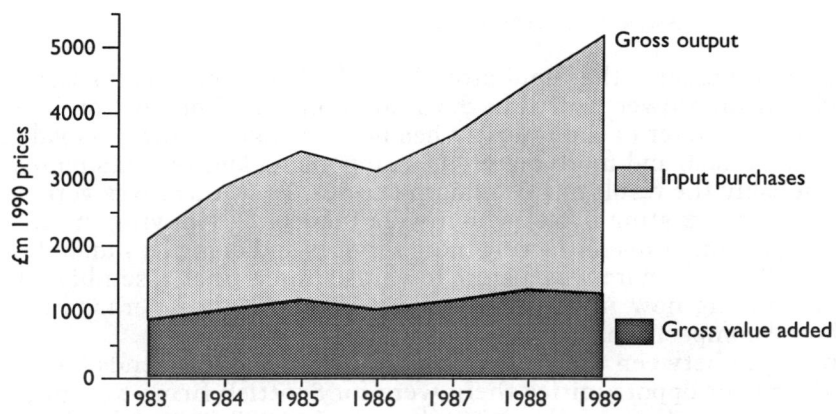

Source: Census of Production. The original figures expressed in current prices were deflated to constant 1990 prices using the UK PPI for electrical engineering and electronics to take account of the effects of inflation.

Gross output is the preferred indicator of official sources, but is a measure of company sales, not production. Value added is a better guide to the amount of work done by firms in Scotland to develop and manufacture the products sold, and hence of the income generated locally. It is in effect the sales value of firms' output less the cost of materials and services bought from other firms and government bodies. So it indicates the degree to which basic inputs are transformed and given real value in the process of production. The share of value added in gross output was only 24.2% in electronics in 1989, compared with 34% in the rest of manufacturing (Census of Production). Furthermore, it had fallen steadily from 39.2% in 1983. There was also a big difference between UK and foreign-owned segments, with the latter falling faster and from a lower starting point in 1983 (Figure 3).

FIGURE 3
Amount of Value Added in Gross Outputs for Electronics.

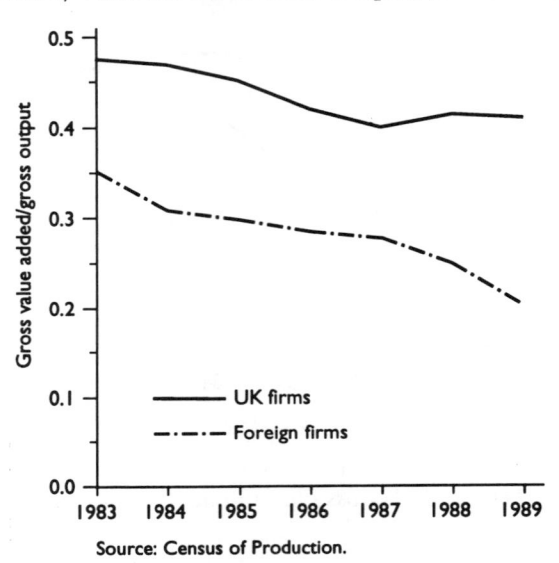

Source: Census of Production.

The widening gap indicates the rapid growth in electronic products shipped from Scotland, but the slower growth in the amount of actual production here. It seems that the character of the industry has been changing, with less value added as sales increased, and more materials, components and services bought in. This was probably the result of two main processes. First, there was vertical disintegration among existing firms, which were increasingly buying-in more ready-made components, sub-contracting more services and doing less manufacturing in-house. Second, there was a shift towards simple final assembly and test operations among new inward investment plants, linked perhaps to a change in sectoral composition.

The widening gap between the gross output and value added trends (Figure 2) indicates the major opportunities there were for Scottish firms to capture a share of the input purchases, at least in principle. In 1989 the total value of these was considerable at over £3,500m. If this had all been spent in Scotland it could have generated up to 50,000 jobs directly. This estimate is derived by dividing the value of purchases by the average gross output per employee for manufacturing in Scotland in 1989 – £69,000 (Scottish Office, 1992b). Furthermore, no less than 85% of all inputs were purchased by foreign-owned enterprises, so their procurement policies were crucial for the prospects of local suppliers.

THE ACTUAL LEVEL OF LOCAL SOURCING

Comprehensive statistics on the extent of local purchasing by electronics firms in Scotland are not available. However, periodic surveys of the industry have been undertaken by the Scottish Development Agency (SDA) (now Scottish Enterprise (SE)) in 1986, 1988 and 1990, and by the author in 1991. The samples were selected in different ways so the results are not exactly comparable. However, the response rates were high, particularly for the largest companies, so the results are likely to offer a fairly reliable indication of purchasing patterns and of the trend over time.

Table 2 shows a consistent picture between 1986 and 1991, particularly in the share of products sourced within Scotland. This seems fairly low at 12%, although it would be helpful if there was more comparative data from elsewhere. The surveys also suggest there has been no increase in the degree of integration or 'clustering' of the industry and its suppliers over time. Some caution may be warranted at this stage bearing in mind that local suppliers appear to have maintained their share of a sharply increasing total volume of input purchases. It may also be early days in the process of supplier development.

TABLE 2
Source of Material Inputs by Value (% of total)

	SCOTLAND	REST OF UK	REST OF EUROPE	ASIA	USA	REST OF WORLD
SDA 1986 survey[1]	12	23	9	8	38	5
SDA 1988 survey[2]	15	25	9	30	9	9
SDA 1990 survey[3]	12	30	16	25	12	7
Author's 1991 survey[4]	12	30	19	30	8	1

Notes: Figures in rows may not sum to 100% due to rounding or incomplete reporting in SDA surveys.
Services inputs are not included but are generally only a fraction of the value of material purchases.
1. Data available for 101 firms (85% of total jobs in electronics).
2. Data available for 60 (73% of companies employing over 50 people).
3. Data available for 35 (57% of total expenditure by electronics firms).
4. Data available for 106 (46% of all electronics firms, oriented towards largest).
Sources: SDA, 1986, 1988, 1990; and author's 1991 postal survey.

If the 12% local sourcing statistic is applied to the overall figure for input purchases from the Census of Production, the value of purchases from suppliers in Scotland amounts to approximately £450m in 1989. This implies about 6,500 jobs generated directly. This is derived by dividing the value of local purchases by the £69,000 gross output per manufacturing employee. This is not insubstantial, but amounts to only 14% of total employment in electronics in 1989.

THE PATTERN OF LOCAL SOURCING

To provide further insights into the impact of foreign firm purchases on the local economy it is important to go beyond the aggregate statistics and examine the kinds of products sourced locally and imported. Figure 4 shows the value of key component purchases by 13 of the largest foreign electronics companies in Scotland in 1991. They were selected by SE as the multinationals spending most on material inputs. Eight manufacture data processing equipment (mainly computers) and five electronic consumer goods. The figures exclude expenditure on basic electronic components such as microprocessors, capacitors and resistors. Very few of these are sourced in the UK, except through distributors stocking catalogued products.

FIGURE 4
Main Inputs Purchased by Leading Foreign Firms in 1991.

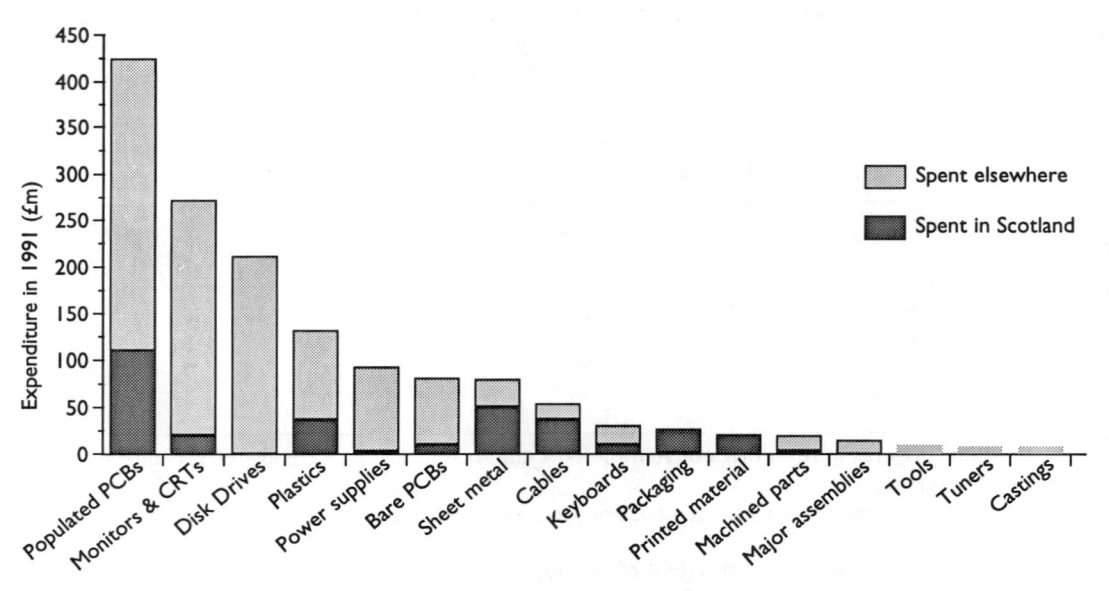

Source: Scottish Enterprise special tabulation.

The purpose of the SE study was to establish the level of spending on key components and the potential for increasing the amount of local sourcing, either by enhancing the capabilities of local suppliers or by attracting suppliers from elsewhere into Scotland to meet particular component requirements. Since the participating firms recognised the potential benefit of the exercise to themselves, they provided a level of detail about their purchasing patterns that is not normally made available because of the political and market sensitivity of this information.

The total value of their product purchases was £1,407m, £319m of which was spent in Scotland. This is a larger proportion than the figures quoted in Table 2, partly because of the above-mentioned omissions. The sample is also slightly untypical in excluding Scotland's seven semiconductor fabrication plants, which have few local purchases because they form part of integrated global production processes. Nevertheless, the 13 sampled firms are clearly a very large and important group in absolute terms. Their £319m of local purchases represents a sizeable share of all electronics purchases within Scotland in 1991.

Several important points emerge from Figure 4. First, populated PCBs are by far the most valuable single type of component, as well as the most important sourced locally. They are the essential building blocks of all electronic products, and incorporate active and passive electronic components mounted onto a bare PCB platform. A quarter (26%) of the populated PCBs procured by these firms were made in Scotland. This is surprisingly low considering the relatively straightforward technology involved in Pin In Hole (PIH) assembly and the substantial productive capacity that now exists here (see below). Surface Mount Technology (SMT) is a more recent and complicated assembly process since everything is miniaturised, but it is still a standard rather than a proprietary technology.

There are three large specialist PCB-assembly plants in Scotland: Avex, Phillips and SCI (a fourth, Timex, was involved in a recent highly publicised dispute and closure). They have highly automated PIH machinery and up to date SMT equipment. All are foreign-owned and they employ about 2,000 people altogether. Two have had long-established plants in Scotland making other things, and diversified into PCB assembly during the 1980s. The other two are recent inward investors which took advantage of the growing market for PCB-assembly work here. So it is foreign-owned rather than indigenous firms that have secured the lion's share of local PCB-assembly contracts.

Second, only 18% of bare PCBs (worth £14m) were sourced locally by the 13 major customers, with an unquantified additional amount by the PCB assembly firms. Scotland has two of the three largest PCB manufacturers in the UK in Exacta Holdings and Prestwick Holdings, as well as a host of smaller specialist producers (Turok, 1993b). Exacta and Prestwick are high volume specialists and employ about 1,000 people altogether. They appear to be competitive internationally: one exports over 50% of its output and the other 15–20%.

In addition, the technology of PCB production is hybrid and less sophisticated than for many electronic components. Barriers to entry were relatively low in the past, although volume production now demands costly equipment. PCBs are also made to order products with much of the R and D carried out by customers. So proximity to suppliers offers considerable advantages for collaboration. For all these reasons one might have expected a higher level of local purchases.

Third, certain kinds of products have distinctly greater local sourcing than the rest. They include keyboards (32%), plastics (45%), cables (61%), sheet metal (65%), packaging and printed material (79%). Most are apparently simple to manufacture, using standard machinery or labour-intensive methods. They also have relatively low price-to-bulk ratios and high transport costs. They are more straightforward than PCBs to make and bulkier to transport. They are the kinds of products that firms responding to the 1991 postal survey said they had bought more of locally in the last three years (Figure 5).

Many of the local suppliers are Scottish-owned or UK subsidiaries, including Fullarton Fabrication, Simclar, Lithgow, Kinloch, Mimtec, TFC and Turnkey.

These seven employ over 3,000 people altogether. They are simple sub-contractors without their own technology and products. Some are labour-intensive assembly operations with little plant and machinery. Many were started within the last decade and have grown quickly. Some of their customers provide all the materials and equipment they need on free issue, which reduces cash flow difficulties and alleviates the financial constraints small growth firms face.

FIGURE 5
Change in Products Sourced in Scotland in the Last Three Years.

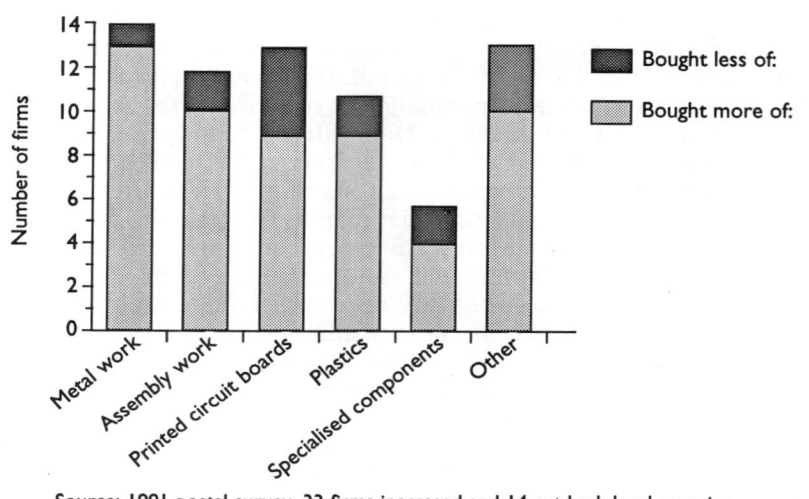

Source: 1991 postal survey. 33 firms increased and 14 cut back local sourcing.

Plastics are slightly different. Much of the recent increase in local sourcing has gone to newly opened branch plants. Companies such as Tenma (from Japan), Tilling (Middlesex), Plastic Engineers (Wales) and Silleck Mouldings (Teeside) have invested in substantial automated plastic moulding equipment. The high cost of investment and inexperience may have deterred Scottish suppliers.

Fourth, more sophisticated, higher value components such as disk drives, monitors and power supplies are almost completely imported into Scotland. Until recently there were no significant manufacturers in Scotland. The indigenous disk drive producer Rodime was an exception. It enjoyed great success early on and expanded to 550 local employees in 1987, but then declined and went bankrupt in 1991. A small firm called Domain Power started manufacturing power supplies in the late 1980s, but was taken over by a foreign company after struggling to survive and grow. There have been several inward investments in these sectors since then, such as Conner Peripherals and YE Data, which make disk drives.

The evidence suggests that local sourcing is fairly low overall, with an eighth of electronics inputs acquired in Scotland, but the pattern is also diverse. A sizeable share of relatively bulky components is bought locally, resulting in extensive growth of a fair number of indigenous firms. There is less purchasing of technically sophisticated products, although there are some signs that this may be beginning to change, mainly through foreign suppliers establishing local branches. Some are 'capacity sub-contractors' that have invested in high volume equipment, as in plastics and PCB assembly. Others are 'specialist suppliers' with their own product technology, as in disk drives.

On the whole, indigenous firms seem to be restricted to making relatively straightforward products, with some exceptions.

TOWARDS AN EXPLANATION: DEMANDING CUSTOMERS AND SUPPLIER WEAKNESSES

The full explanation for the pattern of sourcing is complicated and would require detailed analysis of the characteristics and policies of customers, the performance of suppliers and the relations between the two groups. This would be a major undertaking with several hundred diverse electronics and related enterprises in Scotland (SE, 1991), and in view of their sensitivity about discussing these issues. In the absence of a comprehensive study the following account is exploratory. The postal survey provides useful preliminary insights. It incorporated questions about the difficulties faced by buyers and suppliers. On the whole, major customers were inclined to blame weaknesses in the supply base for limited local sourcing, whereas suppliers accused customers of stringent purchasing procedures.

Seventy-seven firms had tried to increase local procurement. Figure 6 shows the difficulties encountered. Unavailability of materials such as special metals and chemicals, products such as power supplies and monitors, or basic components such as resistors and capacitors, emerged most often. The scale of this response suggests that the supplier infrastructure in Scotland is not as extensive as sometimes alleged.

FIGURE 6
Difficulties Encountered in Increasing Local Sourcing.

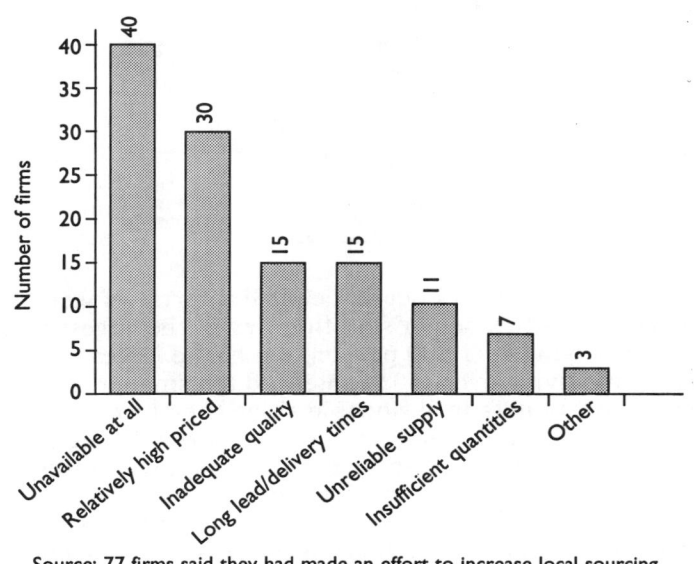

Source: 77 firms said they had made an effort to increase local sourcing.
61 firms mentioned specific difficulties in doing so.

The main reservation about existing suppliers concerned prices. Half the respondents said local firms were more expensive than suppliers elsewhere. Price has become increasingly important as conditions in electronics get more competitive and pressures to cut costs mount. Other drawbacks of local suppliers include inadequate quality, long delivery times and unreliability, which I return to later.

Turning to suppliers, the same kinds of difficulties emerged with customers, but from a different perspective. Twenty-three said they encountered problems in meeting the requirements of major customers, including low price expectations, irregular orders, short-term contracts and short lead times (Figure 7). Price and general short-term behaviour were most important: suppliers felt that unwarranted pressure was exerted on both. Some blamed their customers' poor organisation for the short notice they were often given on orders. Others blamed their customers' inefficiency for their attempts to secure cost reductions from suppliers rather than themselves. Some felt customers deliberately kept them on short contracts to maintain pressure and discipline.

FIGURE 7
Difficulties Suppliers Face with Major Customers.

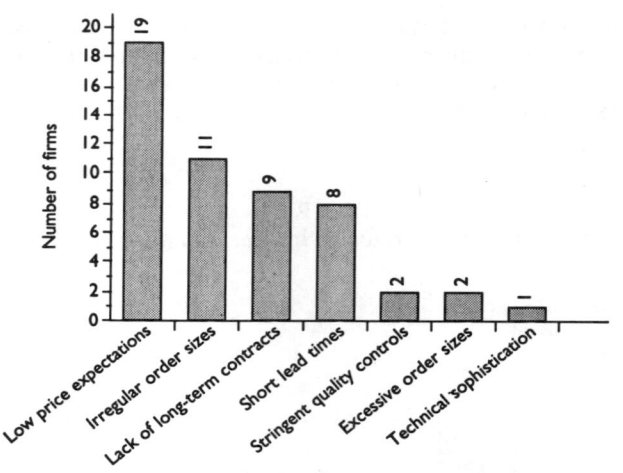

Source: 1991 postal survey. 23 firms said they faced difficulties meeting the requirements of local customers.

To explore these issues in greater depth, detailed interviews were held with the purchasing managers or other senior staff from ten of the largest foreign firms in Scotland (most employing over 500 people), ten of the largest and fastest growing suppliers (all employing over 150 people) and ten smaller, static suppliers. A sample of ten key customers is reasonable since they have a disproportionate share of total purchases. The interviews were supported by an analysis of company accounts to get 'objective' information on growth rates, investment, income distribution and other performance measures (details in Turok, 1993a).

Surprising diversity emerged between the purchasing practices of different firms, reflecting the nature of production processes, the speed of technical change in market segments, the nationality of ownership and global corporate strategies. Yet there were common patterns too, promoted by growing international competition. Leading companies were introducing more advanced procurement procedures and more elaborate supplier evaluation criteria, in order to help reduce the time-to-market of their products, to raise quality standards and to control prices. It is helpful to structure the analysis around four broad factors: technology, quality, responsiveness and price. Their order of importance differs between firms and examples are provided to elaborate and illustrate each. Evidence is presented in this form partly because of the considerable difficulty in securing equivalent information on a wider basis.

Technology

Technology is an important barrier to increased sourcing from indigenous firms. Few are specialist suppliers of technology-based components. This is why many firms in the postal survey stated that certain products were unavailable. They import these components or encourage their suppliers at home to establish branches in Scotland to service them more effectively.

The undeveloped state of indigenous suppliers is linked to difficulties securing financial support, lack of management experience and less risky opportunities in other segments. Firms seeking to develop their own products claim to be hampered by the lack of long-term 'patient' resources from financial institutions or government agencies. Experience shows that technology takes time and is costly to develop, obvious barriers to entry for new small firms. The managers of some suppliers that succeeded in raising funds and enjoyed early success – such as Rodime – made serious strategic errors which jeopardised their existence. Established UK electronics firms in Scotland – such as Ferranti, Marconi and Racal – have been preoccupied with small-batch, high-priced products for protected military markets. This has left them relatively uncompetitive and impeded diversification into expanding markets for high volume civil electronics goods (e.g. McKinsey, 1988).

It is unclear whether technology is becoming more or less important in relation to other factors such as price and quality. On the one hand, the growth of 'open systems' in data processing means a decline in proprietary technology and computers becoming more standard commodities. This should shift the emphasis in component purchasing towards price and away from specialist technology.

On the other hand, technology is becoming important in more subtle ways. It is helpful to distinguish between 'hard' technology – associated with investment in tangible products and processes – and 'soft' technology which is linked with skills and knowledge. Some customers are looking for suppliers offering extra added value beyond simple sub-contracting (e.g. Sun Microsystems – see Turok, 1993c). They want suppliers to have equipment they do not possess themselves, to provide expertise with their own development and production engineers, or to provide knowledge about the market and competitors that stems from operating internationally. These save customers' costs, provide an intelligent resource to assist in problem solving, and help identify ways of increasing quality and cutting waste. It is a moot point how far customers are willing to pay for these resources through higher product prices. Some differentiate between 'preferred suppliers', who are specialists and tend to operate world-wide, and other suppliers of lower value components and simple sub-contractors, whose overheads they are inclined to curtail.

Quality

Most corporations expect rising standards of suppliers in terms of the proportion of defective components and the sophistication of their manufacturing control systems. They expect progressive elimination of 'waste', defined as the amount of equipment, materials, space and workers' time not directly adding value to the product. Quality was the second major drawback mentioned in the postal survey (Figure 6).

'Total Quality Management' implies a company-wide approach focusing on prevention rather than detection and remedial action. Suppliers are expected to introduce techniques to assist monitoring of production, such as Statistical Process Control. They verify the reliability of processes, eliminating the need for incoming inspection of components by customers and so saving them time and money. They also make it easier for suppliers to engineer product and process improvements by providing a complete record of each stage of production and data measuring the effectiveness of efficiency efforts.

It is common for electronics firms in Scotland to require suppliers to operate independently certified quality assurance systems such as BS 5750 or ISO 9000, which specify procedures to ensure consistent standards. They are intended to build in reliability at every stage to reduce defects and cut time spent on modifying designs, correcting faults and re-working products.

Many sub-contractors are critical of these formal systems. They appear simple and straightforward, and are therefore popular for customers to insist upon as a matter of routine. However, they are costly to introduce because of the extensive documentation. They can also be largely irrelevant because of their comprehensive character. For some suppliers, they are little more than marketing tools to ensure they get short-listed for contracts.

Responsiveness

Corporations expect suppliers to demonstrate a high level of commitment to them, including a positive and accommodating attitude, willingness to react at short notice, flexibility in the service provided and on-time delivery. Some also want suppliers to have procedures to utilise their sales forecasts as planning tools and to reduce their lead times once firm orders are placed. The introduction of systems designed to cut stocks and shorten production cycles – such as Just-in-Time – have increased pressure on suppliers. Geographical proximity can reinforce dependability by enabling firms to exert more control over suppliers. The use of Electronic Data Interchange among a few major companies to speed up communication and cut paperwork reduces some but not all of the requirements for physical closeness.

The critical issue for several of the companies interviewed was the attitude of the supplier's owner-manager. This is fundamental to all aspects of responsiveness and is the ultimate safeguard for customers. IBM attaches particular importance to this for some of its purchases (see Turok, 1993c). Its Greenock plant makes personal computers for Europe. Its supplier evaluation scheme assesses the attitudes of key staff as well as their technical capabilities. 'Capacity sub-contractors' are used to manage uneven demand and have to show flexibility in responding to urgent orders of different kinds. They have reserves of people willing to do assembly work at short notice, during evenings and weekends. Their operations are largely reactive: their planning horizons are short, their fixed costs and overheads are minimised, and there is little inducement to invest. Proximity to the plant is an advantage. This is reflected in an unusually large share of inputs sourced within Scotland.

Price

Price has always been important in sourcing decisions. The trend towards increased outsourcing and rising productivity (e.g. Figure 2) helps to explain why the cost of external inputs is even more significant. For individual companies input purchases can represent 85% or more of the gross cost of production.

Sourcing decisions traditionally focused on the 'piece price', i.e. the price quoted by suppliers per component. This put UK firms at a disadvantage compared with those in Asia, in particular, where labour costs were lower and suppliers' time horizons longer. Most corporations now use a measure of the total cost, including freight, import duties, inspection, defects, engineering support to suppliers, delays in delivery and managing stock. One effect is to redress the balance between local and foreign suppliers, particularly for bulky items such as plastics and metalwork with high costs of transport and stock-holding.

Forward-looking companies seek suppliers with the capability to improve productivity continuously in order to secure steady price cuts. Some offer their own engineers and accountants to help suppliers identify ways of improving efficiency. A figure of 15% year-on-year price reductions is often mentioned as a target. This is difficult for labour-intensive sub-contractors lacking machines that can be speeded up or processes that can be upgraded incrementally. There are limits to the productivity increases that can be secured through work intensification.

One way customers achieve price cuts is to compare suppliers against each other and foster rivalry among them. In some cases this is explicit and firms are ranked in 'benchmarking' exercises on detailed productivity and cost criteria. This is also used to identify areas of potential cost-saving. Not surprisingly, some suppliers acknowledge frustration with the demands for price reductions. They say they are expected to submit their lowest possible bid to win the initial contract and then to find scope for further efficiencies subsequently.

Consumer electronics companies appear to attach most importance to price considerations, presumably because price competition has traditionally been fiercer than in data processing or military electronics. In addition, Japanese plants such as Mitsubishi Electric, OKI and JVC have a more disciplined, 'lean' approach to production, apparent even on casual inspection. They are better placed than US firms to compare prices in Asia. Many are part of giant, vertically integrated corporations that manufacture many components in-house, so there is a natural inclination to source them internally. The emphasis on price works against local suppliers, except for bulky items and urgent requirements. EC policy encourages more purchases within Europe than would otherwise occur.

CONCLUSION

The evidence suggests that inward investment in the Scottish electronics industry is not very deeply embedded. About 12% of material inputs are sourced locally. This proportion has at least stayed constant over a period of sharply increased total purchases. Comparative analysis for other regions and industries would help to put this into perspective.

More complete evidence about the nature of local linkages is difficult to collect and further research is needed. The evidence to date indicates that many of the links with indigenous suppliers correspond more closely to the simple dependent model than to the developmental scenario. There are few high value, technology-based linkages, except with the branches of foreign suppliers in Scotland. Their high-level R&D, strategic management and marketing functions are based elsewhere, so local learning and transfer of technology seem limited.

Many links with local firms involve capacity or labour sub-contracting. They serve useful purposes for major corporations, including cost-saving, convenience and less risk. There are clearly benefits for the local economy in terms of job numbers, and some sub-contractors have grown rapidly to employ many hundreds of people. However, the extent to which firms have developed into more rounded enterprises is unclear. It requires further investigation, probably on a sectoral basis. None of the electronic subcontractors interviewed had developed their own products or technology, although some had begun to tap wider markets. Bare PCB manufacturers are good though fairly isolated examples (Turok, 1993b). Overall, the simple conclusion to be drawn from the pattern and nature of linkage formation is that the prospects for self-sustaining, internally-generated growth of the Scottish electronics industry cannot yet be described as promising. Whether it is possible to progress from a dependent situation to a developmental one remains unanswered.

From the point of view of inward investors, the limitations of local sourcing include technological weaknesses of indigenous firms, doubts about their quality and reliability, and their relatively high prices for some products. Other factors include the branch-plant character of many foreign firms, their absence of strong product design and procurement functions locally and their protected supply relationships with parent corporations or global suppliers.

There appears to be scope for some change in the situation. There is certainly a need considering the level of import penetration. It may require policy actions at local and European levels to make a significant difference, and should be directed at the supplier and customer sides of the linkage relation. There is a large potential market in Scotland for components of various kinds. Some inward investors are looking for more local suppliers because of the advantages of proximity. Measures to build up the capacity of the supply base, through targeted investment, training and enterprise development, might prove effective at capturing a larger share of their purchases. Competitive suppliers on price and quality might progress to exploit wider markets in Britain and Europe. Cooperation between focused suppliers could provide the integrated package of products and services that seems to be expected by some corporations.

Scottish Enterprise have a small team of engineers working to improve the management skills and capacity in a group of local sub-contractors. At first sight their Supplier Development Programme appears to be achieving useful results with individual firms. In view of the considerable potential, it ought to be expanded. Many sub-contractors require substantial investment in advanced equipment to compete for high volume contracts, as in PCB assembly work. There is even scope for local firms to secure a larger share of orders for cables, metalwork, keyboards and plastics. Given the tradition of the Scottish mechanical engineering industry with similar basic processes, this should not be infeasible. Some local suppliers need persuasion to reinvest more of their surpluses to raise productivity and shift their activities in the high-income, high-skill direction. Some customers are looking for sub-contractors offering additional value-added services.

The challenge to establish firms with distinctive products is bound to be difficult. This probably requires long-term commitment to an intensive kind of support that has not been acceptable in Britain for years, although it is pursued with apparent effectiveness in some other countries. Established firms such as Ferranti and Marconi with advanced technology experience in military electronics could be good starting points for efforts to diversify into expanding civil sectors. With a ready market for high value components on the doorstep, the potential could be considerable.

Joint ventures with inward investors is another option that has not been seriously considered. They might aim to build the collaborative, technology-based partnerships that many multinationals are seeking to develop. In the past, the struggle to attract inward investment has placed regions in a weak position, reluctant to convey the impression they are making any impositions. Co-ordination by the EC might provide the framework within which localities could begin to negotiate closer, mutually beneficial relationships with foreign investors. The EC could also insist that conditions are attached to regional assistance to support efforts to develop local suppliers. Selective Assistance in the UK already has employment obligations attached and could be extended to include linkage conditions.

NOTES

1. Electronics is defined in the paper to include data processing equipment, electronic components, electronic instruments, telecom, electronic capital goods and consumer goods, i.e. the following 10 activity headings from the 1980 SIC: 3302, 3444, 3453, 3710, 3732, 3433, 3441, 3442, 3443 and 3454.
   The evidence is drawn from an 18-month study of the electronics industry supported by the ESRC (award number 232783), including a comprehensive postal survey of firms in 1991, follow-up interviews with 10 major customers, 10 large local suppliers and 10 smaller suppliers in 1992, secondary survey data from government sources, consultations with industry experts and a review of local and national newspapers for the last decade.

A longer version of this paper has been published in Regional Studies (Vol. 27, No. 5, 1993).

REFERENCES

AMIN A AND MALMBERG A (1992) Competing structural and institutional influences on the geography of production in Europe, Environment and Planning A, 24, pp.401–416.

BEST MH (1990) The New Competition: Institutions of Industrial Restructuring, Polity Press, Cambridge.

CENSUS OF PRODUCTION (various years), from SOID, Glasgow.

HARRISON B (1992) Industrial districts: old wine in new bottles? Regional Studies, 26, 5, pp.469–483.

HIRSCHMAN A (1958) The Strategy of Economic Development, Yale University Press, New Haven.

KENNEDY K (1991) Linkages and Overseas Industry, in Foley A and McAleese D, Overseas Industry in Ireland, Gill and Macmillan, Dublin.
MCKINSEY AND COMPANY INC (1988) Performance and Competitive Success: Strengthening Competitiveness in UK Electronics, NEDO, London.
MORRIS AS AND LOWDER S (1992) Flexible specialisation: the application of theory in a poor-country context: Leon, Mexico, International Journal of Urban and Regional Research, 16, 2, pp.190–201.
PERRONS D (1992) Undefended cities and regions facing the new European order, Report on an international seminar, International Journal of Urban and Regional Research, 16, 2, pp.318–320.
PIORE M AND SABEL CF (1984) The Second Industrial Divide, Basic Books, New York.
SDA (1986) Scottish Electronics Companies Survey, Glasgow.
SDA (1988) Scottish Electronics Companies Survey, Glasgow.
SDA (1990) Scottish Electronics Companies Survey, Glasgow.
SE (SCOTTISH ENTERPRISE) (1991) Electronics and Support Companies in Scotland, SE.
SCOTTISH OFFICE (1990) The Electronics Industry in Scotland, Stat. Bulletin C1.3.
SCOTTISH OFFICE (1991) The Electronics Industry in Scotland, Stat. Bulletin C1.4
SCOTTISH OFFICE. (1992a) Index of Industrial Production and Construction for Scotland, Statistical Bulletin No. D2.4. Edinburgh.
SCOTTISH OFFICE (1992b) Scottish Economic Bulletin, No. 45, HMSO, Edinburgh.
STORPER, M AND WALKER, R (1989) The Capitalist Imperative: Territory, Technology and Industrial Growth, Basil Blackwell, Oxford.
TUROK, I (1993a) Contrasts in Ownership and Development: Local Versus Global in Silicon Glen, Urban Studies, 26, pp. 587–606.
TUROK I (1993b) The Growth of an Indigenous Electronics Industry: Scottish Printed Circuit Boards, Environment and Planning 'A', 25, pp.1789–1813.
TUROK I (1993c) Inward Investment and Local Linkages: How Deeply Embedded is 'Silicon Glen?', Regional Studies, 27,5 pp. 401–417.

CHAPTER 11

Small Firm Autonomy Within a Franchise: A Case of Shifting Fortunes

ALAN FELSTEAD

Today it is commonplace to assume that the main attraction of franchising to potential franchisees is the prospect of 'being one's own boss'. Indeed, there is now evidence to back this up: 30% of franchise exhibition-goers cite independence as the main appeal of franchising (Stanworth and Purdy, 1993, p7; Felstead, 1993, pp80–88). Furthermore, franchising is often promoted as a non-hierarchical form of work organisation. The fact that franchisees trade as legally independent businesses carries the implication that they do not belong to a single hierarchical structure, but that instead they act as autonomous centres of work bound together by a common trade mark/idea/format. The argument of this paper is that in spite of this, the strategic decisions setting out the parameters in which franchisees organise their businesses remain firmly in the hands of the franchisor (cf. Cowling and Sudgen, 1987, Chapter Two). In this sense, franchising simply represents the continuation of trends first identified by Berle and Means 60 years ago:

'Economic power, in terms of control over physical assets, is apparently responding to a centripetal force, tending more and more to concentrate ... At the same time, beneficial ownership is centrifugal, tending to divide and subdivide, to split into ever smaller units ... In other words, ownership continually becomes more dispersed; the power formerly joined to it becomes increasingly concentrated' (Berle and Means, 1932, p9).

There is, though, one important difference: in the case of franchising economic power is exercised not by directly owning and controlling the physical assets of doing business, but by controlling the use to which the intangible assets, such as the trade mark/idea/format, are put.

To substantiate the argument the paper analyses the reshaping of a franchise relationship at close quarters. It examines the reasons why the Coca-Cola Company's original franchised bottler structure in Germany (1) had by the 1980s outlived its usefulness, and why a reshaped franchise structure was put in its place. Two main research techniques were adopted: the collection of documentary evidence, both of an historical and contemporary nature; and a series of semi-structured interviews. The latter were conducted at three levels: the corporate level, where 24 top executives of the company were interviewed (through 26 interviews); the division responsible for Coca-Cola operations in Germany, where 19 personnel were interviewed (through 25 interviews); and at the level of the German franchised bottler, where 9 current (through 10 interviews) and 4 former were selected and interviewed, so as to yield a representative sample of the entire network.

ORIGINAL FRANCHISE STRUCTURE

Almost all producers of carbonated soft drinks manufacture their product not from fruit or other primary inputs but from a syrup or concentrate produced by a specialist firm. At the risk of oversimplifying, the soft drinks industry can be categorised into two distinct kinds of operation. First, there are those producers who purchase syrups or concentrates from specialist firms. The drinks are then bottled and sold under their own labels; such firms are often small to medium-sized firms operating in a local or regional market. Secondly, there are firms which specialise in the manufacture of syrups or concentrates. These firms typically award franchises to local bottlers to produce and market their range of soft drinks over a specific area. Here, the brand belongs to the upstream producer of the concentrate, although advertising and marketing of the brand may be carried out jointly with franchisees. The Coca-Cola Company is the archetypal user of this method of operation. It pioneered the method in its domestic market, and then used it to penetrate other markets worldwide.

Under this arrangement, the Coca-Cola Company manufactures and sells syrup (a mixture of ingredients in liquid form which, when properly mixed with carbonated water, becomes the finished product) and concentrates (a mixture of the same basic ingredients minus sugar) to a bottler who has the exclusive right to bottle according to the company's quality standards and specifications, and distribute the beverage in a clearly defined geographical territory for a finite period (except in the US, where contracts run for perpetuity). The Coca-Cola Company participates, conceptually and financially, in many of the advertising and promotion programmes made in connection with their trade-marked products, provides advice and technical assistance on production, quality control, management and sales problems, and engages in development and test marketing of new products and packages. In the original franchise structure the bottlers, for their part, decided on the plant and equipment to be used, total production by size and type of container, their product mix, the price to be charged, and the manner in which to penetrate the market and secure the widest possible distribution of the product throughout their territory, (as required by contract). By 1970 Germany was covered by 123 franchised Coca-Cola bottlers.

EXPOSING THE CONTRADICTIONS

The franchise structure created a patchwork of 'little kingdoms' throughout Germany. Vertically imposed territorial exclusivity eliminated direct competition between Coca-Cola bottlers, and as a result bottlers enjoyed monopoly power in the filling and distribution of Coca-Cola within their own territorial boundaries. While this proved advantageous to the Coca-Cola Company and its bottlers initially in that it encouraged widespread distribution, over the longer term it was to become the system's 'Achilles heel' (contrary to Katz, 1978, p88). This was vividly exposed by three major developments which came to a head in the 1980s: (1) the addition of new products and packages; (2) the increase in the minimum efficient scale of bottling; and (3) the concentration of retailing.

New Products and Packages

Originally, Coca-Cola was a one product/one package company – the 6.5 fluid ounce (192ml) glass returnable Coca-Cola bottle. However, today Coca-Cola in Germany is sold in many different package types (returnable glass, returnable plastic, one-way plastic, cans), sizes (0.2 litre to 2.0 litre) and configurations (6-packs, 18-packs, 24-packs). In addition, vending units which automatically mix syrup with chilled carbonated water at the point of sale and dispense the beverage into a cup or glass (post-mix) are in place. Extensions to existing brands have been launched, most notably low-calorie versions of existing brands such as Coca-Cola Light (known as Diet Coke in the UK and US). New products, too, have been added to Coca-Cola's range – Fanta Orange, Sprite, Bonaqa, Aquarius and so on (known as allied products) – as well as extensions to these new brands.

However, no bottler was able to produce the entire Coca-Cola range of products, and many did not package all the sizes for which they were authorised. Instead, the company gave bottlers supplementary agreements to their original contract allowing them to sell the complete range, so long as each product and package was furnished by authorised suppliers (either the company's own bottling plants, franchised plants with a toll filling agreement or canning co-operatives). Franchisees, for example, were authorised to distribute cans in their territories following the introduction of cans onto the German market in 1963. However, the right to fill cans for sale within an exclusive territory was never relinquished. Given the high investment costs required to build canning lines and the small size of their territories, few, if any, franchisees would have been able to make the necessary investment. Even if they had, investments expanding the market for Coca-Cola products, such as advertising and marketing campaigns, might have been jeopardised as a result. However, several franchised bottlers combined to form separate canning co-operatives filling cans for Coca-Cola on the basis of a toll filling agreement (cf. Beale and Dugdale, 1975).

Although the addition of each new product and package raised beverage sales (and hence concentrate sales), economic theory suggests that had franchisees been able to produce, package and distribute more of the variations themselves, sales would have been higher still. Products and packages 'bought in' were purchased at wholesale prices (which must at least have covered average costs for the producer to survive). The cost to the purchaser of buying one extra unit must have been higher than the marginal cost of production (since average costs spread fixed and variable costs over total output, whereas marginal costs record the cost of producing one additional unit). The profit maximising distributor of 'bought in' products and packages therefore expanded sales up to the point at which marginal cost equalled marginal revenue (ie, the cost of the extra sale equalled the income received). This point was reached before marginal cost equalled marginal revenue in production (or at an even lower level of sales if the distributor sought goals other than profit-maximisation, see below). In other words, the 'buying in' of more and more products and packages meant that franchisees reached a level of sales which maximised their profits (or other considerations) well before producers, and the company, which supplied the concentrate, reached theirs.

ECONOMIES OF SCALE AND TECHNOLOGICAL ADVANCE

Bottler territories were originally drawn up on the basis of producing and packaging a 6.5 fluid ounce (192ml) returnable Coca-Cola bottle using 1950s technology, and distributing it within a serviceable territory (ie, vehicle-round-trip-in-one-day measurement). Today, the growth of packages and products, technological advances in soft drink bottling and improvements in Germany's transportation system, have all helped to raise the minimum efficient scale of operation. Bottling lines have got faster (today a 100 spout bottling filler can fill a fifth as many bottles again as it could in 1970) and hence production costs have been reduced. Transportation costs have similarly fallen, although traffic congestion is beginning to jeopardise these gains.

However, three factors confined bottlers to production units with higher costs than those attainable in an efficiently-sized plant. First, the most efficient bottling lines required large investments: for example, a new plastic bottling line with an annual capacity of 66 million litres currently costs about DM12 million (Monopolies and Mergers Commission, 1991, p58, Coca-Cola GmbH sources). Second, territorial restrictions prevented bottlers from growing to the minimum efficient scale by expanding the geographical boundaries of the market in which they sold Coca-Cola products. Growth could come only from population increases or higher per capita consumption of brands within their territory. Third, although investment costs could be shared and territorial boundaries enlarged if neighbouring franchisees merged, many resisted doing so voluntarily. Most bottlers were family-owned and run businesses, and many had family members such as wives, grandparents and children working there in some capacity. Although a merger would have increased the financial strength of their businesses, many family-owned bottlers feared that it would also dilute their control – reducing their ability to make family appointments, preventing them giving themselves pay rises, and weakening their economic influence and status within the community. Furthermore, many were content with the level of profits their business was able to generate without the upheaval of organisational change (ie, they had reached their 'comfort level').

These factors held sway until bottling contracts came up for renewal in the late 1980s. Bottling continued to be carried out in plants whose level of production fell below the minimum efficient scale. As a result, higher costs pushed up prices and/or reduced bottler profit margins compared to those of an efficiently-sized plant. Higher prices reduced sales in the short term, while slimmer profit margins narrowed the scope bottlers had to make investments in the market (eg, vending machines), thereby depressing sales over the longer term. In both of these ways, maintaining the status quo reduced volume sales (and hence concentrate sales) from what they might have been. In other words, a franchise network of 100 or so bottlers was increasingly becoming an obstacle rather than a tool for the maximisation of concentrate sales: the Coca-Cola Company had a network of bottlers whose volume sales goals were incompatible with theirs.

RETAILER CONCENTRATION

It is conventional in the soft drinks industry to distinguish between two channels through which products are distributed to the trade: the at-home market and the away-from-home market. The labels given indicate the essential difference between the two: drinks purchased for consumption at home as opposed to those drunk at the point of sale. Most of the retail outlets supplied through the at-home channel are shops of one type or another ranging from supermarkets to corner stores. The outlets comprising the away-from-home market are more varied. These include bars, fast food outlets, clubs, restaurants, as well as leisure parks, sports centres and works canteens.

Concentration has taken place in both channels of distribution. The share of the grocery business won by the German supermarket chains such as Tengelmann, Spar, Metro, Aldi, Karstadt and so on has increased substantially over time. Their growth has largely been at the expense of the independent corner store. Over the period 1970–1989 more than 100,000 retail stores have closed throughout Germany, while the sales of those remaining has leapt by 234%. Even the smaller retailers have joined buying groups in order to buy larger volumes from manufacturers, and have gradually expanded their operations (cf. Pleijster, 1992). The growth of fast food and other restaurant chains such as McDonald's, Burger King, Nordsee, Movenpick and so on has concentrated the away-from-home market in a similar, albeit less dramatic, fashion.

Originally, each franchisee was able to negotiate their own terms and conditions of supply with retailers in their territory: most were single outlet operations, and few had outlets in more than one franchise territory. These negotiations included prices, volume rebates, participation in special promotions, delivery arrangements and the allocation of shelf space. However, while concentration in the retail trade gradually pushed purchasing decisions from the local to the regional and then the national level, the right to sell remained decentralised in the hands of more than one hundred bottlers. At the same time, the buying power of these retail chains increased. For example, 45% of the sales of Coca-Cola brands in Germany currently goes to just ten customers[2].

The initial response of the German Coca-Cola organisation to these changes was the establishment of Key Account Committees consisting of bottler and Coca-Cola GmbH representatives, and central billing of major customer accounts. These committees negotiated with purchasing managers of each major account on behalf of the entire bottling network. However, the committees had no real authority to set pricing and supply conditions with whom they negotiated. Instead, a single bottler could hold the entire network to ransom by refusing to accept the outcome of the negotiations, holding out instead for a better deal. At best this could delay the deal being struck, at worst the entire national account could be lost.

Retailer concentration posed a problem for Coca-Cola's franchise set-up. On the one hand, the retailers to whom bottlers were selling were acquiring more and more buying power – purchasing decisions were becoming centralised, their orders were growing in size, chains were expanding nationally and their own-label products were becoming more acceptable. On the other hand, bottlers' sovereignty to decide the terms and conditions on which they sold the Coca-Cola range remained unbroken, and the network's decision points continued to be fragmented. Despite its national/global image, the franchise structure denied the Coca-Cola Company the power to negotiate with national account customers. Potentially at least, this put some of the largest accounts at risk, and as a consequence jeopardised concentrate sales from which the final product is made.

RESHAPING THE FRANCHISE STRUCTURE

The franchise structure of 100 or so bottlers, which had served both the Coca-Cola Company and its franchisees so well during its formative years in Germany, was beginning to hinder rather than help future growth. The company's own revenue was derived entirely from sales of concentrate to the bottler. The company therefore 'had a near-absolute interest in volume growth, and in keeping retail prices low in order to stimulate further sales of concentrate' (Monopolies and Mergers Commission, 1991, p122). The lower the cost of production, the greater the proportion of the wholesale margin available for non-price marketing, such as promotions, displays, technical sales aids and so on, which also stimulate sales. The German franchise structure, as of the mid-1980s, was making the goal of low cost production increasingly difficult to achieve: small territories were unable to generate sufficient sales to support 'state-of-the-art' production facilities; capacity utilisation was low (few operated round-the-clock production); too many products and packages were purchased from authorised suppliers instead of being produced and packaged in-house; for many family-owned and run bottlers profits were secondary; and the mechanisms through which negotiations with large retailers took place were cumbersome. In each of these ways, bottlers were operating so as to maximise their own profits (or other considerations), but not those of the franchisor. In addition, large national retailing chains were beginning to wield their buying power by refusing to recognise bottlers' territorial boundaries and instead seeking better terms and conditions of supply nationwide. Moreover, the closure of small retail outlets lengthened the distances those who drank soft drinks had to travel to points of purchase, thereby heightening the importance of investment in technical sales aids such as coin-vendors. Without changes to the original franchise structure, competitive brands would have been able to expand their footholds in the market, franchisees would have been squeezed, and would have eventually gone out of business.

Early moves to restructure the bottling network can be traced as far back as the late 1960s. They took two forms: encouraging bottlers to compare their cost structures with others in the network in the hope that economies would be made (through a system known as Bottler Cost Comparison); and encouraging bottlers to merge to form larger, more economic units. In the US, the Coca-Cola Company set up the Bottler Consolidation Department in 1967 for the same purpose (Katz, 1978, p90). However, their success was gradual rather than dramatic: in the US, bottlers declined from 900 in 1968 to about 600 by 1980, while in Germany their number declined only marginally from 123 to 105 (see Figure 1).

However, the bare figures do not tell the full story; they do not record the company's more interventionist stance, especially in the US. There, in the 1980s, the company became active in buying and selling the areas of franchisees who wished to sell up. These were then sold to franchisees who were seeking to expand, were financially secure and had a long-term interest in the business. Over the period 1978–1990, for example, 82% of US volume changed hands. Yet the decline in the number of franchised bottlers in the US was relatively gradual as compared to the experience of the German network during the same period. There, since the mid-1980s, the number of franchised bottlers has fallen more steeply. Instead of waiting for (or encouraging) franchisees to sell at a time of their choosing, the company was able to force the pace of German change as the 'second round' of 20-year bottling contracts awarded after the Second World War approached expiry (contracts were for ten years with a further ten years renewal option – initially issued in the 1940s/1950s and then again in the 1960s/1970s).

FIGURE 1
Number of Francised Coca-Cola Bottlers in Germany and the United States 1899–1992

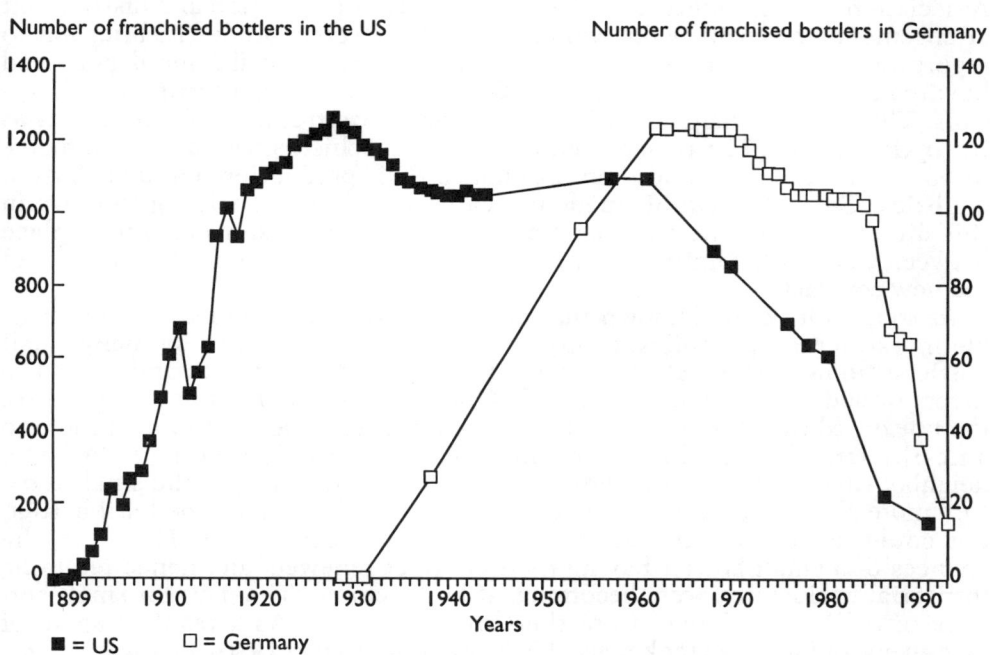

This figure plots the recorded number of franchised bottlers; for some years the number of franchisees is not available. Source: Archives, Coca-Cola GmbH, Essen and the Coca-Cola Company, Atlanta

Three factors were particularly important in the reshaped franchise structure which emerged in Germany:

(1) the consolidation of production through mergers and buy-outs;
(2) contractual changes designed to ensure that economies made are reinvested in generating further sales; and
(3) the creation of a central sales company with the power and authority to negotiate with bottlers' largest customers. Each of these factors is considered in turn.

CONSOLIDATION OF PRODUCTION

Although by 1988, the number of German bottlers had been whittled down to 65, something more drastic was being considered by company executives. The plan was for the Coca-Cola Company to take a 35% interest in a pan-German bottler (3), with the remaining interest being split among existing bottlers (New

York Times, 14 March 1988). This single bottler would then be able to produce the entire Coca Cola range using 10–20 of the most up-to-date production units, maintain round-the-clock production, and set prices and marketing programmes for the whole of Germany. The plan was rejected by bottlers largely on the grounds that it would convert all of them from owner-managers to minority shareholders overnight.

In seeking an alternative solution, Coca-Cola GmbH and the Franchisees' Association commissioned an independent study of production and distribution arrangements in Germany (known as the Weihenstephan Study). Its brief was to report on where best to locate production plants and distribution depots, and how many of them there would be, if Germany was a virgin territory to Coca-Cola. The resulting map identified 14 production centres and 19 warehouses as the optimum mix. Just to approach this ideal, franchisees would have to merge or buy each other out, and then rationalise their production and distribution facilities. Coca-Cola GmbH made it clear that only those willing to move in this direction would be awarded a new contract. Discussions also took place between Coca-Cola GmbH and the Franchisees' Association on the contents of the new contract.

As soon as it became known that rationalisation was favoured, all but tangible investments (eg, coolers, coin-vendors etc) were postponed by many small bottlers: 'some bottlers almost struck, they stopped investment and started to invest outside the system' (Coca-Cola GmbH executive, field notes). Even so, the unexpired franchise of a small bottler continued to be worth much more to a nearby large bottler than to the small bottler actually holding it. A large, neighbouring bottler with underutilised capacity could supply the small territory more cheaply (even with higher transportation costs) than the local bottler, but could not do so without breaking territorial exclusivity. However, the chances of a small bottler having their contract renewed, and hence retaining territorial exclusivity, were becoming, at best, remote. The days for small bottlers unwilling to change were therefore numbered. As a result a spate of take-overs and mergers took place during the mid- to late 1980s.

CONTRACTUAL CHANGES

Franchise contracts are written normally by franchisors, for franchisors, and offered on a take-it-or-leave-it basis to franchisees. It is therefore not surprising to find that franchise contracts impose certain controls which are designed, primarily, to serve the interests of the franchisor ahead of those of the franchisee. In this the Coca-Cola Company's franchise contracts are no different to many others (Felstead, 1993, Chapter Four, Kessler, 1957, Macaulay, 1973, Beale, Harris and Sharpe, 1989). However, many discussions concerning the new contract did take place with the Franchisees' Association and concessions were made; the company wanted to reform not abolish the existing network. Nevertheless, a franchisor (whether they be a manufacturer of soft drink concentrates, a car manufacturer or an owner of a business format) wants franchisees to maximise volume (as measured by units or turnover) since from this their income is derived.

The articulation, and hence strength, of this control varies and, moreover, is subject to change (Felstead, 1993, Chapter Five). A comparison of the early contracts governing the Coca-Cola Company's franchise relationship in Germany with the current one bears this out. Originally, franchisees simply undertook to make every effort and to employ all the means necessary to expand the volume of Coca-Cola products sold. In practice, this commitment had little force during the currency of the agreement since it lacked specifics.

The current contract, on the other hand, gives franchisees precise annual sales and investment targets, with the penalty of termination should both not be met at the end of a five-year period (15 years being the full contractual term).

The sales target commits franchisees to grow 2% faster than the market for soft drink sales in their area. In addition, those whose sales per head fall below the network average have to grow at a faster rate still (the supplement rises in stages to 2%). The annual minimum investment target is similarly specific. It is set at DM4.00 per head and linked to the sales increase required to meet minimum sales obligations (it is also adjusted for inflation). So for every case the bottler has to sell over and above its sales at the beginning of the agreement a further DM0.60 investment is called for. With the exception of production, these investment obligations may be fulfilled in the following areas: advertising; sales promotions; market development; investments in technical sales aids such as coin-vendors, coolers, dispense units and so on; and the funding of rebate conditions for customers.

As planning tools to meet these minimum targets and to go beyond them (the requirement that franchisees 'make every effort and to employ all suitable means to develop and exploit the potential of the business' remains), a three-year plan and an annual working programme must be agreed with the company. The former provides an overarching plan for the development of the business in terms of volume goals by product, package and trade channel, and the means to achieve these ends. The annual working programme provides more detail on the timing and financing of specific programmes: advertising; sales promotion; merchandising; the placement of technical sales aids; the introduction of new packages; and the servicing of accounts. Progress is assessed by the Coca-Cola Company monthly.

The bottling contracts governing the Coca-Cola Company's relationships in the US have also undergone change. However, the change has been more gradual on account of US bottling contracts existing in perpetuity. For example, only from 1986 (ie, under the Master Bottle Contract) has the Company been able to set concentrate prices at its sole discretion, its advertising and marketing expenditures have become voluntary, and the company and bottler must come to an agreement on an annual working programme setting out the bottler's plans for the forthcoming year (see Felstead, 1993, Table 6.2, p242). All of these elements existed in German contracts even before the introduction of the new contract.

However, the new German contract aims to go one step further. It aims to ensure that the gains made in production, occasioned by greater centralisation, do not simply raise profits for the company's, now much larger, German franchisees, but that, in addition, cost savings are reinvested in developing the market for Coca-Cola brands further, hence raising sales of concentrate and ensuring future growth.

CENTRAL SALES COMPANY

One of the advantages to the Coca-Cola Company of establishing 'one bottler for Germany' would have been its ability to negotiate with, and offer a uniform set of prices and supply conditions to, customers with outlets previously located in more than one franchise territory. The existence of more than one franchisee gave each franchisee the right to veto any national agreement reached by negotiating committees which could delay or even threaten the account. Despite the shrinking number of franchisees by the late 1980s, the accounts of Coca-Cola's largest customers – the national chains – continued to be exposed in this way.

Fearing the potential loss of their largest accounts in the face of mounting customer pressure, franchisees agreed to transfer their sales rights for large Key Account customers to a central sales company, Coca-Cola Deutschland Verkauf GmbH & Kg (hereafter referred to as CCDV) which became operational in March 1990. This is owned 50% by Coca-Cola GmbH, 50% by franchisees, and is supervised by a board of four Coca-Cola GmbH appointed directors and four elected by Coca-Cola franchisees (votes weighted according to sales volume). They determine which customers with whom they will deal (as a rule of thumb, their outlets must be located in at least three German states and they must have a central purchasing department), and the general pricing and rebate conditions within which negotiations take place. The inclusion or exclusion of certain customers from the Key Account list is decided by a simple majority, while for the pricing and supply conditions 75% of the votes are needed. Currently, almost a half of total sales of Coca-Cola brands in Germany go through CCDV. Franchisees are still required to produce and distribute the Coca-Cola range of products and packages to Key Account customers within their territories, but only on the terms agreed by CCDV. Those who refuse to comply lose territorial exclusivity for these accounts, and must therefore leave them to others to service.

In practice, CCDV can do something to tilt the balance between bottler and retailer in the bottlers' favour. For example, in 1990 and 1991 CCDV was able to raise prices. However, the bargaining position of retailers remains strong on account of the competition for shelf space, access to high visibility outlets and the prospect (in the away-from-home market) of single sourcing. In fact, the operation of CCDV may simply mean that the conditions of supply are arrived at more quickly and national supply made more certain than in the past.

Safeguarding the sales of Coca-Cola brands to national account customers favours both bottler and the Coca-Cola Company alike. The costs of doing so, though, are unequally shared: the company shoulders the costs of keener prices and more competitive conditions of supply which stronger and stronger retailers are able to demand only to the extent that it also acts as a bottler. Indeed, CCDV provides an institutional device through which prices and conditions of supply can be enforced throughout the network. This is at little cost to the company as a franchisor whose income is derived solely from the sale of concentrate to bottlers (although it pays 50% of the costs of running CCDV).

CONCLUSION

Throughout the 1980s it was becoming increasingly clear that Coca-Cola's previous franchise structure in Germany (as elsewhere) had outlived its usefulness. Small territories were preventing a low cost production and distribution system being established, and the demands of large retailers for better terms and conditions of supply were becoming difficult to accommodate nationwide. Both problems were a product of a franchise structure which gave franchisees monopoly rights in the filling, packaging and sale of Coca-Cola's branded soft drinks within a small geographically defined area. While franchisees operated according to their own goals – profit maximisation, the employment of family members, community status or whatever – these same considerations began to serve the interests of the company – through the maximisation of concentrate sales – less and less. As contracts approached renewal in the late 1980s, the company flexed its hierarchical muscles by demanding changes. In the words of a franchisee:

'Although the conflict between franchisor and franchisee can be more precisely seen in theory than in practice, it became all too obvious during the process of restructuring. We were often told that we should consider ourselves as part of the Coca-Cola family, and that what was good for the company was good for us. Yet Coca-Cola [the company] owned everything of importance and was therefore able to call the shots' (field notes).

As a result, a new generation of Coca-Cola franchisee has emerged. Today, there are fewer franchisees; but with larger territories they are able to support up-to-date, high capacity plants. Existing franchisees were given several options to produce these larger entities. Either way, franchisees must be committed to low cost, high volume production. Underpinning these production changes is a new contract designed to ensure that any economies made do not simply increase franchisee profits, but are also used to develop the market for Coca-Cola brands still further thereby reinforcing the products' 'Acceptability, Affordability and Availability' (known as the three As). Finally, a central sales company was set up to deal with bottlers' largest customers, thereby ensuring that prices and terms of supply can be uniformly applied.

For the time being, the interests of franchisee and franchisor have been brought more into line. At present the emerging group of larger franchisees is committed to much larger production facilities requiring a higher throughput to be economic. Sales, therefore, need to be higher, and investment in the market is the mechanism through which this is achieved. In the absence of a temporary coincidence of interests, however, the Coca-Cola Company's interests predominate. Sales and investment targets ensure that the company's near absolute interest in volume growth (and hence sales of concentrate) takes precedence in guiding how Coca-Cola franchisees must operate if they wish to retain their franchise.

Although legally recognised as independent businesses, in practice the relationship between franchisor and franchisee is a close one. It consists of two interdependent elements. First, it is a market relationship through which franchisees either buy supplies of concentrate to make up the finished product, purchase cars/petrol from a manufacturer/oil company to sell on, and/or operate according to a tried and tested formula. Secondly, the market exchange itself is controlled and is subject to change – a range of contractual clauses govern the use to which these purchases are put. In other words, we really do need to look beyond the legal boundaries of the firm to gauge the true extent of a firm's power and control. As one franchisee put it: 'the cloak of the franchise system is often used to disguise the true situation of them [franchisors] calling all the major shots' (field notes). This includes reshaping the franchise structure to meet a changed commercial environment and underpin the organisational commitment to sales growth, first and last. This may, or may not, be in the interests of franchisor and franchisee, but what is clear is that decisions of this kind remain the sole preserve of those outside the ambit of the superficially autonomous franchisee, thereby placing a ceiling on the level of independence franchisees can expect to enjoy.

NOTES

This paper is a substantially abridged version of a chapter in my book, The Corporate Paradox: Power and Control in the Business Franchise (Felstead, 1993). It appeared in the International Small Business Journal, Vol 12, No 2, January–March 1994, and has been reproduced here with the permission of Professor Clive Woodcock.

1. Throughout this paper 'Germany' before the Second World War refers to the German Empire, while after the Second World War it refers to the Federal Republic of Germany, before and after reunification on 3 October 1990. The former German Democratic Republic is currently supplied by a wholly owned subsidiary of the Coca-Cola Company.
2. The Coca-Cola Company's franchise structure faces a similar concentration of buying power in other advanced industrial economies. For example, in the UK just 5 customers accounted for 21% of total sales of Coca-Cola brands in 1989, 10 accounted for 40% and the top 20 took 60% (Monopolies and Mergers Commission, 1991, p108, p116, p156). Moreover, Coca-Cola's largest customers are becoming pan-European; in 1991 ten customers accounted for 17% of the European sales of the Coca-Cola organisation, and this is projected to rise to 28% by 1994 (Journey – The Magazine of the Coca-Cola Company, September 1991, p10).
3. The Coca-Cola Company has taken up ownership positions in approximately 60 different bottling, canning and distribution operations around the world. Often this entails taking managerial responsibility for the operation, and where, as in many cases, the company's equity falls short of 100% ensuring that the dividend pay-out to shareholders is subject to its approval (The Coca-Cola Company Annual Report 1990, p30). The Company estimates that it has equity stakes in those who generate 38% of its worldwlde volume. This ensures that: 'By working closely with our bottlers to help increase retail sales, we are also boosting our concentrate sales' (The Coca-Cola Company Annual Report 1991, p37).

REFERENCES

BEALE H AND DUGDALE T (1975) Contracts between businessmen: planning and the use of contractual remedies, British Journal of Law and Society, vol. 2, no. 1, Summer, pp45–60.

BEALE H, HARRIS D AND SHARPE T (1989) The distribution of cars: a complex contractual technique, in Harris D and Tallon D (eds.) Contract Law Today: Anglo-French Comparisons, Oxford: Clarendon.

BERLE AA AND MEANS GC (1932) The Modern Corporation and Private Property, New York: Macmillan.

COWLING K AND SUDGEN R (1987) Transnational Monopoly Capitalism, Brighton: Wheatsheaf.

FELSTEAD A (1993) The Corporate Paradox: Power and Control in the Business Franchise, London: Routledge.

KATZ BG (1978) Territorial exclusivity in the soft drink industry, Journal of Industrial Economics, vol. 27, no. 7, September, pp85–96.

KESSLER F (1957) Automobile dealer franchises: vertical integration by contract, Yale Law Journal, vol. 66, no. 8, July, pp1135–1190.

LEIGHTON P AND FELSTEAD A (1992) (eds.) The New Entrepreneurs: Self-Employment and Small Business in Europe, London: Kogan Page.

MACAULAY S (1973) The standardized contracts of United States automobile manufacturers, International Encyclopaedia of Comparative Law. vol. 7, chapter 3, pp18–34.

MONOPOLIES AND MERGERS COMMISSION (1991), Carbonated Drinks: A Report on the Supply by Manufacturers of Carbonated Drinks in the United Kingdom, Cm 1625, London: HMSO.

PLEIJSTER F (1992) Towards full-scale business integration? The development of business co-operatives in Dutch retailing, in Leighton P and Felstead A (eds.) The New Entrepreneurs: Self-Employment and Small Business in Europe, London: Kogan Page.

STANWORTH J AND PURDY D (1993) The Blenheim/University of Westminster Franchise Survey No 1, September 1993, London: International Franchise Research Centre.

CHAPTER 12

Supporting Inner-City Firms: Lessons from the Field

J MARK FORD AND MONDER RAM

INTRODUCTION

Reviving inner-city areas has become a European and national preoccupation. The characteristics of inner-city areas – high long term unemployment and poor opportunities for school leavers in areas of severe industrial decline mirror three of the five objectives of the European Regional Development Fund and Social Fund. From a national policy perspective, concern about inner-city areas is manifest in the City Challenge initiatives which demonstrate how policy thinking has shifted from a general emphasis on urban areas to a specific emphasis on certain inner-city areas.

Despite an apparent burgeoning of measures, small firms appear to be exhibiting a marked reluctance to take up business support services. Why external actors often fail to become a part of the small firm owner's milieu has been a question discussed at length in Curran et al. (1991, 1992) studies.

They offer a comprehensive explanation which includes factors like the individualistic disposition of owner-managers, the perceived lack of knowledge and expense of professional advisors and the work and family commitments of owner-managers. However, small firms' centrality to the discourse of inner-city regeneration (Bannock and Albach, 1991; Stanworth and Gray, 1991, Ch2) has prompted many influential agencies, particularly local authorities, to attend to the issue of supporting small businesses.

This paper reports on a local authority sponsored initiative which stemmed from a concern that firms in a particular West Midlands inner-city area were not utilising support services. Information on the owner-managers themselves is presented: for instance, their particular problems and preoccupations; their views on business support; their experience of the consultancy exercise; and their views on follow-on support. But particular emphasis is accorded to assessing the initiative itself. To this end, the following questions are considered: was the type of support provided appropriate?; was it well marketed?; will these firms benefit from the support given?; could more effective intervention be developed and delivered?; what type of follow-on support is needed?

Chapter 12

THE INITIATIVE

The inner-city area where the initiative took place is characterised by densely packed, row or terrace housing. Its residents traditionally tended to look for employment in adjacent areas which contained a number of large scale manufacturing and utility industries. In recent years these industries have declined, thereby reducing employment opportunities for people in the surrounding areas.

As a result of the severe industrial decline in the locality, the area in which the initiative took place is now one of the most deprived in England and Wales (local authority 1991 census) and is characterised by high unemployment, overcrowding, a lack of basic facilities, pensioners living alone and single parent families.

Of the area's 20,000 residents, 60% of the population were Asian, particularly from the Mirpur and Kashmir districts of Pakistan and from Bangladesh. African-Caribbean residents represented only 5% of the population; 35% were white-European. Of children leaving school at sixteen, 89% were either black or Asian.

The project was sponsored by the local authority; they were concerned by the poor take up of business support services by local owner-managers. Its principal aims were to raise awareness of business support services to firms in the area and to provide, through independent consultants, support to 50 small businesses in the locality. Secondary aims of the project were to gather information on the business support needs of small firms and identify gaps in existing services.

There were two stages to the project: the first stage, marketing, consisted of a mail-shot of 1250 owner-managers. One of the five consultants working on the initiative either visited or telephoned 274 owner-managers and identified firms for the second stage of the initiative. In this second stage the consultancies were delivered to 50 firms. These aimed to provide owner-managers with a business health-check, which is essentially an overview of the business with recommendations for further action.

The project was managed by a local authority officer and coordinated by a local enterprise agency. Five freelance consultants, some with associates, were involved in marketing and delivering consultancies.

MARKETING

Firms with under 50 employees were eligible to participate in the project and no limits were set as to the minimum number of employees, age or sector of participating businesses.

It was originally intended that door to door canvassing or cold calling should be done by the consultants. During the planning process (after some pressure from consultants who felt that an amount of marketing support would be needed) the door to door canvassing was replaced by a 'database mail shot–telephone follow up–appointment' marketing process.

A database was provided by the local Training and Enterprise Council, which listed businesses with under 25 employees in the target postal districts. This was used to identify potential clients for the project.

The database needed extensive editing since it contained organisations which were outside the scope of this project – schools, doctors' surgeries, community centres and branches of larger firms such as Barclays Bank and Swinton Insurance for example. Many businesses on the list had closed or moved and an unquantifiable number of businesses were missing from the database. Some firms which took part in the project, because they had been canvassed by consultants, were not on the database.

One thousand, two hundred and fifty firms from the database were contacted by letter. This letter informed owner-managers of a free two-day consultancy in which an independent business advisor would be assigned to the business to advise and make recommendations. Recipients of the letter could take up the two-day consultancy by responding positively either by reply slip or by telephone to the project's managing organisation.

Twenty-two firms sent back reply slips indicating that they were interested in the consultancy. Fourteen of these were passed to the consultants – the remaining eight could not be accommodated since the target number of fifty businesses had already been reached by the time reply slips were received by the project managers. The consultants were each allocated firms drawn from the database and were asked to follow up the mail shot until they had reached their quota of consultancies.

Different sales and marketing methods appeared to work for different consultants. One consultant was not able to sell at all by telephone but experienced a 100% conversion rate once he was able to talk with the owner-manager in a door to door sales campaign. Another consultant, once he was able to speak directly with the owner-manager on the telephone, was able to sell consultancies to one in every two prospects. A third consultant was not able to sell on a door to door basis at all but achieved his target sales figure from subsequent telesales.

Contrary to expectations at the beginning of the project, marketing and selling the consultancies proved to be relatively easy. The response to the mail shot was better than anticipated and four out of five consultants admitted that the marketing stage had taken less time than anticipated. Three adjusted the amount of effort spent in the consultancy stage of the project accordingly.

The quality of marketing information received back from consultants about why owner-managers did not opt for business support was not as comprehensive as had been hoped for. This may have been due to pressure to identify recruits to the second stage of the project rather than catalogue detailed research information. Relevant and useful information about why firms did not take up the offer of support remains, at best, indicative. However, always bearing in mind that the consultancy was offered free, experience in the marketing process seems to suggest that a substantial proportion of owner-managers do perceive a value in some kind of business support.

WHY DO OWNER-MANAGERS OPT FOR – OR REJECT – BUSINESS SUPPORT?

Owner-managers' reasons for opting for the consultancy were analysed for two reasons: to check whether the consultancy, when delivered, provided the service for which clients were asking and to gain information which would be useful in future marketing exercises. It was clear that owner-managers' participation in the consultancy process was for a number of reasons rather than one predominant factor. The following reasons for opting for the consultancy were given:

26% need help due to present economic climate.
24% need general advice.
15% need help and advice with further development.
13% need financial assistance with development or expansion.
10% need help with developing business skills.
7% need help with internal aspects of finance.
5% need help with extending customer base.

If the quality, appropriateness and take up of business support is to improve, it is important to note the reasons why owner-managers did not opt for the consultancy.

These reasons for rejecting the offer of consultancy were recorded:

31% business is fine as it is.
14% more information about the consultancy is needed before making a decision.
11% too busy.
9% previously received unhelpful advice.
9% support will not be of any use to the business.
7% decision-maker unavailable.
6% already using a consultant or advice agency.
6% would consider advice in the future but not convenient now.
5% a waste of time.
2% retiring/selling/liquidating business.

In analysing why owner-managers rejected the offer of consultancy one needs to question whether the responses given were genuine or deployed as a convenient way to reject a canvassing consultant. Although it is apparently enlightening to discover that the most frequent reason for rejecting the consultancy was that business was 'fine', the negative reasons for rejecting consultancy require some scrutiny.

Of the owner-managers who wanted more information, some wanted to know how the consultancy would benefit their business but others were wary and sceptical about the offer of free help: 'I am wary of outside people looking at my business – there must be a catch.' This type of sentiment frequently accompanied requests for more information.

A real issue facing people involved in enterprise support activities is the high frequency (23%) of wholly negative replies – 'previously received unhelpful advice', 'support will not be of any use to the business' and 'a waste of time'.

Some owner-managers who had previously received business support were worried that, sooner or later, the consultant would try and sell further services to which a charge would be levied. Others felt that what had been sold to them as support resulted in little more than a consultant telling them what they already knew, albeit articulated in a different way, and offered no relevant advice.

Of the owner-managers who did opt for the consultancy, we identified six who had previously approached at least one business support agency for assistance. However, only two of these owner-managers felt that they had received any kind of substantive help from these organisations.

A recurring theme of owner-managers, even if they did opt for further consultancy support, was that the consultant did not understand or relate to the particular problems faced by the owner-manager or the dynamics of the small business.

DELIVERING THE TWO-DAY CONSULTANCIES

The fifty businesses which participated in the project carried on these trading activities:

Engineering	7
Retailing	6
Building trades	6
Restaurants, cafes, clubs and public houses	6
Financial, consultancy and professional services	6
Food manufacturers	4
Motor trades	4
Transport and distribution	3
Clothes manufacture	2
Printers	2
Care home	1
Furniture manufacturer	1
Hairstylist	1
Exhibition contractors	1

The age of businesses which participated in the project was as follows:

1–2 years old	10
3–10 years old	27
over 10 years old	13

The number of employees in participating businesses was as follows:

1–4 employees	33
5–9 employees	11
10–19 employees	3
20–50 employees	3

The ethnic origin of participating owner-managers was as follows:

African Caribbean	1
African Caribbean/white-European	1
Asian	17
Chinese	1
Greek	1
White/British	29

No accurate figures on the ethnic origin of owner-managers in the area existed. But the experience of those working on the initiative suggests that ethnic businesses (particularly Asian-owned) constitute a significant majority of those firms in the locality. The experience of some of the Asian firms involved in the initiative is discussed elsewhere (Ram 1993).

Format

Each consultant was asked to produce a report based on a model 'health-check' format for the fifty owner-managers participating in this stage of the project. The reports thus provided an overview of the firm's activities, provided recommendations which proprietors could take on board and suggested what support services may be useful in furthering the firm's development.

Although this documentation generated useful information on the firms, it is acknowledged that the health-check format may have been inappropriate. The 'health check' is essentially a functional and compartmentalised document which views individual aspects of a business (marketing, finance, production etc) one by one and, by separating these aspects, tends not to take a holistic view of the firm. Yet it is this holistic view which the owner-manager sees most clearly and on which he will make management decisions. If an owner-manager thinks and acts from a holistic perspective – and this may be necessary in a firm where the boundaries between, for example, marketing, finance and personnel management are blurred – then to produce an overview which defines unrecognisable boundaries will be of limited use to the owner-manager. Put another way, if the health-check does not relate to the owner-manager's Weltanschauung it will not be perceived as relevant. The advocacy of a more process-based consultancy approach in small firms (Taylor et al 1991) is often predicated on a recognition of this feature.

A further constraint of the health-check-style consultancy is that it tends to overestimate the ability of small firms to cope with external influences by internal management changes. We could concur with the view that generally, in comparison with some larger organisations, small firms are inherently less able to cope with pervading external influences (Curran et al. 1992).

Consultants working on this initiative often expressed the view that it was difficult to fit the consultancy into the suggested format, especially where financial information was not forthcoming. The imposition of these model guidelines prompted the view that efforts were being oriented towards the needs of the project manager rather than the owner-manager.

BUSINESS PROBLEMS AND PREOCCUPATIONS

Employers experienced a wide range of interrelated problems. Rather than presenting an extensive catalogue of these here, some of the most commonly experienced problems are noted. Many were similar to those facing small firms per se (Stanworth and Gray 1991; 1992) – finance, marketing and people – but it is interesting to note that the problems as perceived by owner-managers were very often different to those identified by the consultant.

From the owner-manager's perspective, the problems faced often tended to be concerned with external influences. The single most commonly perceived problem highlighted by owner-managers was a lack of customers caused by recessionary trading conditions.

A range of problems concerned with other organisations was also cited by owner-managers. This included problems with banks and other financial institutions, landlords, the local authority, government agencies involved in public works which affected access to premises, Inland Revenue and Customs and Excise.

Owner-managers frequently pointed out that it was not simply the problems with external organisations but the time spent on these problems which concerned them. They felt that their time could be better spent promoting or developing their business.

Problems concerning the lack of suitable staff were also frequently mentioned. This concern tended to be expressed as the fault of prior and external educational and training provision rather than the business's internal training approach.

From the consultants' perspective the problems faced by small businesses tended to relate to internal rather than external matters. An analysis of the problems most frequently identified by consultants reveals a range of internal management faults which could be addressed:

23% insufficient business strategy/plan.
22% insufficient sales and marketing strategy.
21% insufficient management information systems.
16% insufficient market knowledge and research.
 7% insufficient attention to quality issues.
 5% insufficient attention to diversification.
 5% premises are insufficient/unsuitable.

Clearly there is a difference between the owner-managers' perception of problems being external influences and the consultants' perception of internal management problems. This discrepancy can probably be explained by the divergent expectations of the parties involved. It was noted earlier that many of the owners requesting the consultancy did so because they believed it would be of assistance in improving relations with external actors and the wider environment. The consultants' brief, however, was to focus more on the internal aspects of the business. Furthermore, given the relatively short period of time that they were actually with owner-managers, it seems unlikely that they could come up with anything more detailed or substantive than comments on obvious departures from text-book notions of 'good management practice', like the absence of business plans, poor management information systems, inappropriate organisational structures and so on and so forth. This is a frequent criticism of traditional approaches to consultancy (Taylor et al 1991).

A further explanation of the differing perceptions of need may have been the trading experiences of the owners. As the figures on the age of the businesses indicated, many had been in existence for some time and were apparently trading successfully. Moreover, they had often reached this position without any form of external assistance. Hence, it seemed that owner-managers were quite prepared to avail themselves of a service which may assist with the problems of negotiating a wider business environment. This could take the form of ideas on new markets, applications for grants, dealing with the local authority and so on. But what they were often less willing to countenance were suggestions relating to the alteration of a modus operandi that had served them sufficiently well for a number of years.

This point has important implications for policy-makers since the perception of need will be a critical factor in shaping owner-managers' use of business support. If firms in the inner-city context do not perceive internal matters as priorities for the development of their firms then the utility of discrete initiatives of this genre is likely to be limited.

The attraction of 'free' expertise may persuade owners to participate, and this could conceivably lead to further development work. But this seems an indiscriminate and unfocused way of allocating scarce resources and smacks of the 'programme-led' approaches that have often been utilised by support providers (Ram and Sparrow 1992).

Chapter 12

EMPLOYER FEEDBACK

A number of owner-managers were interviewed after the consultancy in order to elicit feedback on how useful they thought the process had been. The partners in a food manufacturing business hoped for a continuation of the level of service that they had received in this project but intimated that they 'expected' a mixture of good and bad service from the business support agencies which had been recommended to them by the consultant.

They pointed out that they had contacted some of these agencies and were frustrated by the mixed and confusing signals sent by them. The clients had acted upon recommendations made by the consultant but they had made neither negative nor positive comments about the report, despite considerable prompting.

Another participant in the project felt that the consultancy had been valuable insofar as he had received information on a local grant scheme and had been put in touch with an organisation which could help him build his network of business contacts.

A shop owner who participated in the project did so because he had heard that business support was available but was confused by its nature and apparent diversity – he wanted someone to 'help them through this maze'. He was quite happy with the service which he had received so far but hoped for a longer relationship with a consultant to help him address some of the issues raised in the report and to help him apply for (public sector) funding.

We asked the owner-managers who participated in the initiative a number of questions about how they felt about the consultancy itself and the subsequent report. Their replies to our questions were perhaps of less significance than their unanimous reaction, which was to persistently question us about what might happen next – sometimes they asked for further support and sometimes for assistance with funding applications for example – but the notable suggestion may be that they all seemed keen to perpetuate a relationship with some kind of business support organisation.

None of the owner-managers we talked to professed to being dissatisfied with the consultancy which they received. However, a common theme did emerge from our conversations with owner-managers in the feedback process – they all felt that the health-check style consultancy was a prelude to further assistance of one kind or another. This seems to add weight to the view that simple 'one-off' consultancies are of limited use to the small firm.

CONCLUSIONS

In this project, fourteen requests for further assistance were made within days of the consultancies being delivered, particularly from owner-managers, concerned with funding expansion plans or, conversely, people with financial difficulties. These all seem to be 'complex' problems often to do with a root problem in sales and marketing, symptomised by immediate financial problems.

The nature of these complex problems suggests that formal packages of business support or the 'selling' of programme-led approaches are not likely to meet with an enthusiastic reception from owner-managers. More success is likely to be achieved in providing practitioners who relate well with owner-managers in the small business environment, who can act as advisor within the firm and as advocate and mediator with external commercial and public sector organisations. This type of role is similar to that of the relationship counsellor supported by Stanworth and Gray (1992); within a process consultancy paradigm, the emphasis in this model is toward the development of a relationship over time and the client's ownership of problems,rather than quick-fix solutions provided by an 'expert'.

The project raised participating owner-managers' expectations so that they believed that there was a range of support services available to them. Since it was some four months before any suitable follow-on support was available it is perhaps not surprising that some owner-managers' expectations were raised when they felt that support was available to them but were then disappointed when follow-on support was either slow in appearing or inappropriate. Resources need to be available to follow up client enquiries whilst demand for services is still 'warm'.

Our experience in this project has led to serious concerns about the efficacy of using a health-check-style consultancy as an appropriate tool for analysing small businesses. A modified, three-stage approach is suggested:

1. An initial meeting between consultant and owner-manager should concern itself with the collection of key data which will be needed by the business support agency and consultants.

   A pro-forma model should be developed for recording information about new client businesses. The pro-forma should contain: standard data such as the age, size, sector and levels of employment; some limited financial information about the business, where this is obtainable; information about specific issues which are affecting the firm; information about the needs and wants of the owner-manager for his or her business regardless of support services available and information about what the owner-manager expects from the business support services.

2. The second stage in this approach would be a more full consultancy period – typically one day – in which the consultant should seek to summarise the key issues in the business and, at the same time, obtain an overall picture of the business in its environment. It is at this stage that the agenda for a process-based consultancy is set. Consequently, the skills of the consultant must be appropriate for the type of intervention (Taylor et al 1991).

   Depending on the nature of the issues revealed in this stage of the process, suitable actions should be agreed between the consultant and the owner-manager and would form the basis of the third stage in the consultancy process.

3. The third stage of the consultancy is the most difficult to define and to predict since it will need to relate as much to the short term consultancy needs of the owner-manager as it does to the medium and long term actions which the client may wish to take.

   We feel that medium to long term problems can be dealt with through a mixture of training and development. These would sometimes include issues such as business planning, consideration of quality issues and installing management information systems. More likely however, if the whole consultancy process is to be worthwhile from the owner-manager's perspective, the final part of the consultancy should be outward looking and could concern itself with tasks such as helping the owner-manager sell into wider markets or develop business 'networks', or it could focus on particular problems the firm has with external actors.

Moreover, by this last stage of the consultancy, the relationship between the firm and business support providers should be consolidated so that the owner-manager clearly understands where, and how, he can access further relevant support.

It is likely that this three-stage model would be a more long term and process oriented relationship between consultant and owner-manager and, if it is to be effective, should not have a binding time scale attached to it. The length of the consultancy should be determined by the time taken to complete a task which has been agreed between the support provider, the consultant and the owner-manager.

Although this might cause difficulties in terms of quality control, verifiable outputs and the 'timing' of public sector funding, these factors should not – if the principle of customer demand is held at all – mitigate non-provision of services which businesses clearly need and owner-managers want.

REFERENCES

BANNOCK G AND ALBACH H (1991) Small Business Policy in Europe, London: Anglo-German Foundation.

CURRAN J, JARVIS R, BLACKBURN RA and BLACK S (1991) Small Firms and Networks: Constructs, Methodological Strategies and Preliminary Findings, Paper presented to the 14th National Small Firms Research and Policy Conference, Blackpool.

CURRAN J, JARVIS R, BLACKBURN RA AND BLACK S (1992) Small Firms and Networks: Constructs, Methodological Strategies and Preliminary Findings. ESRC Centre for Research on Small Service Sector Enterprises, Kingston University.

RAM M (1993) Intervening in Small Firms – A Case from the Inner City, Paper to the 16th National Small Firms Policy and Research Conference, Nottingham.

RAM M AND SPARROW J (1992) Research on the needs of the Asian business community in Wolverhampton, Report to Wolverhampton TEC.

STANWORTH J AND GRAY C (Eds)(1991) Change and Continuity in Small Firm Policy since Bolton (Ch. 2), Bolton 20 Years On. London: Paul Chapman.

STANWORTH J AND GRAY C (1992) Entrepreneurship and Education: Action Based Research with Training Policy Implications in Britain, International Small Business Journal, (10): 2, pp 11–23.

TAYLOR J, ABSALOM W, AND EVANS D (1991) The Development of Consultancy Skills Appropriate to Small and Medium-Size Enterprises. Paper presented to the 14th National Small Firms and Policy Conference, Blackpool.

CHAPTER 13

TEAMSTART – Overcoming the Blockages to Small Business Growth

SHAILENDRA VYAKARNAM AND ROBIN JACOBS

INTRODUCTION

The Business Start-up Scheme currently operating in the UK began as a scheme to support unemployed people through a transition into 'self-employment'. In order to do this, candidates had to be unemployed for at least 6 weeks and be able to put up £1,000 into the venture. Very high failure rates and a recognition that business support could assist economic recovery have changed the scheme into a more purposeful business start-up programme, requiring business plans, more training and information and latterly counselling support allied to monitoring visits. However, these efforts continue to be unsegmented and according to Storey (1992) somewhat questionable in their value.

The ambition of most of the TECs in the delivery of Business Start-up targets is that the enterprise must be trading at 52 or 78 weeks (IFF Research, 1992). There is no mention that they must be growing successfully. Indeed if existence is sufficient criteria and the enterprise makes it to 78 weeks from the time support begins, all contact ends as the next tranche of support is delivered from a different government department (DTI, Block 3 funds) which focuses its attention on somewhat larger, more established, businesses.

The outcome is that a vast proportion of resources is expended on supporting 'replacement income entrepreneurs' under the assumption that they will grow. In other words the acorns of today will grow into oak trees of tomorrow. There has been considerable discussion about how to 'pick winners', which carries with it an underlying assumption that by picking winners, ie individuals, growth businesses are likely to result. However, there is evidence to suggest that growth businesses are started by teams and not by individuals, therefore it is time to take another look at the start-up process and see if it is possible to redesign the delivery of support.

The next section reviews literature on entrepreneurship development, especially those articles which have been so influential in establishing the frameworks used in current forms of enterprise support.

LITERATURE REVIEW

Much research into the explanation of entrepreneurship, in other words the creation of economic wealth by the development of new products (Schumpeter,

1934) or the discovery of unexploited market opportunities (Kirzner, 1973) has gone into the attempt to isolate individual entrepreneurial characteristics (McClelland, 1967; Kaish and Gilad, 1991). These characteristics (innovativeness, resilience, perseverance, creativity, information seeking and so on) are thought to enable people to identify those individuals with the best chances of success. However, the search for a unified theory has not so far succeeded for a number of definitional and methodological reasons (d'Amboise and Muldowney, 1988).

More recent research in the area of small business development has moved to growth as a key determinant of entrepreneurship (Sexton and Bowman, 1985; Birley, 1989; Kanter, 1989; and Chell, 1990). However these authors are not agreed about how to define growth or to measure success.

Growth theories in enterprise research have a long history originally commencing with the cell division model of Starbuck (1965) and subsequently the metamorphosis models of growth where the small business was thought to change form and shape as it grew from one size to another (d'Amboise and Muldowney, 1988). Perhaps the most interesting element about these growth theories is not that they exist or that they might be incomplete, but they have not been translated into effective training and development models which can be applied by entrepreneurs to move from one state of being to another (Hendry, 1993).

Indeed, many of the local initiatives from the Department of Employment and various consultancy-based programmes have attempted to deal with growth issues largely based on the functional changes which are required to grow a business. Since the theories are incomplete, solutions based on these theories are therefore also likely to be incomplete.

Business growth programmes have not taken the issue of personal development of the entrepreneur into account when assessing viability for growth. For example, Vyakarnam and Jacobs (1990) found that high technology entrepreneurs encountered a transition from being scientists to becoming entrepreneurs. This transition is primarily one of mind-set and requires careful management with the help of learning methods appropriate to their styles and the use of a mentor to tackle particular issues and personal development.

Indeed, the hesitation of individuals to make this transition has been noted by other researchers who have attempted to re-define the entrepreneur with labels such as owner-manager, small business owner and so forth, each carrying with it the implication that these new definitions offered alternative views to the notion that every entrepreneur was 'growth oriented'. Indeed the notion that everyone must pass through linear growth stages was challenged by Churchill and Lewis (1983) and Chell (1990).

It may be more helpful to move away from growth paradigms which have little to offer in the field of enterprise development during a recession and instead consider definitions based on organisation type or to concepts such as small business competence.

Filley and Aldag (1978) suggested three types of organisation structure: Craft, Promotion and Administrative, in which the first was non-growth, the second experienced S-curved growth and the third experienced linear growth. The staffing issue in the first is 'housekeeping', the second is based on technical-personal and the third technical-coordinative.

We suggest that the vast majority of enterprise promotional activity which has taken place in the UK over the past twenty years has generated businesses run by 'craft oriented' individuals. We label them as 'Replacement Income Entrepreneurs'. The forecast for 1993/94 is that some 350,000 businesses will be started throughout the UK creating an average of 1.5 jobs in addition to the entrepreneur (Bradford,1993). Alongside this forecast is that of business failures which is averaging 50,000 per year (Guardian, 1992). Although we should not decry the impact this is likely to have on the economy we must wonder if all the resources available to small business promotion should be targeted only at this sector of replacement income entrepreneurs.

Indeed Storey (1992) argued that Business Start-ups should be halted as part of government provision due to the minimal impact it was having on the economy. Although there is some sympathy for this view, we do not think that the 'baby should be thrown out with the bath water'. A response is required to the needs of wealth and employment creation which can address the issues of new venture creation and effective long term growth. The concept of TEAMSTART is one such response.

WHY TEAMSTART?

One is reminded of the story of the Emperor's new clothes, when dealing with the justification for helping to start self-employed businesses. For many years after Bolton most of the enterprise industry has been putting forward the myth that the stimulation of small businesses today will lead to big businesses tomorrow. Somehow everyone has accepted this notion, perhaps based on the original belief that small is beautiful. However, the experience twenty years after Bolton (Stanworth and Gray, 1991, p7) is that this is just not happening, because 99% of businesses are still small. While this may deal with unemployment, how does it deal with wealth creation, especially when so many of the 'businesses' are in the service sectors?

Brockaw (1993) states that in the USA, during the 1980s, of the youngest of the Inc. 500 companies, the 306 which were founded in 1985, 1986 and 1987, almost two-thirds were started by teams. He also quotes a study of 1709 businesses which found that only 6% of hypergrowth ventures were founded by a single person; 54% had two founders and 40% had three or more. This contrasted with low-growth companies where a full 42% were started by individuals. He goes on to say:

'After stripping away the folklore, it is apparent that companies that grow begin differently from the ones that do not, in a handful of starkly identifiable ways. One of these is that they rely on team effort.' (pp 56-64)

Attempts to help start team-based ventures are not new. Timmons, Smollen and Dingee (1977) set out a framework in their book on New Venture Creation. More recently, Kamm and Aaron (1993) have put forward a framework for establishing and maintaining teams in new ventures. A more complete discussion of this work is presented in the concluding section of this paper.

In addition to the growing evidence that successful firms rely on teams, other literature on constraints to growth has identified that it requires a major upgradation of skills, increased variety of personnel, new competencies, wider networks and so on (Greiner, 1972; Hendry, 1993). Indeed de Carlo and Lyons (1980) questioned if the entrepreneur is capable of moving through the stage of development to the delegation stage anyway.

A number of people have begun to experiment with the idea that rather than stimulating small businesses, which stay small, it might be better to help start truly growth oriented businesses in the first place. There are at least four such programmes at various stages of development; three in Ireland (Shannon, Dublin and Belfast) and one in Nairobi, Kenya.

The authors of this paper have become increasingly aware of this area of literature and the apparent gap both in practical terms of providing support to team-based ventures and in the academic sense that so little is known about this phenomenon, especially in the UK. Therefore two studies were carried out. The first was at Hertfordshire TEC with the redundancy programme at British Aerospace in Hatfield. The findings and outcomes are very particular to one firm and no generalisable lessons can be drawn. The second study involved Essex TEC in the development of awareness seminar-based research activity with the general public and the findings from this study are reported on next.

THE ESSEX STUDY

Essex TEC had carried out a study during 1992, where one of the key recommendations indicated that Essex should capitalise on its historical strength in manufacturing and attempt to stimulate growth oriented entrepreneurs in order to create growth in the county.

Within this framework TRANSITIONS devised research and awareness seminars, which were jointly conducted by Frances Hoare of Essex TEC and Shailendra Vyakarnam and Robin Jacobs of Transitions, to elicit potential candidates for small growth oriented businesses.

The concept of TEAMSTART (business being started by individuals with complimentary skills coming together to form a team) was branded as Superstart in Essex as it was felt that a TEAMSTART label might limit the scope of the key objective to stimulate growth oriented enterprises. Therefore for reasons of consistency, the term Superstart will be used through the rest of this paper.

OBJECTIVES

The underpinning vision for Superstart is to find growth orientated entrepreneurs who would operate in production-based sectors of industry with a view to export. Therefore awareness seminars were designed and run in the form of focus group discussions, so that the following questions could be addressed:

1. The strengths and weaknesses of the concept.
2. The interest, if any, in taking up the concept of Superstart.
3. To identify the assistance potential participants of such a scheme might wish from the TEC and indeed from an overall support infrastructure.

METHOD

Six research seminars were scheduled in total, including two for key business influencers and four for potential Superstart candidates. The target groups for the seminars were as follows:

1. 'key business influencers' including managers of banks, local accounting firms, local authorities and trade associations, who may have important contacts and ideas.

2. personnel managers of large companies, who may be looking for solutions to problems arising from redundancies.
3. people who have been or were being made redundant.

The method of generating interest and recruiting key business influencers included direct mail, telephone follow-up and personal networks. Potential candidates were targeted through media campaigns including press releases, advertising, direct mail and radio interviews. The concept of Superstart was put over with a 35mm slide presentation.

The next section sets out the findings from the seminars, based on verbal and written feedback from key business influencers and potential candidates. A total of 90 people attended the seminars.

FINDINGS

Key Business Influencers – Summary of Comments

1. The key issue raised by most of the audience at the key business influencers seminars was to do with pulling teams of people together. Many questions were raised including: the concept of an introduction service, the issue of how one builds trust amongst the various members of the team, how these would be pulled together to form an effective working group and indeed how, if at all, business teams could be built up in the long term.
2. The second issue raised was concerned with how to provide information about business opportunities and how market data could be brought to the notice of potential Superstart candidates.
3. The third issue was concerned with how to help existing businesses to grow through team formation and improved team effectiveness. It was felt by some people that start-ups in teams may be over-ambitious whereas accelerating growth may be more achievable.
4. The fourth issue was to do with the level of support that should be provided for service businesses in addition to that given to production-based businesses.
5. The fifth issue concerned the implementation of Superstart in terms of how it would be managed and whether or not the TEC was perhaps being too ambitious and taking on too much.

Summary from Feedback Forms

1. The key business influencers offered support in the form of advice and guidance with initial contact being free of charge.
2. In addition to support, all of them wanted to be kept informed of further progress.
3. The most disappointing aspect of this group was their apparent lack of a network. For example only 38% said they knew potential candidates; only 28% stated they might have business contacts. These low figures may be due to the fact that:
   a) they actually have a narrow contact base
   b) they are reluctant to answer the question on a form
   c) the question itself could not be answered at short notice.

Potential Candidates – Summary of Comments

The key issues in the minds of the Superstart candidates were as follows:

1. Team formation issues
   How, if at all, can teams be formed at an early stage of the business? There are so many inherent risks due to issues of trust, ambition, financial commitment etc.
   Discussions included examples of successful team formation mechanisms, ideas of a shared vision, short and long term teams. Formation of teams based on assignments and those built on 'marriage broking' or introductory services. There were likely to be both formal and informal mechanisms for team formation.
2. Business viability issues
   Assessing business viability did not appear to be a major concern to a small group of candidates as they had already begun their own assessments. However it was clear from discussions after the main presentations that many of the delegates had a long way to go with regard to:
   - assessing market size, segments etc
   - assessing benefits rather than describing features
   - calculating break-even points and pay-back periods
   - developing a marketing strategy.
3. Access to finance
   Almost all the delegates echoed their frustrations with the lack of access to finance. It would appear that this one key element is a major obstacle to the formation of growth oriented businesses. However, we need to be cautious in reaching an explicit conclusion that finance is a constraint, since we have not seen viable business proposals from any of the candidates.
   There were a few candidates who appeared to have excellent business propositions but were themselves not motivated or lacked the necessary competencies to translate their idea into a full business proposition. Superstart may be the only form of help realistically available to these individuals.
4. Access to support services
   There was a very clear message from the audiences that support was needed during the early stages of their business development to clear away some of the ambiguity. The data collected from the feedback forms identifies the nature of the desired support, although there is not a clear signal for any one specific service. The central issues of team formation, marketing and access to finance were themes which emerged during discussions.

Findings from Candidate Feedback Forms

Classification of all delegates into four sections

1. Information from the feedback forms enabled us to classify the respondents into four categories:
   a) Production based
   b) Service but large scale
   c) Replacement income (self-employment ideas) entrepreneurs
   d) Resource pool candidates where people thought they might join enterprises soon after they were started.

There were two main objectives in using this classification. The first was to independently validate the targeted phone follow-up, the short-listing of which was completed by Frances Hoare (Essex TEC) and Robin Jacobs (Transitions). In all but a handful of cases, the two separate initiatives have linked closely together, ie to focus phone calls on groups (a) and (b) above.

The second purpose was to provide a list of candidates to Essex TEC so that they could follow up with other forms of enterprise provision.

An analysis of the sources of ideas indicated that 53% were from their former business/employer. This is encouraging as it suggests that they may have some knowledge of the product and their markets.

3. Sixty-four per cent of respondents indicated their desire to locate in Essex and a further 13% on its borders.
4. The vast majority of candidates had not discussed their ideas with anybody beyond their immediate family. Indeed the results were similar to those on the Herts TEC/British Aerospace project, which suggested that the vast majority of potential candidates had not talked to many people about their ideas.

We have summarised our understanding of the Training and Development needs.
 i) Assessment of viability of the business idea with a focus on
    - marketing, buying and selling
    - raising finance
    - developing business contacts.
 ii) a) For those with prior experience – explore experiences through focus groups and examine growth ambitions. For example, how big a business do they want to create?
     b) For those with no previous experience in small business run a 'start-up' self-awareness workshop.
 iii) 'Managerial skills' is used frequently as a generic term but detailed clarification will be required to determine exactly what people mean by it.
 iv) Target Group
There appeared to be three main categories from the data on the forms:
a. Production based
b. Second year sales turnover in excess of £250,000 of which there were 14 ventures, although some were service based
c. Second year turnover £100,000–£200,000, especially if they were production-based.

However, these categories were defined more precisely through the telephone follow-up.

6. Envisaged support required by candidates included:
   a) Legal/Financial
   b) 50% want a business plan panel
   c) Desired on-going support. The table below summarises the percentage of candidates who specified the support they most needed:

	%
Marketing	60
Business development	60
Access to other support	49
Legal	47
Sales/negotiation	37
Financial	34
Premises	34
Product development	34

7. It was not possible to establish the willingness of candidates to pay for the services with any degree of accuracy.

FINDINGS FROM THE TELEPHONE FOLLOW-UP

The telephone follow-up was conducted after a few days of the final candidate seminar. A group of 26 potential candidates were selected from the short-list of 30 on the basis of information gleaned from the feedback forms and judgements made by the three presenters following the conversations with candidates at each seminar. A key influence on the decision to include a candidate on the follow-up list was their level of ambition in terms of estimated sales figures for their business over the first two years.

From the list of 26, a recommendation was put forward to Essex TEC to provide support for 13 candidates on the basis that they displayed the following characteristics:

1. They had a high level of ambition.
2. They had a strong business idea.
3. They had already put in considerable effort.
4. They had already started their market research and business planning.
5. One had already begun to form a team.

DISCUSSION

The literature review points to the need for a new initiative and the survey findings indicate the potential to segment the start-up sector of enterprise support in a new way. The question is whether it is worth while doing it and how one would set about implementing the process. The section below sets out to examine the cost benefit analysis in some detail and concludes with two potential frameworks for implementation.

COST BENEFIT ANALYSIS

The data from candidates and information regarding the costs of enterprise development and promotion have been brought together in this section in order to provide a framework for reaching conclusions on the viability for further support to Superstart.

There are a number of key assumptions which have to be made in order to carry out the calculations. These are:

For Business Start candidates (Business Start-up candidates receiving allowances):

1. The average candidate generates a turnover of £40,000 and one extra job in the second year.
2. The survival rate at 18 months (approx) is 90%.
3. The average direct cost of support is £1,500 and the cost of indirect support is a further £1,000, thus a total of £2,500.
4. Approximately 400 candidates were due for support in Essex in the following year.

For Superstart candidates:

5. The estimated total sales from the 13 who wished to go forward was approximately £7,000,000 in the second year.
6. Allowing for gross margins, other fixed costs, the sales per individual employee in a Superstart business was estimated at £80,000, thus the total sales represents approximately 90 jobs.
7. From the follow-up phone calls there appeared to be a high degree of probability of success for most of them.
8. The cost of supporting Superstart candidates will be higher than Business Start (due to the fact that they are teams as opposed to single individuals). At this point an estimate of £5,000 per business in both direct and indirect costs should suffice.

We have tried to examine the data from several different perspectives. The first is the level of ambition displayed by the candidates. Thirteen Superstart candidates forecast nearly £7,000,000 in sales. This is the equivalent of 175 replacement income entrepreneurs. This is a clear indication of the importance of Superstart. (See Tables 1 and 2.)

TABLE 1
Sales forecasts of candidates in year two

Table I sets out the candidates' sales forecasts for the second year. Only one person has been deleted from the calculations as is distorts the whole picture. Those who wished to go forward with Superstart are in the left column and those who did not wish to proceed with Superstart are on the right.

Respondent Number	Candidates Going Forward Year 2 £	Respondent Number	Candidates Not Going Forward Year 2 £
002	750,000	003	–
021	–	006	20,000
023	600,000	008	500,000
027	–	011	–
030	1,000,000	022	4,500,000*
040	120,000	024	500,000
045	1,000,000	025	–
049	–	042	–
053	250,000	044	–
060	2,000,000	046	1,200,000
062	300,000	047	–
063	500,000	050	–
064	200,000	055	40,000
TOTALS	£6,720,000		£2,280,000
3 non-replies		6 non-replies	
		* 1 dreamer ignored	

TABLE 2
Comparison of Wealth Creation

	£
Business start: £40,000 each × 13	520,000
Superstart × 13	7,000,000

A second index might be the level of job creation potential of Superstart. This is a measure of the level of equity in society in terms of income distribution. It would hardly be worth while if a huge amount of sales were generated without any concomitant benefit to the local economy through job creation.

It would appear from the data that Superstart candidates have the potential to create a total of 90 jobs in the second year when compared with the 26 from Business Start candidates. The benefit appears to be three times as great. (See Table 3.)

TABLE 3
Comparison of Job Creation Potential

	JOBS
Business start: 13 × say 1 extra each	26
Superstart at £80,000 cost each, from sales of £7 million	90

The benefits outlined above can be set against the costs which have to be incurred. In other words what is the size of the 'bang for the bucks' being put in?

On the wealth creation index it would appear that Business Start type programmes could cost £485,000 compared to Superstart's £75,000 to achieve the £7,000,000 in sales. (See Table 4.)

TABLE 4
Comparison of costs involved in Estimated Wealth Creation

Business start £7 million/£40,000 = 175 starters
If 175 = 90% then 100% = 194 receiving support.
Therefore support for 194 × £2,500 = £485,000.
Superstart £7 million from 13 businesses. Assume 13 = 90%, then 100% say 15 starters.
Therefore support for 15 × £5,000 = £75,000

On the job creation index, based on 90 jobs, the equivalent costs appear to be £250,000 for Business Start and £75,000 for Superstart (See Table 5).

If these estimates are sustained it will be necessary to consider the allocation of budgets for the future. For example, perhaps by reducing support for 30 Business Start candidates, funds can be re-directed at Superstart. The loss of support for 30 however has the potential of creating 90 jobs, which may be construed as a more secure route forward in stimulating production-based, growth oriented businesses.

TABLE 5
Comparison of costs involved in creating 90 jobs

Business Start, assume 2 jobs per business.

45 starters = 90% thus support for 50 × £2,500 = £125,000.

If only 1 job per business then costs are £250,000.

Superstart, the 90 jobs would be generated from the 13 businesses, with 15 starters costing £75,000.

It can be clearly seen from several perspectives that the level of ambition and indeed the amount of progress candidates have already made suggests very strongly that segmentation of business support to enable a Superstart form of programme to be created would be worthwhile. The question that arises now is really about implementation. The next section examines two models, the first built largely on literature based concepts and the second on empirical work in the UK.

It can be clearly seen from several angles that the level of ambition and indeed the amount of progress candidates had made suggests very strongly that a segmented effort aimed at a Superstart form of support would be worthwhile. The question which results from this point is how does one go about implementing this form of support. The next section examines two models, the first built largely on literature-based concepts and the second on empirical work in the UK.

MODELS FOR IMPLEMENTATION

Two models are considered, the first developed by Kamm and Aaron (1993) and the second by Jacobs and Vyakarnam (1993).

First Model

Kamm and Aaron have conceptualised the formation of team-based businesses in two broad stages; idea generation and implementation. At the idea stage, one of two processes is thought to occur. An individual may get an inspiration for an unmet market need. Thus a 'lead entrepreneur' begins to process the idea through a feasibility stage, perhaps involving social networks, as well as personal experience at work, at school or at home. Alternatively, a group of people may come together, regardless of whether or not there is an entrepreneurial idea. They value the potential to work together and begin to form an idea as a result of networking.

This rather loose undefined start is characteristic of many starts, but is soon followed by a series of decisions which begin to formalise the venture creation process. It is this decision-making process which they believe provides a clue to a better understanding of team formation. According to Yukl (1989) groups tend to be most effective at problem solving when they (1) take enough time to thoroughly consider alternatives; (2) include the participation of all members; (3) avoid polarisation; and (4) carefully develop action plans.

The decision stages, according to Kamm and Aaron (1993) are:

1. Partner recruitment decisions, involving sources, criteria and inducements.
2. Team maintenance decisions, involving an assumption that at least one person in the team is interested in human relationship issues, the team must be cohesive at least till the venture is launched and that group maintenance does not imply that all members of the team are retained.
3. The model they put forward assumes that decision-making authority is a major team maintenance issue and this is addressed by successful teams through openly agreeing roles and using the common goal as a primary criterion for resolving conflict.
4. There are boundary issues such as who is in the group and who is allowed in or required to leave (eg family members). Teams resolve these conflicts by allowing everyone some degree of participation in recruitment, termination and reward decisions.

In summary the Kamm and Aaron model has some useful insights into the team formation and maintenance issue. However, their picture is incomplete as they do not adequately address the requirements of complementary skills and competencies, their model is built on bold assumptions and is untested as a developmental process. Liberal use is made of insights from other studies to try and close the gaps.

Second Model

We believe that the main gaps which remain in building enterprising teams must include a substantial personal development component at the very beginning at an individual level. Unless people have a clear understanding of their own motivations and why they want to be in business, let alone be part of a team, it is unlikely that they can make an effective contribution.

Based on the small business competency study (Jacobs and Pons, 1993) the authors argue that this model provides a more holistic approach to team-based venture start-ups. In brief the model suggests that at the heart of a successful business, the core competence required is the ability to build and manage relationships. This core competence, which has been derived from empirical research, is supported by five other areas of competence; technical, financial, marketing being the three functional areas and two at a personal level being self-awareness and personal skills.

It is suggested that a full understanding of these competencies would help in team formation and maintenance, both in the short term and the long term.

In addition, the development model for team-based businesses must include further input; business viability assessment which is achieved through assignments. The primary questions at this stage are:

- Will the business stack up in its own right?
- Will the team be able to function in any form of enterprise? (ie is the team viable)
- Will the team be able to function in its chosen business?

Assignments can provide powerful learning vehicles to move team members through to greater business skills, mutual understanding in non-threatening situations and building of mutual trust. As a result of the assignments, it should also be possible to develop a clear strategy which can provide the framework and the common goal on which teams can judge future performance, both in business terms and as teams. This second model is in fact being implemented by the authors. A more complete description has been provided elsewhere (Jacobs and Vyakarnam, 1993).

CONCLUSION

We believe we have demonstrated a gap in the business start-up activity, where considerable resources are poured into replacement income activity, creating little or no value-added, merely replacing income.

We have also demonstrated:

- considerable cost/benefit advantages in segmenting this sector
- that the idea is not new
- that almost all hypergrowth businesses were team-based
- that there are mechanisms to resolve ideas generation, team formation and team maintenance issues
- that potential candidates are clearly aware of their infrastructure needs (eg finance, advice etc.)
- that there is support from key business influencers.

Therefore it only remains for policy makers to develop an initiative to stimulating growth oriented businesses, perhaps through helping to start big business – small.

REFERENCES

BIRLEY S (1989) (Ed) European Entrepreneurship: Emerging Growth Companies, European Foundation For Entrepreneurship Research.
BRADFORD J (1993) Speech at Venture cash presentation 27.9.1993. Head of Small Business Services, National Westminster Bank plc.
BROCKAW L (1993) The Truth About Start-Ups, Inc., Vol 15 No 3, pp 56–64.
CHELL E (1990) The Characteristics of Entrepreneurs and Entrepreneurial Firms: A Fresh Approach, paper given at 13th Small Firms Policy and Research Conference, Harrogate, 1990.
CHURCHILL N AND LEWIS V (1983) Growing Concerns, Harvard Business Review, May.
D'AMBOISE G AND MULDOWNY M (1988) Management Theory for Small Business: Attempts and Requirements. Academy of Management Review, Vol 13 No 2, pp 226–240.
DE CARLO JT AND LYONS PR (1980) Toward a Contingency Theory of Entrepreneurship, Journal of Small Business Management, 18, 3, pp 37–42.
FILLEY AC AND ALDAG RJ (1978) Characteristics and Measurements of an Organizational Typology, Academy of Management Journal, 21, 1978, pp 578–59.
GREINER LE (1972) Evolution and Revolution As Organisations Grow, Harvard Business Review, July.
GUARDIAN THE (1992) The Dun and Bradstreet survey showed 62,767 business failures in Great Britain during 1992, against 47,777 in 1991, 31st Dec p 12.
HENDRY C (1993) Group Training for Small Firms Growth, International Workshop on Innovations in Training for Entrepreneurship and Small Business Development, Entrepreneurship Development Institute of India.

IFF RESEARCH LTD (1992) Enterprise Allowance/Business Start-up Schemes, A study of TEC schemes for TEC Research and Evaluation Branch, Employment Department, Nov.

JACOBS RC AND VYAKARNAM S (1993) The need for a more strategically led, research based approach in management development, British Psychological Society Conference.

JACOBS RC AND PONS T (1993) Developing a new model of individual and team competence in small business, 16th National Small Firms' Policy and Research Conference, Nottingham.

KAISH S AND GILAD B (1991) Characteristics of Opportunities Search Or Entrepreneurs Versus Executives: Sources, Interests, General Alertness, Journal of Business Venturing.

KAMM JB AND AARON NJ (1993) The stages of team venture formation: a decision making model, Entrepreneurship: Theory and Practice, Vol 17 No 2, Jan pp 17–27.

KANTER RM (1989) When Giants Learn To Dance, Simon and Schuster, London.

KIRZNER I (1973) Competition and Entrepreneurship, University of Chicago Press.

MCCLELLAND DC (1967) The Achieving Society, Free Press, New York

SCHUMPETER JA (1934) The Theory of Economic Development, Harvard University Press.

SEXTON D AND BOWMAN N (1985) The Entrepreneur: A Capable Executive and More, Journal of Business Venturing, Winter, pp129–40.

STANWORTH J AND GRAY C (1991) Bolton 20 Years On: The Small Firm in the 90s, Paul Chapman, London.

STARBUCK WH (1965) Organizational Growth and Development, in J.G. March (ed) Handbook of Organizations, Rand McNally, Chicago, 1965, pp 451–533.

STOREY D (1992) Should we abandon support for start-up businesses?, in Caley K, Chell E, Chittenden F and Mason C (eds) Small Enterprise Development: Policy and Practice in Action, Paul Chapman, London.

TIMMONS JA, SMOLLEN LE AND DINGEE ALM (1977) New Venture Creation; A Guide to Small Business Development. Irwin, Illinois.

VYAKARNAM S AND JACOBS RC (1990) Transitions from Scientist to Business Owner, proceedings of symposium on Growth and Development of Small High-Tech Businesses, (eds) Millman and Saker, Cranfield School of Management, April.

YUKL GA (1989) Leadership in Organizations, 2nd ed., Prentice Hall, Engelwood Cliffs, NJ.

CHAPTER 14

From Entrepreneurship to Professional Management: An Examination of the Personal Factors that Stunt Growth

ANITA MACNABB

BACKGROUND

From 'entrepreneurship' to 'professional management' – is this a meaningful concept? The answer will depend on one's definition of entrepreneurship and the perspective one takes on the study of the subject.

From a 'behaviourist' perspective, one would expect an examination of the differences in behaviour and management practices which are viewed as necessary to enable the business to move from an 'entrepreneurial' organisation to a 'professionally managed' organisation. The behaviourists would view the organisation as the primary focus for investigation and the entrepreneur or small business owner is examined in the light of the behaviour he or she displays as part of that process. The upsurge in interest in attempts to identify a generic list of competencies required for successful business growth emanates from a behaviourist perspective (Kakabadse 1991; Lindsay, Stuart and Thompson 1993).

Others have described the progression from entrepreneurship to professional management as a life-cycle or a developmental process. This longitudinal view of the development of the business has resulted in a number of stage-models. Stage-models purport to predict the necessary changes in the behaviour and management practices of the owner to enable the progression of the business from one stage to another stage. They draw attention to the different problems encountered at each stage and the abilities required to deal with them. Flamholtz (1986), for example, sees stages 1 (New venture) and 2 (Expansion) as the entrepreneurial phases beyond which the company must make the transition to a professionally managed business. Stage 3 is referred to as 'Professionalisation' and Stage 4 'Consolidation'. While there is little doubt that behavioural changes do occur as a result of the different problems facing the small business owner/manager at the various stages of the business life-cycle, the identification of discrete stages is controversial and there is no inevitability of progression from one stage to the next (Chell et al 1991). While these arguments are indeed valid, the underlying justification for the stage-model approach is one that needs to be taken into account, namely: the context in which the owner-manager is operating cannot be overlooked if we are to fully understand their behaviour.

Taking a different perspective, some researchers have built upon the work of personality theorists. They have sought to find either single characteristics or traits, or interacting characteristics, which predispose the entrepreneur to act in a certain way. Personality theories can be broadly categorised into (i) traditional trait approaches (ii) psychodynamic approaches (iii) socio-psychological approaches and (iv) owner typologies. The differences between the 'entrepreneur' and the 'professional manager' have largely been addressed by the work on owner typologies, which is based on the premise that small business owners are not all the same. Owner typologies had their origins in the work of Collins, Moore and Unwalla (1964) who distinguished the personality type 'entrepreneur' from salaried managers whom they labelled 'business hierarch'. This typology is criticised mainly because it is a 'fixed' categorisation and ignores the propensity to change. This early work on typologies used personality traits and ignored situational factors. Later work took account of personal goals (Woo, Cooper and Dunkelberg 1988; Hornaday 1987). However the question of progression or changing types has not been given much attention. Hornaday (1987) states that business owners can change types but it will be difficult for them to do so.

This raises the question 'Do professionally managed firms have to be less entrepreneurial?' Drawing on recent leadership research, we see an emphasis on the need for transformational leaders who show many entrepreneurial qualities: vision, being proactive rather than reactive. However, rather than act independently it is said that these leaders will have to motivate, empower and inspire staff. (Bryman 1992; Leich 1992). Following this, the influence of management style and organisational structure and their impact on the type of firm is a critically important area of study in this field. Slevin and Covin (1988) differentiate organic versus mechanistic structures. They demonstrate that increases in top management's entrepreneurial orientation will positively influence the performance of the organically structured firm, concluding that 'a strong entrepreneurial orientation . . . is only warranted when other elements in the organisational structure provide a supportive context.' (Chell et al 1991).

On examining the variety of perspectives drawn on to study the progression/transition from the entrepreneurial business to the professionally managed business, there would seem to be limited research on the value systems and cognitive frameworks which the small business owners use to make sense of their environment. STRATOS (1990) made the link between business owner types and their personality profile which was based on an assessment of their value orientation. Kakabadse and Dainty's recent work (1993) identified executive values as one of the two key drives distinguishing successful executives (the other being 'shaping the future'). While there has been increasing emphasis on cognitive frameworks (Calori, Johnston and Sarnin 1992; Gimenez 1993), there has been little application to small business research and to the developing small firm. The justification for such an approach emanates from the following argument:

'the strategies of organisations are the product of managerial decisions whilst they, in themselves, are influenced by the cognitive frames of reference of managers. If we are to understand how strategies come about it is, therefore, important to understand these frames of reference.' (Calori, Johnston and Sarnin 1992:75).

The argument becomes even more potent when we substitute manager for small business owner or entrepreneur, given, in most cases, his/her key role in the development or otherwise of the business.

To date, research into cognitive frames of reference and value systems has been limited by research methods and tools which are complex and are of limited practical use to those working in the small business support environment. This paper introduces a relatively new framework called Identity Structure Analysis (ISA) and shows how it can be applied to small business owners who are making the progression towards a professionally managed business.

THE STUDY

The research was divided into two stages:

- the first stage investigated the value and belief systems of 62 business founders/owners at different stages of the business life-cycle
- the second stage used explanatory case studies to understand and explain how self-image, values and beliefs influence the way in which the business is managed.

WHY CHOOSE ISA?

ISA (Weinreich 1980, 1986, 1988) was chosen as the most appropriate method of investigation as it provides a comprehensive means of investigating people's value systems and their identifications with others. It is underpinned by Erikson's (1959) identity theory, the symbolic interactionist approach (Kuhn 1964), cognitive affective theory (Festinger 1957; Weinreich 1969) and Kelly's construct theory (1955) and differs from current psychometric methods of assessing entrepreneurship by examining the entrepreneur in a social and familial context. Individuals develop notions of their identities and characteristic ways of thinking about themselves through a complex of social and developmental processes. Such processes include those of forming identifications with others, internalising ascriptions of self by others, comparing self with others in relation to various skills and competencies and assessing self in terms of one's desires and aspirations.

ISA allows for the complexity of individual entrepreneurs, allowing entrepreneurship to be viewed as a developmental process rather than an end in itself. It does not assume that entrepreneurs are an homogeneous group and allows for the fact that individual characteristics may not be static over time.

ISA consists of analytic psychological concepts, which are explicitly defined so as to be 'etic' (culture free/universal) but nevertheless also to incorporate 'emic' (culture specific) content. Chief among these are role-model identification (in both positive – idealistic-identification – and negative – contra-identification – modes), empathetic identification and conflict in identification with others. 'Role-model' identification refers to aspirational orientations (positive or negative) and 'empathetic' refers to de facto identification. ISA does not use psychometric scales: it has the virtue of combining the qualitative (idiosyncratic values and beliefs of the person) with the quantitative (metrics that can be compared across individuals). It is sensitive to subtle changes in people's values and beliefs, as it is to people's inconsistencies in evaluating themselves and others in terms of their beliefs. Hence it is eminently suited to investigating changes and development in people's values and beliefs during transition or redefinitions of identity such as may happen when a person makes the progression from the entrepreneurial business to the professionally managed business. It can therefore be most useful in a diagnostic and counselling capacity as well as for research purposes.

One of the major features of ISA, as mentioned above, is that it not only provides a hierarchy of personal constructs (derived from Kelly 1955) but also allows us to ascertain the consistency of their usage (based on the theories of cognitive-affective inconsistency; Rosenberg and Abelson 1960; Festinger 1957). This is achieved through measuring the extent to which people consistently attribute favourable and unfavourable characteristics to those they approve and disapprove of respectively. The measure is called 'Structural Pressure' (SP). Very high net structural pressures (70+) indicate constructs that are used with extreme evaluative consistency and are labelled 'core evaluative dimensions' of identity. Constructs with low values of structural pressure are indicative of a possible point of stress, depending on its degree of importance to the individual. Core evaluative dimensions of identity are more resistant to change than those used inconsistently.

Unlike most psychometric tests which are not specifically designed to assess entrepreneurial attributes, the ISA instrument is tailor-made for the individual or group under investigation. The instrument is similar to a repertory grid in that it consists of a series of scales by means of which the respondent construes various people, facets of self-image and other 'entities', using a series of 'bipolar constructs' one at a time. For this study 15 bipolar constructs were used. These were elicited by carrying out in-depth interviews with 10 small business owners who had survived the post-start-up stage.

The instrument takes about 30–45 minutes to complete. The highly flexible computerised analysis programs enable both in-depth analyses of single case studies to be made (as in Stage 2 of this study), as well as intricate analysis of large groups of people in terms of the criteria set by the investigator (as in Stage 1 of this study).

STAGE 1: GROUP STUDY FINDINGS

The business groups were categorised into clearly differentiated stages of development: Pre-start-up, Post-start-up, Established and Professionally managed businesses. The findings are reported in detail in MacNabb and McCoy. 1992.

They are summarised as follows:

- Growth, as a prerequisite for the success of the business, becomes a stronger value among owners as the business develops with 88% of the established group and 93% of the professionally managed group choosing 'Believes that continued growth is necessary for success' as a core value. Indeed, it is significantly more consistent value for the professionally managed group (ANOVA SP across groups p=0.04).
- 12% of respondents from the established business group use the construct 'believes that growth should be restricted in the interests of maintaining control' consistently, indicating that this is a core value to them and as such is resistant to change. This belief is likely to hamper the growth of these businesses as the owner will consistently restrict growth in the interests of maintaining control.

- There was split consensus among the life-cycle groups on their choice of polarities on the construct 'Likes to spread responsibility and control as part of a team/ Feels happier to take full control and responsibility'. Forty-one per cent of the established business group appraises self and others in terms of 'feels happier to take sole control and responsibility' consistently indicating that it is a core value and therefore more resistant to change. This value could hamper the growth of the company as the owner will avoid delegating control and responsibility.
- There was unanimous consensus among the professionally managed group that 'building a strong management team is essential to grow one's business'. However, the structural pressure was less than 50% indicating that self and others were inconsistently evaluated by means of this construct and therefore it was not a core value. This is indicative of a value which is causing respondents some stress.
- 5 members of the established business group selected the bipolar opposite value, namely 'Believes that a strong leader can grow the business just as effectively'. However the low structural pressure on this value indicates that it is not a core value and could change over time.
- All business groups were split over the issue as to whether 'priority should be given to family or business'. Eighty-five per cent of a comparison group of non-business owners would emphatically give priority to family over business.

The group results provided an indication of some of the values and beliefs which could prevent the continued growth of the businesses. However this, the first stage of the study, was limited because it didn't provide the link between value systems and behaviour. The following case studies examine this relationship.

STAGE 2: THE CASE STUDIES

The case studies were used to explore the interaction between the owner's personal qualities and the way he manages the business. The case studies were drawn from participants of NISBI's Growth Programme. This 18-month programme is aimed at small business owners who have the motivation and potential to grow their business significantly.

A number of tactics were used to ensure the validity of interpretation, correctness of inferences and reliability of the results. Multiple sources of evidence were used. In each case, the respondent was given feedback on the results of the analysis and asked to comment on the accuracy of the findings. Growth counsellors (who had built up a relationship with the respondents) also sat in on the feedback sessions and verified the researchers' interpretation. Secondary data was also gathered on personal background, motivation for entering the business and on business performance.

Case 1: Michael

Michael comes from a tradition of self-employed business people. His father and grandfather were building contractors. He is one of six sons and, his father, realising that the family business could not support all of them, gave each of them some property as an incentive for them to be independent and self-employed.

Chapter 14

Michael, aged 18, saw the opportunity of starting a building supply business based on high quality service. He founded the business in 1982 with his two brothers who are equal shareholders. The company has grown steadily each year, initially by 40–50% per annum, slowing down to 20% per annum 2–3 years ago. The turnover is currently over £12m per annum and it employs 70 full-time staff.

The ISA analysis revealed Michael to be a confident, self-assured individual. It came as somewhat of a surprise for us to find that Michael had no strong aspirations for the future. Unlike many on the Growth Programme, Michael did not see the need to change personally. His evaluation of 'me as a business owner now' was 93% of 'me as I would like to be'. While discussing this, Michael revealed that he had changed quite a lot over the last few years, having been quite autocratic in the early years of the development of his business. He now feels quite content and while wanting the business to continue to consolidate and grow, he felt he didn't need to change personally.

Examining Michael's core values, it is evident that Michael has very strong family values, commonly found in a traditional family firm. This is evident from the consistency of his use of the constructs 'Would prefer to hold on to the business even if offered a good take-over deal' (SP: 79.42), 'Feels that family support for one's business is essential' (SP:77.96) and 'Would give priority to family interests and commitments' (SP 75.75). Michael's strongest core value 'Would only sell/make goods that reflect good taste' (SP 83.90) is evident in his commitment to quality which runs into every aspect of the business.

Michael's core values (see Table 1) are reflected in the way he manages the business. Three years ago, he recognised the need to move towards a more professionally managed business and undertook an extensive in-house staff training programme using experienced consultants. His management team now comprises seven managers (including his two brothers who are fellow directors). Family support and loyalty, a growth orientation and involving others in decision-making are his core values and are reflected in the operation of the business. Michael's role has changed from day-to-day operations to the strategic management of the business.

TABLE I
Case One: Stable or Core Evaluative Dimensions of Identity

CONSTRUCT	STRUCTURAL PRESSURE
Would only sell/make goods that reflect good taste	83.90
Would prefer to hold on to the business even if offered a good take-over deal	79.42
Feels that family support for one's business is essential	77.96
Would give priority to family interests and commitments	75.75
Would seek the opinion of others before making a decision	71.07
Believes that continued expansion is necessary for the success of the business	61.72

The fast growth of the company has no doubt been aided by Michael's self-confidence. While admiring his father and empathetically identifying with him, he disassociated from his father's non-risk-taking values. This explains the inconsistency (evident from the low structural pressure) in the use of the construct 'Would take a challenging job that offered high remuneration based on performance' (SP:8.50). (Table 2.)

TABLE 2
Case One: Inconsistently Evaluative Dimensions of Identity

CONSTRUCT	STRUCTURAL PRESSURE
Would take a challenging job that offered high renumeration based on performance	8.50

Regarding the future growth of this company, one could infer that continued success will be dependent on:

- the continued support and loyalty of family members.
- Michael understanding that self-confidence, while a positive attribute, needs to be tempered with realism.
- Michael's propensity towards risk-taking needs to be supported by good quality information.
- Michael does not have any aspirations to change or develop personally. This may indicate the need for a new challenge.

Case 2: Brian

Brian and his brother Bill run an engineering business which has 28 employees and a turnover of approximately £650,000. The business was started in the early 1970s by Brian's father who only let go of the reins two years ago.

Brian and Bill recognise that the organisation relies too heavily on them and they work long hours to keep it ticking over. They recognise the need to build a simple yet effective management structure.

The ISA analysis (Table 3) reveals that Brian prefers to behave independently and in an autocratic manner and to hold characteristically entrepreneurial rather than managerial characteristics.

These values coupled with a high degree of self-confidence make it difficult for Brian to delegate, trust and build a good management team. Brian realises that their key line managers need to be replaced. One is nearing retirement and the other is not committed to the business. Brian's own inability to delegate and empower his staff has probably reinforced their lack of commitment. (Table 4.)

Case 3: Giles

Giles also is an entrepreneur. Not only did he found his own business but he displays classical entrepreneurial characteristics. Giles held a management position in a successful international company. He was being 'groomed' for a top position when he decided to seize an opportunity and start up his own business.

TABLE 3
Case Two: Stable or Core Evaluative Dimensions of Identity

CONSTRUCT	STRUCTURAL PRESSURE
Feels comfortable making most decisions without consulting others	78.78
Likes to be in charge or direct others	73.35
Would take a challenging job that offered high remuneration based on performance	72.55
Prefers to create, rather than respond to, opportunities	58.62
Believes business profits should be used to reward individual/s	55.67
Would give priority to business commitments over family	44.75

TABLE 4
Case Two: Inconsistently Evaluative Dimensions of Identity

CONSTRUCT	STRUCTURAL PRESSURE
Believes that building a strong management team is essential to grow one's business	13.72
Feels that family support for one's business is essential	−19.31

The ISA analysis revealed that Giles disassociated from the values he perceived his father to have. He explained that his father was an unambitious labourer who handed over his wages at the end of each week to his wife who handled the household budget. Giles, on the other hand, evaluates self and others on the basis of achievement, autonomy and internal locus of control. This is evident from the ISA analysis which revealed Giles' core evaluative dimensions of identity to be as shown in Table 5.

TABLE 5
Case Three: Stable or Core Evaluative Dimensions of Identity

CONSTRUCT	STRUCTURAL PRESSURE
Would sell a business for profit which one had built from scratch	96.57
One shapes ones own future	86.93
Likes to be in charge or direct others	85.29
Would take a challenging job that offered high remuneration based on perfomance	83.01
Believes business profits should be used to reward the individual/s	80.51

One of Giles' core values was 'Likes to be in charge or direct others'. It is evident that this core value has been a barrier to the growth of the firm as he finds it difficult to delegate and spread control and responsibility (see Table 6).

TABLE 6
Case Three: Dual Morality Evaluative Dimensions of Identity

CONSTRUCT	STRUCTURAL PRESSURE
Feels that family support for one's business is essential	−27.78
Likes to spread control and responsibility as part of a team	−47.87

Giles' autocratic management style has not encouraged his key staff to show initiative, which in turn has reinforced his leadership style. This is an obvious area of stress for Giles as he tries to balance being a strong leader and building a management team. This construct is inconsistently evaluated (see Table 7).

TABLE 7
Case Three: Inconsistently Evaluative Dimensions of Identity

CONSTRUCT	STRUCTURAL PRESSURE
Believes that building a strong management team is essential to grow one's business	8.33

A further barrier to the growth of the company lies in Giles' own lack of a ambition for the company. The ISA analysis revealed that he was more preoccupied with his past than with his future. He explained that he regrets leaving behind the high flying image associated with his former senior executive position. While his business is successful, he does not derive the same degree of satisfaction from it.

Giles realises that he needs to reassess his position in relation to the business as it would seem that he requires a new challenge and would be more amenable to selling up rather than building the business for long-term growth.

DISCUSSION

One might assume from the title that the author believes that 'entrepreneurship' and 'professional management' are two discrete entities – that the entrepreneur has to leave behind his or her 'entrepreneurial qualities' in order to become a 'professional manager'. This would be a wrong assumption – the concern of the paper is how the entrepreneur manages growth. Continuous growth requires the entrepreneurial role to change and develop as the business moves from sole reliance on the founder/owner for ideas and management to the development and involvement of the management team. Rather than a mutually exclusive transition, this is seen as a necessary progression if continuous growth is to be achieved. However, the entrepreneur needs to maintain many of his or her entrepreneurial qualities in order to successfully compete in today's and tomorrow's market-place. An awareness of his or her own value and belief system can help the entrepreneur develop the business, avoiding the uncomfortable and stressful feelings associated with acting against one's core values.

The research suggests that some of the entrepreneur's core values will act as barriers to the continued growth of the business. These are 'believes that continued growth should be restricted in the interests of maintaining control', 'feels happier to take sole control and responsibility', 'believes that a strong leader can grow the business just as effectively (as a strong management team)'.

The case studies reveal further potential constraints to the continued growth of these small businesses. These include:

- heavy reliance on family support (often epitomised by employing family members and giving them key positions in the management team)
- lack of aspirations to change (which often indicates a lack of vision for the future of the business)
- an autocratic management style coupled with unrealistically high degree of self-confidence which resulted in an inability to delegate, motivate and empower staff and build an effective management team.

The research to date however has its limitations in that it is not a longitudinal study. Future research will use qualitative techniques to examine whether the Growth Programme has helped to overcome these potential barriers and whether the participants' values and beliefs have changed over the 18-month period of the programme.

CONCLUSION

The findings of this research add further evidence to the view that some entrepreneurs find it difficult to empower staff, delegate responsibility and build an effective management team. ISA allows one to identify these potential barriers by examining the stability of values and beliefs and the consistency with which they are applied in judging self and others. It also provides a quantitative means of measuring changes in a person's self-image and value system over time.

The in-depth analysis of the person's self-image and value system provided by ISA can be a useful starting point for growth counselling. It can provide the framework for a personal and business development plan as it situates the individual in terms of where he/she is now in relation to where he/she would like to be. Rather than providing solutions, it provides the diagnosis – a first step in helping people to find a means of building a professionally-managed business based on their own personal value and belief system.

REFERENCES

BRYMAN A (1992) Charisma and Leadership in Organisations. London: Sage.
CALORI R, JOHNSTON G AND SARNIN P (1992) French and British top managers' understanding of the structure and the dynamics of their industries: a cognitive analysis and comparison. British Journal of Management, 3(2), pp61–78.

CHELL E, HAWORTH J AND BREARLEY S (1991) The Entrepreneurial Personality. Concepts, Cases and Categories. London: Routledge

COLLINS OG, MOORE DG AND UNWALLA DB (1964) The Enterprising Man, East Lansing: Michigan State University Press.

ERIKSON EH (1959) The problem of ego identity, Journal of the American Psychoanalytic Association, 4, 56–121.

FESTINGER L (1957) A Theory of Cognitive Dissonance, Evanston, Ill.:Row,Peterson.

FLAMHOLTZ EG (1986) How to make the transition from an entrepreneurship to a professionally managed firm, San Francisco: Jossey Bass.

GIMENEZ F (1993) 'Small firms entrepreneurs' views of competition: a cognitive approach. Paper presented at the EFMD European Small Business Seminar, Northern Ireland.

HORNADAY RW (1987) Dropping the E-words from small business research. Journal of Small Business Management, 28,4:22–33.

KAKABADSE A (1991) The Wealth Creators: Top People, Top Teams London: Kogan Page.

KAKABADSE A AND DAINTY P (1993) Executive Competencies Research Programme, Cranfield School of Management, Resources Group Internal Working Paper.

KELLY GA (1955) The Psychology of Personal Constructs New York: Norton.

KUHN MH (1964) Major trends in Symbolic Interaction in the Past Twenty-Five Years, in Manis JG and Meltzer BN (eds) (1970) Symbolic Interaction: A Reader in Social Psychology. Boston: Allyn and Bacon.

LEICH CM (1992) Entrepreneurial Leadership: Transforming Enterprises for the Twenty-First Century, paper presented at the Forum for Research on Enterprise Education. NISBI-The Small Business Institute.

LINDSAY P, STUART R AND THOMPSON J (1993) Development of the top team: the definition of a competence framework for small to medium-sized enterprises. Paper presented at the EFMD European Small Business Seminar, Northern Ireland.

MACNABB AI AND MCCOY J (1992), Growth Orientation and Control Issues from the Small Firm Owner's Perspective, paper presented at the 15th National Small Firms Policy and Research Conference, Southampton, England.

ROSENBERG MJ AND ABELSON RP (1960) An analysis of cognitive balancing, in Rosenberg M. and Turner RH (eds) Social Psychology: Sociological Perspectives New York: Basic Books.

SLEVIN DP AND COVIN JG (1988) Entrepreneurship and organicity: two key variables in small firm success. Paper presented at the 11th National Small Firms' Policy and Research Conference, Cardiff.

STRATOS (1990) Strategic orientations of small European businesses. Aldershot: Avebury.

WEINREICH P (1969) Theoretical and experimental evaluation of dissonance processes. PhD thesis. London: University of London

WEINREICH P (1980, 1986, 1988) A Manual for Identity Exploration using Personal Constructs, Social Science Research Council, now: Economic and Social Research Council.

WOO CY, COOPER AC AND DUNKELBERG WC (1988) Entrepreneurial typologies: definitions and implications, Frontiers for Entrepreneurship Research, Wellesley, Mass.: Babson Centre for Entrepreneurial Studies: pp165–176.

CHAPTER 15

Habitual Owners of Small Businesses

PETER J HALL

INTRODUCTION

Habitual owners, those entrepreneurs who are involved in multiple business start-ups (McMillan 1986), are a significant phenomenon though little researched. It has been proposed that habitual owners 'have had the opportunity to learn how to efficiently and swiftly overcome the stumbling blocks they encountered in the first place.' (Anonymous 1986). 'However, there is, as yet, no evidence to support the hypothesis that 'habitual' entrepreneurs are any more successful than their colleague owner-managers' (Birley and Westhead 1992).

This paper is in three parts. The first part critically examines the current state of knowledge about habitual owners, the second part examines how different strategies might be selected by an owner and the third part proposes a model linking the owner to owner outcomes.

The first part, including the second and third sections, examines recent papers on the subject concentrating on definitions, the frequency of the phenomenon, and the relationships that have been found. This is followed by an empirical critique highlighting the lack of an accepted definition of 'habitual' for research purposes and the absence of a definition of a business. The lack of definitions and the measurement of only one business has led to a lack of comparability in the studies and reduced the significance of any findings.

The second part, comprising the fourth section, examines the key decisions made by novice owners (those who have established only one business) when contemplating habitual ownership in order to further their personal materialistic aspirations. It is proposed that different decision paths lead to different types of habitual ownership; voluntary serial ownership where businesses are owned sequentially and portfolio ownership where businesses are owned concurrently. Motivation, ability and industry structure are suggested as the key factors affecting owner strategy and thus owner outcomes.

The third part, comprising the fifth section, develops a model linking the owner's personality traits to owner outcomes, through behaviour. Owner outcomes are the aggregation of business outcomes. Behaviour is influenced by personality traits, motivation, ability and the situational context. In turn owner outcomes are influenced by behaviour and the situational context, two key components of which are industry structure and strategy.

CURRENT STATE OF KNOWLEDGE

Definitions

'Habitual' has been coined as a phrase to describe those entrepreneurs who are involved in multiple business start-ups (McMillan 1986). This has not been developed into an accepted definition for research. Each research paper has defined its own terms as the following examples show.

'Multiple business starters are entrepreneurs who, after having started a first company, set up or participate in the start-up of (an)other firm(s).' (Donckels et al 1987).

'A habitual entrepreneur is defined as a person who has had experience in multiple business start-ups, and simultaneously is involved in at least two businesses.' (Kolvereid and Bullvag 1992).

'Novice' founders were defined as those individuals with no previous experience of founding a business, whilst 'habitual' founders had established at least one other business prior to the start-up of the current new independent venture.' (Birley and Westhead 1992).

These definitions encompass several different concepts of multiple business ownership which will be explored in detail in below.

Frequency of the Phenomenon

A surprisingly small number of UK research projects allow for the possibility of habitual owners considering the following findings.

Birley and Westhead (1992) have reported the following studies with the percentage of owners with prior business founding experience.

- 34% in Wales (Westhead 1988, p.732);
- 32% in Cleveland (Storey 1982, p.116);
- 28% in East Anglia (Keeble and Gould 1985, p.205);
- 25% in Northern Ireland (Hisrich 1988, p.34);
- 25% in Northern Ireland (Birley et al 1990, p.28);
- 16% in Cleveland (Storey and Strange 1992, p.19);
- 15% in West Lothian (Turok and Richardson 1989, p.29);
- 11.5% in Scotland (Cross 1981, p.219)'

Gray (1993) reports that 40% of the respondents of a Small Business Research Trust survey had run another business previously and many of them more than one. In addition, 10% of the total sample were still operating the other business.

Storey et al (1989) found that the majority of directors of fast employment growth companies were also owner/directors of one or more other small companies.

Birley and Westhead (1992) report that 37% of their sample were habitual owners. In other countries the incidence of habitual owners is perhaps more prevalent.

Kolvereid et al (1991) report 34% of Norwegian entrepreneurs.

Rondstadt (1986) reports 63% of currently practising US entrepreneurs.

Chapter 15

RELATIONSHIPS FOUND

Personal Characteristics

Few relationships have been found between personal characteristics and owner type, classified by habitual and novice.

'The results suggest that very few women become habitual entrepreneurs. Habitual entrepreneurs tend to have higher education and start their first business at a younger age than their novice counterparts. Social background does not seem to influence whether to become a habitual or not.' (Kolvereid and Bullvag 1992).

'Habitual founders were younger than their counterparts when starting their first business although they were older than 'novice' founders when starting their current new businesses. Also, 'habitual' founders had gained experience and developed business contacts in a large number of organisations, had a greater tendency to have been self-employed and had worked in their own business prior to start-up.' (Birley and Westhead 1992).

'The background of both groups of starters give a different picture:

- relatively more multiple business starters stem from an entrepreneurial background, while this is true for the working-class background of the other starters;
- the hierarchical level of the multiple business starters who were employees before starting-up was often higher than that of their counterparts in the other group of starters.' (Donckels et al 1987)

Venture Outcome

'all seven measures failed to show significant differences between habituals and novices with respect to the performance of the ventures they start.' (Kolvereid and Bullvag 1992).
(last business started – measured)

'A pattern has emerged. There is no evidence from this study to suggest that those new businesses established by 'habitual' founders with prior experience of business venturing are particularly advantaged compared to their more inexperienced counterparts.' (Birley and Westhead 1992)
(last business started – measured)

'Most jobs are created by the multiple business starters. In 1985 28.5 per cent of the multiple business starters employed five people or more. This figure amounts to 8.2 per cent for the other starters. At start-up these figures were respectively 12.1 per cent and 5.1 per cent.' (Donckels et al 1987)
(First business started – measured.)

Few factors were found to differentiate habituals from novices and only Donckels et al (1987) found a significant difference in outcome.

EMPIRICAL CRITIQUE

Overview

The variability of the findings and their relative lack of significance tend to indicate that perhaps this is not a fruitful field for research. However the large proportion of owners found to be habituals shows that they are a very important part of the small business community, yet the research shows that we know very little about them. The lack of consistent findings can be explained entirely by inconsistent definitions and the methodology used.

Definition of Habitual

Being an habitual is about founding or owning businesses. Although the concept of habitual initially concerned start-ups it has grown to encompass owning businesses as well. In the small business context starting or buying a new business may not be significantly different processes and might not be capable of being differentiated by owners. This is further explored in the next section. It is necessary first to consider business outcomes before considering owner outcomes. Too much research is simplistic in terms of the dichotomy death or survival. In habitual situations the death of one business in the form of a sale or an insolvency may lead to the founding of another business, but different outcomes could lead to differing foundings. A sale may provide the funds for a further founding or purchase whereas a legal outcome, such as company liquidation or personal bankruptcy, is likely to leave the owner resource poor, in terms of funds and contacts. In habitual ownership situations the quality of prior events is likely to be significant.

The definitions considered earlier already provide us with two types of habitual. There are those owners who own one business after another but effectively only one business at a time. Previous businesses may have been sold, closed or had a legal outcome. These owners can be classified as serial owners. There is another category of habitual owner in which the owners own more than one business at a time. These are portfolio owners.

Serial owners
Portfolio owners

Donckels et al (1987) and Birley and Westhead (1992) include both of these in their definition of habituals whilst Kolvereid and Bullvag (1992) only include portfolio owners in their definition. This is the first factor that leads to lack of comparability in studies of habituals. If Kolvereid and Bullvag (1992) found 34% of Norwegian entrepreneurs were portfolio owners, how many serial owners would they have found, and therefore how many habitual owners in total?

When measuring outcomes of the latest business founding, or purchase, Kolvereid and Bullvag (1992) and Birley and Westhead (1992), it may be important to consider what has happened to the previous business or businesses, if the quality of prior events is significant.

This would indicate that there are two types of serial owner and a multiplicity of possible portfolio combinations. The serial owners can broadly be classified as those who sold their previous business or businesses, voluntary serial owners, and those who have had their previous business closed for them through force of circumstance, involuntary serial owners.

Serial owners   – voluntary
                        – involuntary
Portfolio owners – many permutations

The studies cited above all recognise another category 'novice' or 'other starter'. This category – 'other than habituals' – may have led to a lack of significance in many research results since this is not a unique category. All potential serial and habitual owners will be in this category. A significant proportion of respondents in the novice category may have habitual personal characteristics. Novice owners are therefore a stage rather than a category and therefore make an unsatisfactory comparison group.

There is one final category labelled 'one shot' by Anonymous (1986). These are owners who only ever have one business.

The complexity of research observation is characterised in the following owner hierarchy:

Portfolio
Voluntary serial
Involuntary serial
One-shot.

This hierarchy does not relate to potential outcomes but to the complexity of observing the current situation. Portfolio situations are likely to be the most complex to observe since there are many possible permutations and complexity will arise from the potential overlap of activities between concurrent businesses. Voluntary serial is likely to be more complex than involuntary serial because of the difficulty in measuring the outcome of a voluntary disposal. One-shot represents a unique business situation and is likely to be the least complex to observe.

The Definition of a Business

The postal questionnaire, SARIE – Society for Associated Researchers in International Entrepreneurship – used by both Kolvereid and Bullvag (1992) and Birley and Westhead (1992) poses the following two questions.

Q1. 'How many businesses have you established prior to this current one?'
Q2. 'If you have established/owned another business, what happened to the most recent business?'

Storey et al (1989) pose the following questions.
Q3. 'Is the key individual the director or owner of any business other than this one?'
Q4. 'How many other operating businesses?'

Without an explicit definition of 'business' these questions all rely on individual respondent's concepts of a business. These concepts are unlikely to be the same, so common variables are not being measured. These concepts may be different in different cultures and may explain some of the inter-country differences.

In addition Q2 confuses owning and establishing a business so the definition of a habitual owner as an owner of several businesses has to be accepted rather than the given definitions, is identified above under 'Current State of Knowledge', involving start-up or founding. Another factor to be considered is that Q3 combines directorship and ownership and there is not necessarily a relationship between the two.

These questions show that there is a lack of objectivity in the definition of the variable being measured, and this will influence any findings. Research into 'serial' and 'one-shot' ownership do not depend on a definition of business since the events being researched are discrete. However when 'serial' and 'one-shot' ownership have to be differentiated from portfolio ownership then the definition of a business is crucial. The transition event from serial or novice ownership to portfolio ownership takes place when a subsequent business is founded or bought and the other business is still owned.

Legal definitions of businesses, in terms of sole traders, partnerships and limited liability companies, are inadequate since many limited companies never trade. Also the same business is capable of being subdivided into separate legal entities in different ways. For example in many service industries expansion is achieved through additional branches. In one instance these branches could be part of the original company, in another instance they could be separate companies and in another they could be subsidiary companies. In all three cases the measurement of outcome must be the same if a consistent model linking owners to outcomes is to be established, since only the legal situation is different not the business situation. Outcome can be defined as a measurable result of the business activities.

There may be no universally acceptable definition of a business. However, within any one study a definition needs to be made explicit, especially with regard to calculating the number of businesses owned, if this is the basis for segmenting the sample.

Measurements of Venture Outcome

All the studies cited earlier measured only one business of the habitual owner. Kolvereid and Bullvag (1992) and Birley and Westhead (1992) measured the last business started. Donckels et al (1987) measured the first business started.

If an understanding of outcomes is to be achieved, all businesses of both serial and portfolio owners would have to be measured. First business started or last business started is probably irrelevant. An owner who has sold a business for a large sum may no longer be motivated in the development of other businesses owned and they may not perform well. Conversely if the owner is still highly motivated the large sum may be used to found a new business that would start at a larger size than might otherwise be possible. In another case a subsequent business that is growing rapidly may take resources from the original business and may even cause it to decline.

Since only one business was measured in each of the three studies it is not known if habitual owners performed any differently from other owners. It is only known that their latest businesses did not perform significantly differently from novice owners' businesses. However, Donckels et al (1987) show that when comparing first businesses, habitual owners created more jobs than novice owners.

Birley and Westhead (1992) sum up this empirical shortcoming in their own paper as follows:

'Nevertheless, this empirical evidence reinforces the view (Scott, 1990) that if the business is the sole unit of analysis there is a threat that the value of the new venturing event will be underestimated. It also indicates that future attempts to explain business growth should incorporate the possibility that owner-managers may attempt to resolve their personal materialistic aspirations through the growth of further multiple business operations, which may not be directly related to the single unit of analysis being studied.'

Data Collection Relative to the Founding Event

It follows from the above that owner characteristics are unlikely to be linked to individual business outcomes but to owner outcomes, the aggregate of all business outcomes related to an owner. These outcomes are only likely to be observable after a significant time period. Also if segmentation by owner type is required, one-shot owners cannot be positively identified until they have given up business, although their status can be inferred given a sufficiently long time frame.

Gestation Period of a Portfolio

As proposed above, additional businesses may be an essential element of strategy for certain categories of owner. Whilst it is known that individual businesses can reach two-thirds of their assumed ultimate employment level within three years (Storey, 1985) and more than half never change their employment profile from start-up (Birley, 1987), it is not known how long it takes to acquire a portfolio or at what stage a portfolio stops growing.

There is very little research information about habitual owners and even less about portfolio owners. Kolvereid and Bullvag (1992) give an average age of 29.6 years for portfolio owners when starting their first business. Birley and Westhead (1992) found that habitual owners had an average age of 30 years when starting their first business and an average age of 39.39 when starting the current business.

This would indicate that at least ten years should elapse from the original founding event before any data relating to habituals are collected. Any prior measurement could give spurious results. Most of the studies of habitual owners have researched businesses that are new ventures and often less than five years old.

THE KEY DECISIONS

Portfolio Owners

Donckels et al (1987) suggest that additional businesses are founded as a means of the owner achieving his/her growth objectives. Gray (1993) suggests that portfolios are a means of the owner maintaining control. Stanworth et al (1992) suggest that only 2% of small firms grow to 50 employees. Presumably these owners have the highest motivation and ability. Other owners have to adopt other means if they are to achieve significant growth.

Birley and Westhead (1992) conclude that attempts to explain business growth should acknowledge that owners may attempt to resolve their personal materialistic aspirations through further business operations, which may not be directly related to the single unit of analysis being studied.

The Key Issue

The above sections have described what happens when a novice owner becomes an habitual owner. The types of habitual owner, voluntary serial, involuntary serial and portfolio have been classified.

The time taken for this change to take place has also been estimated. It is proposed that at least ten years should elapse between the founding event and measurements of habitual ownership.

The reasons as to why the transition takes place from novice to habitual ownership are proposed as growth and control to satisfy personal materialistic aspirations. However, this does not illuminate the key issue as to why an owner founds or acquires additional businesses to achieve these objectives rather than expand the existing business.

In the next sections the decisions that need to be made in expanding a business and the sequence in which they are taken are explored in order to offer an explanation of the habitual phenomenon.

HABITUAL DECISIONS

At any time an habitual owner can be faced with one or all of the following decisions.

1. Expand an existing business/do not expand existing business.
2. Sell or close a business/do not sell or close business.
3. Start a new business/do not start a new business.

Portfolio owners can be faced with all three decisions simultaneously.

Voluntary serial owners are faced with decision 2. Decisions 1 and 3 would be subsequent decisions dependent on decision 2.

Involuntary serial owners are only faced with decision 3.

Novice Decisions

Owners in the novice stage have not yet metamorphosed into 'habituals' or 'one-shot'. The question is what decision does the owner face and what factors influence the decision? 'One possible explanation may be that habitual entrepreneurship becomes more common in settings where opportunities for growth are restricted. This may force the entrepreneurs to substitute growth of one venture with the creation of multiple companies.' Kolvereid et al (1991).

Changes have been observed in business owner motivations when additional businesses are started. Independence seems to be a strong motive when starting the first business but more materialistic motives, high income and enlarging business property for the family, seem to come to the fore when subsequent businesses are founded. (Donckels et al, 1987; Gray, 1993)

FIGURE 1

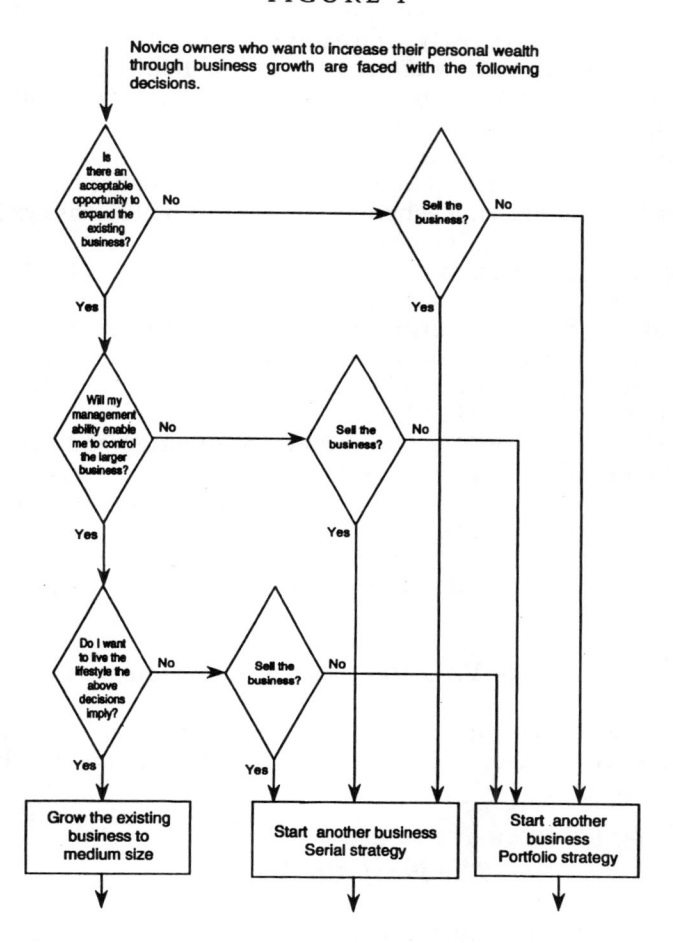

Novice owners who want to increase their personal wealth through business growth are faced with the following decisions.

```
        ┌─────────────┐
        │ Is there an │
        │ acceptable  │  No      ┌──────────┐  No
        │ opportunity ├────────→ │ Sell the ├──────┐
        │ to expand   │          │ business?│      │
        │ the existing│          └────┬─────┘      │
        │ business?   │               │ Yes        │
        └──────┬──────┘               ↓            │
               │ Yes                               │
               ↓                                   │
        ┌─────────────┐                            │
        │ Will my     │                            │
        │ management  │  No      ┌──────────┐  No  │
        │ ability     ├────────→ │ Sell the ├──────┤
        │ enable me   │          │ business?│      │
        │ to control  │          └────┬─────┘      │
        │ the larger  │               │ Yes        │
        │ business?   │               ↓            │
        └──────┬──────┘                            │
               │ Yes                               │
               ↓                                   │
        ┌─────────────┐                            │
        │ Do I want   │                            │
        │ to live the │  No      ┌──────────┐  No  │
        │ lifestyle   ├────────→ │ Sell the ├──────┤
        │ the above   │          │ business?│      │
        │ decisions   │          └────┬─────┘      │
        │ imply?      │               │ Yes        │
        └──────┬──────┘               ↓            ↓
               │ Yes
               ↓
   ┌──────────────┐    ┌──────────────────┐   ┌──────────────┐
   │ Grow the     │    │ Start another    │   │ Start another│
   │ existing     │    │ business         │   │ business     │
   │ business to  │    │ Serial strategy  │   │ Portfolio    │
   │ medium size  │    │                  │   │ strategy     │
   └──────┬───────┘    └────────┬─────────┘   └──────┬───────┘
          ↓                     ↓                    ↓
```

The decision to sell the business is in two parts. First, does the owner want to sell the business? If the owner does want to sell the business then the second part depends on the opportunity to sell the business at an acceptable price.

The cycle of decisions repeats itself until the owner's business growth aspirations are satisfied.

In the above decision sequence all positive decisions lead to a voluntary serial strategy. Any negative decision or constraint leads to a portfolio strategy.

FACTORS AFFECTING DECISIONS

The Three Primary Level Decisions

The first decision, assessing the opportunity to expand, must also include the assessment of the risks involved in alternative strategies. This decision can be illustrated by a service industry example. If a small service business develops a new concept and expands on a geographical basis (branch by branch), it will only be able to expand slowly, if the owner wants to retain ownership. Competitors imitating the new concept will establish themselves in adjacent geographical areas before the original business. If the growth objectives of the owner of the original business have not been fulfilled, expansion can now only be achieved against competition. Expansion into these areas will now be perceived to carry a higher risk. The owner may now consider additional new businesses within the existing geographical area to be less risky. The opportunity to expand is therefore influenced by the industry structure.

The second decision assesses the owner's ability to control subsequent situations. If the owner wants to continue in a role that does not match the future business situation then the decision may be taken not to expand the existing business with its implied potential loss of personal control. An example would be an owner who behaves as a worker and is not willing to cross the threshold of delegation of supervision (Hall 1992).

The third decision depends on the owner's motivation and desire to live the lifestyle that a decision to expand the existing business to a larger size may imply. Distance is a control problem for small businesses as it is for large. Townsend (1970) suggests that the management difficulty increases with the square of the distance measured in hours travelling between locations. This may also inhibit geographical spread that is essential for service businesses to grow.

The Voluntary Serial Decision

This decision is dependent upon the owner's willingness and the opportunity to sell the business at an acceptable price which in turn is likely to be influenced by the industry structure.

The Portfolio Decision

Given the owner's desire to increase personal wealth through business growth, any negative decision becomes a constraint on expanding the existing business. A negative decision at the secondary level concerning selling the business excludes the voluntary serial option. If the owner is unwilling to grow the existing business and unwilling to sell it, the only alternative, in order to achieve the growth objective, is to start another business. Lack of opportunity to sell the original business, lack of management ability and lack of motivation can individually or in combination lead to negative decisions that result in a portfolio strategy.

Chapter 15

FACTORS AFFECTING OWNER OUTCOMES

Industry structure, owner ability and owner motivation all play a part in deciding owner outcomes in terms of portfolio, serial or one-shot strategies.

The relationship between these factors needs to be explored in order to understand their influence on owner outcomes.

Modelling the Factors Affecting Owner Outcomes

Building a model of the factors affecting performance begins with Maier's (1965) proposal that job performance is a multiplicative function of ability and motivation. Hollenbeck and Whitener (1988) developed this by proposing that the effects of personality traits on job performance are mediated by motivation and moderated by ability. In other words, motivation is the driver that brings about job performance and ability is the regulator that constrains job performance. In this context job performance is the evaluation of a set of behaviours. The model at this stage is sufficient to explain why there is no observable link between personality traits and job performance. A causal link exists but it is heavily moderated by other variables.

Behaviour is a function of environment as well as people factors (Ekehammer 1974) and this element is introduced into the model by Herron and Robinson (1993) as a variable called context. They show these relationships in Figure 2 below.

FIGURE 2
Herron and Robinson (1993)

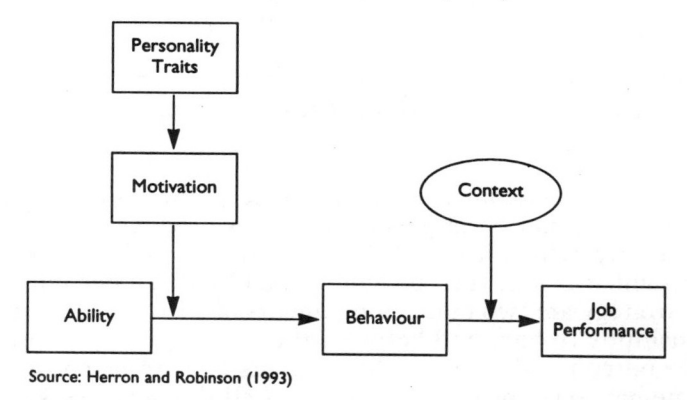

Source: Herron and Robinson (1993)

This model shows behaviour that results from personality traits brought about by motivation but constrained by ability. This behaviour within a context leads to job performance.

However, the correct behaviour for a desired job performance, in a given context, would depend on that behaviour having been selected as suitable for the context. So not only is job performance influenced by context but so also is behaviour. The subsequent preliminary value creation performance (VCP) model by Herron and Robinson (1993) does not take this into account.

Hall (1992) proposed a model of owner attributes that influenced owner behaviour, the key attributes of which were managerial ability and entrepreneurial inclination. The measurement of ability in terms of prior management ability is supported by Milne and Thompson (1992), Chell et al (1991) and Leigh, North and Smallbone (1992). Motivation is not directly observable or testable but can be measured in terms of the amount of time during which a behaviour takes place, or the strength of desire for a goal, or a combined measure such as GET (General Enterprising Tendency) (Caird 1988, Cromie and O'Donaghue 1992).

Sandberg (1986) proposed a model that showed new venture performance (NVP) as a function of the characteristics of the entrepreneur (E), the structure of the industry (IS) in which the venture competes, and its business strategy (S).

NVP = f (E,IS,S)

Combining this model with Herron and Robinson (1993) Figure 2, the model shown in Figure 3 can be derived.

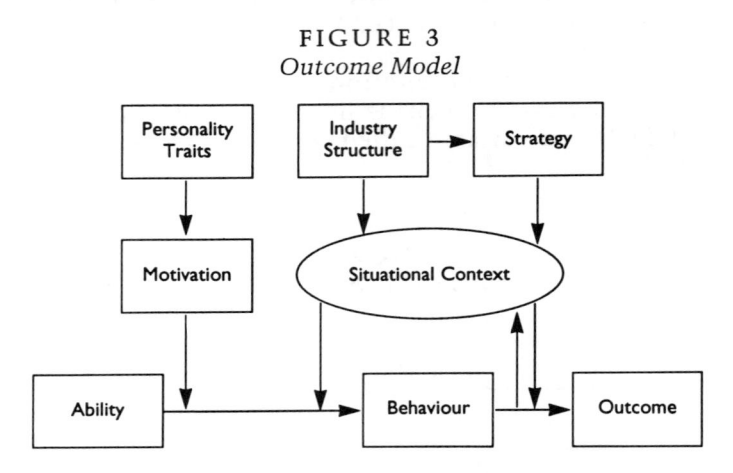

FIGURE 3
Outcome Model

This model shows that outcomes, job performance, new venture performance or other measures are a function of personality traits mediated by motivation and moderated by ability, which lead to behaviours that are selected in relation to a given context, which can in turn be determined by those behaviours. Industry structure and strategy are two of the components of situational context.

If a relationship is to be found between the entrepreneur, or small business owner, and the outcome, then all of these factors have to be considered. In particular outcome has to be measured in terms of all the businesses relating to an owner and not just one of them. In certain circumstances other career activities of the owner may also have to be taken into consideration.

CONCLUSION

A significant proportion of business outcomes, approximately 40% (Gray 1991; Birley and Westhead, 1992), are influenced by habitual owner strategies, owning more than one business, yet few small business research projects take this into consideration.

It is proposed that for novice owners who want to increase their personal wealth through business growth there are two distinct habitual strategies, voluntary serial and portfolio, in addition to the one-shot option. The voluntary serial strategy involves the disposal of the existing business before the founding or purchase of a subsequent business. The portfolio strategy leads to the simultaneous ownership of more than one business. An analysis of the decisions that lead to these two distinct habitual strategies suggests that positive decisions lead to voluntary serial outcomes whereas negative, or constrained, decisions lead to portfolio outcomes.

The factors that influence the decisions, given the owner's desire to increase personal wealth through business growth, are assumed to be: industry structure which influences the ability to expand the existing business as well as the opportunity to sell the business at an acceptable price; ability to manage and control a business with an increased size; and motivation to lead the lifestyle necessary to achieve a larger business rather than to start another business.

This paper proposes that owner characteristics are related to owner outcomes and not to the outcome of any one business. Owner outcomes can be regarded as the aggregation of individual business outcomes related to that owner.

Finally a model is developed showing that personality traits, mediated by motivation and moderated by ability lead to behaviour which within a situational context that the behaviour also influences, leads to owner outcomes. It is proposed that industry structure and strategy are two of the key components of the situational context.

REFERENCES

ANONYMOUS (1986) To Really Learn About Entrepreneurship Let's Study Habitual Entrepreneurs, Journal of Business Venturing 1.
BIRLEY S (1987) New Ventures and Employment Growth. Journal of Business Venturing 2.
BIRLEY S AND WESTHEAD P (1992) A Comparison of New Businesses Established By 'Novice' And 'Habitual' Founders In Great Britain. Unpublished.
CAIRD S (1988) A Review Of Methods Of Measuring Enterprising Attributes, Durham: Durham University Business School.
CHELL E ET AL (1991) The Entrepreneurial Personality, London: Routledge.
CROMIE S AND O'DONAGHUE J (1992) Assessing Entrepreneurial Inclinations, International Small Business Journal, Vol 10 No 2.
DONCKELS R, DUPONT B AND MICHEL P (1987) Multiple Business Starters Who? Why? What? Journal of Small Business and Entrepreneurship, 5.
EKEHAMMER B (1974) Interactionism in Personality from a Historical Perspective, Psychology Bulletin, 81,12.
GRAY C (1993) Stages of Growth and Entrepreneurial Career Motivation in Chittenden F et al (eds) Small Firms: Recession and Recovery, London: Paul Chapman.
HALL P (1992) Small Business Portfolios, 15th National Small Firms Policy and Research Conference, Southampton.
HERRON L AND ROBINSON R (1993) A Structural Model Of The Effects Of Entrepreneurial Characteristics On Venture Performance, Journal of Business Venturing, 8.
HOLLENBECK J AND WHITENER E (1988) Reclaiming Personality Traits for Personnel Selection, Journal of Management, 14 (1).

KOLVEREID L, SHANE S, STARR J, WESTHEAD P AND BULLVAG E (1991) Novices versus Habitual Entrepreneurs: A Three Country Survey, 21st European Small Business Seminar, Barcelona.

KOLVEREID L AND BULLVAG E (1992) Novices Versus Habitual Entrepreneurs: An Exploratory Investigation, Second Annual Global Entrepreneurship Conference.

LEIGH R, NORTH D AND SMALLBONE D (1992) Growth Characteristics of Mature, Small Medium Sized Manufacturing Enterprises in Robertson M Towards the Twenty-First Century, London: Nadamal/Paul Chapman.

MAIER N (1965) Psychology in Industry (3rd ed.). Boston: Houghton Mifflin Co.

MCMILLAN L C (1986) Executive forum, Journal of Business Venturing 1.

MILNE T AND THOMPSON M (1992) Patterns Of Successful Business Start Up, Unpublished.

RONDSTADT R (1986) Exit, Stage Left: Why Entrepreneurs End Their Entrepreneurial Careers Before Retirement, Journal of Business Venturing, 2.

SANDBERG W R (1986) New Venture Performance: The Role of Strategy and Industry Structure, Lexington, MA: D.C. Heath and Co.

SCOTT MG (1990) The Entrepreneurial Life Cycle: Some Preliminary Results from a 20 Year Study of New Scottish Independent Businesses and Their Founders, 13th Small Firms Policy and Research Conference, Blackpool.

STANWORTH J, PURDY D AND KIRBY D (1992) The Management of Success in 'Growth Corridor' Small Firms, Small Business Research Trust Monograph.

STOREY D J (1985) Manufacturing Employment Change in Northern England 1965–78: The Role of Small Businesses, In D J Storey (ed.), Small Firms and Regional Economic Development; Britain, Ireland and the United States, Cambridge: Cambridge University Press.

STOREY DJ, WATSON R AND WYNARCZYK P (1989) Fast Growth Small Businesses: Case Studies of 40 Small Firms in N.E. England. Department of Employment Research Paper No. 67.

TOWNSEND R (1970) Up the Organisation, New York: Knopp.